ALSO BY JIM APFELBAUM

*Golf Etiquette*
(with Barbara Puett)

# GOLF ON $30 A DAY
## (or Less)

# GOLF

# ON

# $30

# A

# DAY

# (or Less)

## A BARGAIN HUNTER'S GUIDE TO GREAT COURSES AND EQUIPMENT

# JIM APFELBAUM

VILLARD BOOKS

NEW YORK

1995

Library of Congress Cataloging-in-Publication Data

Apfelbaum, Jim.
Golf on $30 a day (or less): a bargain hunter's guide to great courses
and equipment / by Jim Apfelbaum.
p. cm.
ISBN 0-679-75071-1
1. Golf courses—United States—States—Directories. 2. Golf—United States—States—
Equipment and supplies. I. Title. II. Title: Golf on thirty dollars a day (or less)
GV981.A83   1995        796.352´06´873—dc20        94-36537

Manufactured in the United States of America on acid-free paper
9 8 7 6 5 4 3 2
First Edition

Book design by Jo Anne Metsch

FOR
NANCY ABEL
AND
JESSIE KREMPASKY

We must beware of trying to build a society in which nobody counts for anything except a politician or an official, a society where enterprise gains no reward and thrift no privileges.

—Winston Churchill

Not everyone can afford to join a country club.

—Michael Jordan

# CONTENTS

# INTRODUCTION

At a nine-hole state park course (it happened to be in Texas), the pro was showing me around. The facility had been built by the Works Project Administration during the Depression. Inside the rustic stone clubhouse, above the homey fireplace and on the enormous wood beams, hung photos of his grandfather, who had helped build the course, and his father, whom the young pro had succeeded.

The course that had been a part of his family for three generations, he said, "teaches you everything you need to know." This beautiful description has served as my measure for a "good" course ever since. The best of the eminently affordable courses in this country offer the same comprehensive golf education.

This book is not meant to disparage those who charge more than $30 to play golf or those who willingly pay that and more. The author bears no grudge against fine courses or first-class treatment.

The fact is most of us rarely play the crème de la crème. Somewhere along the way golfers have come to believe that golf must be expensive to satisfy. Golf requires many things: fortitude, determination, imagination. Pots of money are merely optional.

Why $30? Because that's the average cost for eighteen holes of golf in America. Why nothing about travel packages? Because statistics bear out the obvious. Golf junkets are pie in the sky. When we travel, we usually know where we're going to stay. Finding accommodations is not a problem. The problem is finding the time, the money, and good value. Most of us squeeze our golf in on the run, around business and family obligations. We're much more likely to head to Memphis or Minneapolis than Maui or the Monterey peninsula.

Wherever you travel—even if you don't—this book will increase your enjoyment of golf. (And it will even save you money if you ever get to Maui, Pebble Beach, or other top-shelf golf destinations.)

At many of the courses noted, $30 will cover both your green fee and a cart, often with enough left over for a dog and a beer. Without getting feisty, I must point out that, with only a few exceptions, courses that don't allow walking missed the cut. Walking is on the way to becoming an act of defiance in golf. It only shows how far we've strayed from golf's roots. The game was meant to be played on foot. Besides, we can all use the exercise.

Every effort has been made to keep to the title's mandate. My apologies for the inevitable intercession of inflation, time, circumstance, or greed. There are some terrific courses along golf's blue highways and some terrific people. Thanks to everyone who made the trip so memorable. Happy Trails!

Jim Apfelbaum
P. O. Box 402101
Austin, TX 78704

apfel@bga.com

# GOLF ON $30 A DAY
## (or Less)

# SAVING THE GREEN

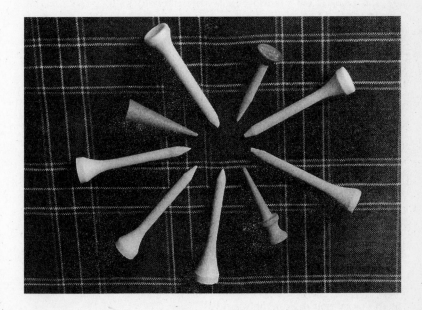

*Everything in this section is meant to save money, time, equipment, sanity, face, or, in modest measure, the environment. Assembly is rarely required. When it is, even the extremely impatient—or all thumbs—should be able to make ends meet without damaging one's self-esteem. In the rare instances where it does appear, golf instruction is left to the capable care of professionals. This is as it should be. Instruction in the hands of amateurs is a very dangerous thing.*

*Information on products and companies listed in "Saving the Green," appears in the Appendix.*

## TO WEATHER THE ELEMENTS

His clothes may continue to luminesce in staunchly bright colors and fabrics. Still, the stereotypical image of the never-need-ironing golfer is thankfully fading. The look of the bygone greats has been rediscovered. Only this time around, it features a logo.

Whichever way the trendwinds blow, it seems safe to say, on the golf course as off it, classic style never embarrasses. The wardrobe shortlist remains topped by old standards of style, function, and comfort, not to mention price. Until golf moves indoors, common sense will always be more important than fashion sense.

One needn't eat granola nor wear Birkenstocks to recognize that clothing made to withstand the elements offers far longer wear and better value. The Patagonias, Bogners, L.L. Beans, Eddie Bauers, et al.—innovators who cut their teeth making tough but still attractive outdoor wear—always seem to outdrive the strictly golf clothing makers.

Sure, they can be expensive. But like everybody else, these guys, and their growing list of competitors, still have to move merchandise. They have clearance and seasonal sales. Many have factory-outlet stores.

For all the basics, and especially whenever inclement weather is involved, these companies manufacture superior products (often 100 percent Made in America). Who knows what the professional golfers would wear left to their own devices, if the endorsement dollars and the long arm of the tours weren't so strident. (Funny thing is, Payne Stewart in slacks is nearly unrecognizable.)

These fiercely competitive retailers also bust their butts on service. Most pride themselves on their willingness to satisfy customers before and after the sale. The customer complaint that ends happily is the story that makes the rounds.

These companies are also innovative in seeking out and even developing new products. The space-age fabric Gore-Tex, for example, was long a backpacking standard before golf discovered its superior rain protection.

What Gore-Tex did for rain gear, Capilene is now doing for long underwear. When Ben Hogan won the British Open in 1953, his secret weapon was tailor-made cashmere long johns. Capilene is soft, pliable, designed to wick perspiration from the body while still providing warmth. It's also a lot less expensive than cashmere, and it doesn't *look* like long underwear. The top can be worn as a separate, ideal for layering as a windbreaker under a golf shirt. They even make Capilene bras (The Boundary Waters Catalog).

Sierra Trading Post puts out a nifty catalog of name-brand outdoor clothing (Sierra designs, North Face, Sportif USA) discounted from 35 to 70 percent. The catalog is stocked with seasonal artillery: cotton turtlenecks ($9.95), wicking turtlenecks ($14.95 instead of $28), a great selection of windbreakers, even fancy clip-on sunglasses ($17.50) with 100 percent UV protection.

### GETTING COLD FEET

The course can be a bayou, my shoes absorbent as wet cardboard, but if my feet are dry, everything's great. Waterproof golf shoes are wonderful (guaranteed for increasingly longer terms and dropping in price). Even if you play in Pro Keds, dry feet are not an impossibility.

Unfortunately, Gore-Tex socks are now over $30 (see "Finding the Green in Delaware" for a shopping tip). Two less-expensive alternatives are WigWam's Sealskinz MVT Waterproof Socks ($24.99 at better camping stores) and Neoprene socks ($19.50). Neoprene works like a wet suit for your foot. Designed for truly wet conditions, winter canoeing, for instance, they will more than suffice for golf at its sloshiest (The Boundary Waters Catalog).

### OUTLETS FOR SERIOUS SHOPPING

In our family, it's known as "having a fire in your pocket." An enthusiasm akin to auction fever, the urge may be closer to a shopping Saint Vitus' dance brought on by the lure of a bargain. Factory-outlet stores play on this weakness, like a drum. If it seems as if they are growing exponentially, that's because they are. Brooks Brothers, for example, has immediate plans for opening one hundred new stores filled with discounted apparel.

Traditional outlet stores were once little more than basements filled with boxes of seconds and rejects with sizes crossed out in

Magic Marker. Hit or miss was putting it mildly. But if you weren't too picky, and had some time to kill, you stood a good chance of walking away with two shoes that were never meant for each other or the coveted "rare" buy.

Let's not kid ourselves. The modern outlet store is typically nowhere near the factory (which may require a passport and several updated immunizations to visit). The typical store bears little resemblance to its predecessors, the true factory stores that once dotted New England mill towns.

The thrill of the hunt for bargains notwithstanding, prices seem no different from what you'd find at a department store during a major sale. This is admittedly the view of someone who shops only under duress.

What you may not know is that there are some big names in the golf apparel world, *very* big names, who would rather not let on that their outrageously high-priced sportswear ends up in outlet stores. One manufacturer asked specifically not to be included. Another never returned calls. Just so you know, the big game is out there, and it is discounted big-time.

A typical Reebok outlet had Greg Norman shirts for $14.99, marked down from $40 and $24.99, down from $60. Next door, a pair of those Polo trousers with the embroidered crest on the butt were $29.99 instead of $70. More of the same was nearby at Izod, Brooks Brothers, J Crew, and Nike, to name just a few of the major outlet players.

Check the clothing carefully to avoid disappointments. Better yet, ask about the merchandise. Employees can be surprisingly candid about the quality of the stock. They also have the scoop on upcoming new arrivals and sales. Although it is not well known, many outlets will take orders over the phone. Finally, visit an outlet mall around the holidays and you've got no one but yourself to blame.

Cursory outlet information can be found in this book under the heading "shopping," within each state in the Finding the Green section. *Outlet Bound,* a national guidebook, is another resource ($6.95 from 800/336-8853). There is also *Fabulous Finds, the Sophisticated Shopper's Guide to Factory Outlet Centers* ($12.95). For New England coverage, A. Miser and A. Pennypincher's *Factory Outlet Guide to New England* ($9.95) provides useful strategy (keep a notebook with family sizes and birthdays) and store profiles to tell an Athletic Outlet from an Amherst Sports. Two newsletters of interest to outlet aficionados, *The Best for Less* and *Factory Outlet Newsletter,* are included in the Appendix. Should you miss the billboards, any self-respecting visitor center has brochures to steer you to the bargains.

## A BRAND-NEW BAG

Golf fashion may lag somewhat behind the times. Equipment, however, rides the cutting edge, and that includes accessories. Cellular-phone pockets are another in a long line of novel innovations for golf bags; although this strikes me as a dubious improvement.

The hallmarks of sound backpack design—lighter, sturdier frames and fabrics, thicker padded straps, and more ergonomic designs—have markedly improved golf bags. Some aren't so much carried as worn.

Light on the shoulders, high tech is anything but on the wallet. Many golfers endure bags as energy-efficient as a '76 Chrysler New Yorker. Fortunately, there are a number of inexpensive adaptors to help save your bag, your back, and a few bucks.

Sun Mountain sells the Loop (about $25), an attaching strap that converts any bag into a backpack for better weight distribution. Izzo has a similar Velcro-affixed adaptor. In the same price range, it converts any bag except a Sun Mountain.

Moderately priced tripods are also available. Golf Day has one for $12.95 that weighs 6 to 7 ounces. The GolfWorks has one for $15.95 that weighs "under a pound." A catalog of primarily reconditioned and factory-closeout camping equipment, Leisure Outlet offers the Paxton Crosswalk Bag Stand (no straps or buckles) for $14. It weighs seven pounds.

The day may not be far off when remote-controlled trolleys sufficiently drop in price, to become as familiar as today's handcarts. One imagines fairways filled with mechanical rolling stiffs not unlike the stridently ill-mannered beings infesting low-budget horror flicks. The effort expended to customize equipment is welcome nevertheless. Now, if they're really looking for significant peacetime applications for the military, how'z about some affordable ball-finding sonar?

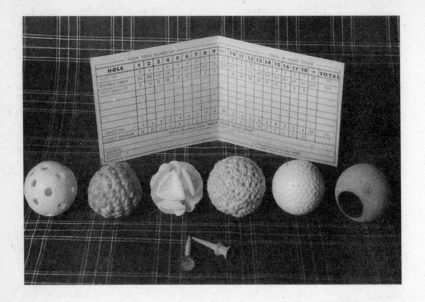

## A BETTER PRACTICE BALL

Reminiscent in shape of the Death Star from *Star Wars,* ProShot by Exclusive Design Products is the sturdiest of the plastic practice balls. They are not indestructible. Metal will eventually win out over plastic as surely as good triumphs over evil. Unlike competitors, ProShot will withstand repeated blows from a driver. The novel geodesic shape allows the ball to be fitted onto a tee. In packs of three, they retail for $4.99. How you keep them off the roof is your problem.

I once overheard Lee Trevino say he practiced chipping balls into a chair while watching a game on TV. Hardwood floors and an inaccurate stroke proved more than my household could bear, so the search began for an alternative.

Decades before Nerf, the Practo-Ball, made by the Reliable Knitting Company of Milwaukee, Wisconsin, was a popular alternative. Further inspiration came from the irrepressible sleuth Rumpole of the Bailey. The venerable barrister Uncle Tom often passes the days chipping with a ball of yarn.

These facts were relayed to the talented team of Mrs. Alice Melanson of Baton Rouge, Louisiana, and her son, David. They have created a crocheted practice ball that will not break windows or damage blinds. (They are, with the author, however, hereby absolved from any liability resulting from improper use.) With the aid of a small throw rug, the Melan-Ball offers substantial relief from spells of indoor antsiness. It also performs admirably outdoors, holding its shape and taking flight surprisingly well. I'm assured they are not hard to make for crocheters of intermediate ability and up. Each takes about an hour each to make, and the costs are minimal.

### MELAN-BALL INSTRUCTIONS

*Glossary:*

ch = chain
hdc = half double crochet
sl st = slip stitch

Ch 4, join with sl st in first ch to form ring.
Round 1: Ch 2, 7 hdc in ring, sl st in top of ch.
Round 2: Ch 2, 2 hdc in each hdc, sl st in top of ch.
Round 3: Ch 2, hdc in each hdc, sl st in top of ch.
Round 4: Ch 2, hdc in each hdc, sl st in top of ch, fasten off.

Repeat rounds 1–4 to make second half of Melan-Ball cover/outside. Wind thread into a ball to use as the center/stuffing. Sew together the two halves around the wound ball using a whipstitch of an overcast stitch.

NOTE: The ball in the photo is made of 100 percent mercerized cotton thread on a size F crochet hook. The size and weight of the finished Melan-Ball will vary depending upon the thickness of the thread or yarn and the size of the crochet hook used.

## BETTER LIVING THROUGH LEAD TAPE

Several better hardware stores had no idea what I was talking about, but all the golf-supply houses carry rolls of adhesive-backed lead tape. At about $3 for one hundred inches, that's more than enough for hours of good clean fun fooling with the swing weight of your clubs.

In *And If You Play Golf, You're My Friend,* Harvey Penick notes that Mickey Wright has "a touch of lead tape on the toe and another bit of lead on the heel" of her putter. To make a putter less whiffy, or just to tinker, the enterprising should dig out Guy Yocum's insightful treatise on the subject, "Get the Lead Out," in the May 1992 issue of *Golf Digest.*

Lead tape will also make a serviceable practice club. Take an old seven iron. Wrap some lead tape around the face (leave it on the backing so you can use it later). Wrap some masking tape over it and some sealing tape over the whole thing. Presto. Instead of eighty bucks for a store-bought model, you've just created a serviceable, hybrid weighted club, just right for working those golfing muscles. Just don't hit any balls with it.

Several years ago, *USA Today* ran the following recipe for a practice club designed by Tennye Ohr, pro at Connemara Golf Club in Kentucky. Here it is:

Take a 36 in. metal pipe with a 3/8″ diameter. Put a screw cap on one end. Add powdered lead to desired weight. Stuff the pipe with aluminum foil to keep the powder in place. Place a size .600 golf grip over the open end.

### LOW-IMPACT (ON THE WALLET) CLUB-FACE MARKERS

Label-on Impact tape will show you where the club face strikes the ball. To a lesser extent so will masking tape, chalk, or talcum powder, and for a heck of a lot less than $14.50. (The catalogs really roll out the markup on these babies.)

Consumer Advantage sells fifty LongShot Impact Recorders with a correction/instruction booklet for under $10, as cheap as the commercial stickers run, if you're hankering for the real McCoy.

Even better, how's 120 impact decals for about $8? Head on down to your local office-supply superstore and get a box of Avery Clear Label Printer Labels, #4151 (1 1/8″ × 3 1/2″). They're not the exact size to cover the entire club face (they're a little longer), but the fit over the sweet spot is close enough. The impact shows up clearly in black on the tape. Despite the permanent-adhesive notation on the box, the stickers peel off easily. No muss, no fuss. For some reason that I can't explain, the labels work perfectly on irons, but a shot with a wood won't register on the tape.

## NOTHING BUT NET

For those who insist on practicing at home, here's a novel approach: Buy your practice netting directly from the manufacturer. This may not be front-page news, but it will get you more net for the buck than from other, more widely advertised sources (leaving you better equipped to pay for the inevitable damage).

Memphis Net & Twine will do you up with an 8′ × 10′—just the net, no frame—for $26, including twenty feet of hanging cord. Make sure to request the sports net and equipment catalog or you may end up with something better suited to snaring yellow fin tuna; Memphis also makes fishing nets.

## DRIVING-RANGE MATS

Reasonably priced range mats are a little harder to come by. Surely there must be scraps and seconds. I finally found a genuine, honest-to-goodness range mat (not one of those flimsy, cheesy ones readily available) on the cheap. It never occurred to me that a driving range would sell mats and potentially threaten its own till, but some do.

Sure you can pay $30 to $70 for a much smaller mat that's not nearly as tough as the genuine article *or* you can buy one right from a range as I did for an unbelievable $15 new. It even came with a rubber tee. No, it doesn't make sense; I still visit the range out of a sense of allegiance (and anytime the dents in the garage door from missing the net get me down). Some ranges and courses simply sell their old mats. Even beaten up, the price and durability still make them a good deal.

## THE FINE PRINT

Reading the side of a sleeve of balls can be rewarding as well as educational. The following guarantee, for instance, appears on boxes of Titleist DT 90s:

NO-CUT GUARANTEE
   If a Titleist DT is cut through the normal course of play with a golf club, Titleist will replace each ball returned with three new DT

golf balls free of charge. Please return golf balls to Titleist for replacement.

This is not an exclusive offer. Read the label.

The same goes for all your equipment. When something was clicking inside my driver (it was loose foam), Taylor Made offered to replace the head for free. All I had to do was take it to a Taylor Made account (a local muny) and have it returned. The hardest part was finding out the club was covered in the first place. You never know. If something goes wrong with a club, a pair of shoes, a bag, it can't hurt to call. All manufacturers have 800 customer-service numbers. As *Golf Pro* magazine noted in an incisive cover story: "No single standard warranty exists throughout the golf club industry." That said, the parties of the first part are united with respect to abused equipment. Every manufacturer reserves the right to inspect returned merchandise for evidence of malfeasance. In other words, if you've wrapped a club around a tree and now want a replacement: Don't bother.

## X-OUTS

There are golfers who would sooner concede a putt than tee up an x-out (no doubt to the relief of manufacturers). Social ostracism notwithstanding, the savings clearly outweigh any risks. Just how popular are these not-ready-for-prime-time balls? Consider the experience of Bridgestone, which makes the popular Precept line. The company has manufactured golf balls for decades. Traditionally, it eschewed the x-out market altogether. Any ball less than perfect was destroyed. Increasing demand for x-outs, however, and a subsequent rise in market share became so apparent that after thirty-five years of destroying rather than selling its imperfections, Bridgestone quietly joined the fray for the duffer's dollars. Even with the introduction of new "breakthrough" balls, manufacturers today know that some pros won't stock the top-of-the-line ball without an x-out.

The best advice, according to sources, is to stick with logoed balls. There is no guarantee with any x-out, granted—something's off, that's why it's an x-out—but remember this distinction. X-outs are not the orphans filling fishbowls on pro shop counters. The uncertain heritage of these "experienced" balls brings them into question.

They may have been underwater for who knows how long or subjected to other detrimental conditions.

Logoed balls, on the other hand, are victims only of circumstance, typically overruns or canceled orders. They have not been hit, lost, or submerged. An x-out's most common failing is generally accepted to be cosmetic rather than substantive. Without specific standards, however, there is no way of being 100 percent certain.

The USGA does not test x-outs as it does pedigreed balls, although it would be interesting to see what might turn up if it did. In the course of a conversation with a technical advisor at the USGA, he mentioned that he, personally, had no reservations about playing them. In fact, he did play them. Unscientific and unofficial as that may be, it's good enough for me.

Cayman balls, increasingly in vogue—so named for the islands where the "short-distance" ball was introduced—also make great range balls. The Cayman Golf Company sells them for $8.95 a dozen.

## A PEN FOR YOUR THOUGHTS

Sharpies ($1.09), in your choice of eight colors, are excellent indelible markers. Repeated ball washings during a round? No problem. The mark won't come off. You'll lose the ball long before then. Any office supply store has them.

## TENNIS ANYONE?

Once an old tennis ball sufficed. Now there are any number of squeezable and squishy products on the market to serve the same purpose, presumably strengthening the hands and wrists.

The poor man's alternative is much harder than it sounds. Take a full page of the newspaper in one hand. Using only that hand, crumple the page into a ball as tightly as you can.

## PUTTING TIP: TEN CENTS

You can pay Dave Pelz, very much in demand for his short-game expertise, $2,500 to attend his school, or you can cull the substantial benefits of his research on the critical role of putter-head stability—improving your putting in the process—for the princely sum of ten cents.

Dave details his entertaining quest and incisive findings in *Putt Like the Pros* ($12).

One of his training tips for repeatedly hitting the sweet spot on the putter remains to my mind one of his most clever, simple, and effective. He now markets a little plastic doodad that slides over a putter, but two nickels serve nicely.

Tape the nickels to either side of a putter's sweet spot. Leave enough room so the ball, when putted precisely on the sweet spot, cleanly avoids the nickels. Should it touch the nickels in the course of the putt, the ball will careen off weakly.

(Determine the sweet spot by holding the putter by the grip off the ground between your thumb and forefinger. Tap on the face of the club until it doesn't waver. That's the sweet spot.)

Putting with the nickels on the putter face is maddening at first, but with practice it will definitely improve your stroke and your powers of concentration over the ball.

## TWO-BY-FOUR YOUR SLICE

Most driving ranges place two-by-fours every few feet as station dividers. The board makes a convenient and effective antidote to common swing faults. Line up parallel to the two-by-four, placing a ball between you and the board. Put it an inch or so from the board. Physics will insist that should you swing too much inside out, or outside in, you will strike the board during the swing. Swing cleanly and, with other elements in harmony, you should have a good result.

## THE SMOOTH SWINGMAKER (PATENT PENDING)

To truly drive someone batty, consider the Smooth SwingMaker ($12.95) from Sports Products. No doubt well intentioned, it seeks to promote a still head with diabolical simplicity. A Wiffle-type ball with a bell inside, it attaches to a cup via a string. The cup is Velcroed to the front of a visor.

The object is to swing a club while keeping the head down and still. Doing so prevents the ball from bouncing out of the cup.

"Your friends may laugh when they first see your Smooth SwingMaker (TM)," begins the instruction booklet. Laugh? Come now. How about roll around in hysterics?

I tried the Smooth SwingMaker. Of course I did. Desperate times call for desperate measures. Would I incur the humiliation of others to develop a repeatable draw? Willingly.

Not two minutes with the Smooth SwingMaker and it was one #@%&*! worm burner after another. But dagnabbit, that @#$%*! *ball stayed in the $%&$*! cup!*

This is the kind of practice aid that should come with a warning from someone in a position of authority, the USGA perhaps, in cooperation with the Surgeon General. DANGER: Prolonged Unsupervised Use of the Smooth SwingMaker Can Induce Erratic Behavior. Consult Your PGA-approved psychologist.

No question. This is lethal. Pure TNT. Buy several for your friends. Over 4,800 served. (The SSM also makes a compelling but potentially hazardous cat toy.)


## 1,001 USES FOR HOME AND GOLF SWING

A comb, two rubber bands, a phone book, and an extension-cord holder. These are some of John Rhode's favorite teaching tools. One of the most respected instructors in the game, John delights in finding simple and effective alternatives to commercial (i.e., more expensive) practice aids.

You've seen that plastic wrenchlike thing that links the forearms to promote a consistent putting stroke. It's $29.95. John found an alternative at the hardware store for around a buck and a half. You can too. It's called an extension-cord holder. The idea is to keep the club in front and the pieces of the triangle (the forearms and upper body) moving in unison through the stroke.

The fruits of John's forays through toy and hardware stores work well enough to attract a client list that reads like a *Who's Who* of the pro tour. His ideas also are a lot of fun. Familiar household items provide concrete images that simplify the complexities of the swing. The imagery provides reminders that you and I can take to the course.

The comb and rubber bands convey the importance of a firm wrist through the putting and chipping stroke. Place the comb along the left wrist (for righties). Hold it in place with the rubber bands, as shown in the accompanying photo. Now putt or chip. The comb prevents the right hand from flipping or turning and spoiling the shot. The wrist stays flat and firm all the way through the stroke without breaking down.

Here's another from John's creative arsenal. Take your stance holding a not overly thick phone book. Press it between your palms. The palms should evenly face each other. Take a slow backswing, bringing the book back at a forty-five-degree angle over the shoulder. At the top, it's as if you are holding the book like a tray resting upon your right hand.

Swing your arms back down on the same forty-five-degree angle. As you return to where you started, your hands should slowly rotate so that the palms again squarely face each other.

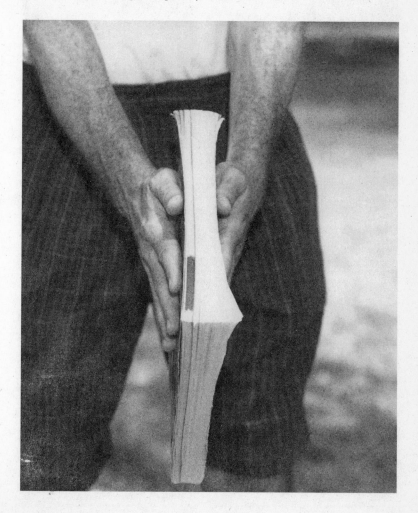

Should the right hand end up underneath as you approach where
the ball would be on the downswing, that would produce a slice. If
the right hand is on top as you move through the ball, that would
produce a hook. What you're doing is simply practicing what John
calls squaring up your hands at impact.

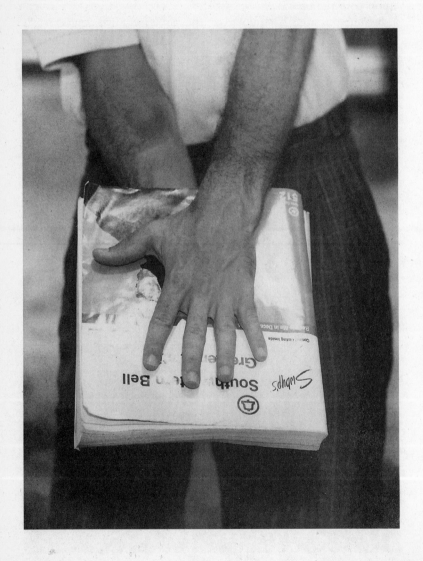

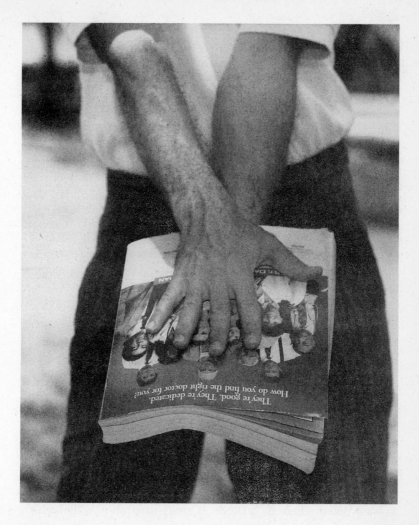

## FOLLOWING THROUGH

Hell can take many forms. Rather than fire and brimstone (or even several hours closeted with the Smooth SwingMaker), I see a course shimmering at dawn. The stillness is invigorating. No one's here! So high are the spirits, the emptiness arouses no suspicions. Neither does a primo parking space. Golf shoes, putter, and wallet have not been forgotten. Practice putts fall crisply. Cool thoughts suffuse the brain. Today, a tantalizing thought percolates, could be the day.

Then comes word of the tournament, the temporary greens, the rototilled fairways, the frost, the locust infestation, the hostage situation or any of a dozen other unforeseen events that explain why the place is practically deserted. Usually, though, it's a tournament. On the worst of days—surprise! The course is closed. Arghhh.

Does it really need to be said that this appalling tragedy can easily be avoided? All it takes is one simple act of civility and prudence. Pick up the phone and call ahead.

## THE THREE BEST DAYS TO PLAY GOLF

In all fairness the following advice is prefaced with the understanding that in portions of the country, late January and even April are inhospitable to golf for all but fundamentalists or amphibians, or both.

That said, here are the suggested three best days of the year to play golf:

Super Bowl Sunday
Easter Sunday
Mother's Day

I didn't say it would be easy.

## ON WALKING

No one to my knowledge has formally quantified the widely held assumption that carts speed up play or, conversely, that walking slows it down. There is, however, a study that confirms the benign attributes of walking while playing golf.

Edward A. Palank and Ernest H. Hargreaves, Jr., surveyed twenty-eight male golfers, ages forty-eight to eighty, average age of sixty-one. The control group was composed of sixteen sedentary nongolfers between the ages of thirty-eight and sixty-eight (median age of fifty). The participants were told not to alter their diet or deviate from their normal smoking or drinking habits during the course of the study.

The golfers played three times a week. The findings detailed in "The Benefits of Walking the Golf Course: Effects on Lipoprotein Levels and Risk Ratios" determined the golfers walked approximately eight thousand yards, or about four and a half miles. They burned an estimated 470 calories each time they played. (No details were provided on their handicaps. Your mileage may vary.)

Palank and Hargreaves determined, "the extent of reduction among golfers was quite significant, as was a decrease in some low-density lipoproteins, a concomitant increase in high-density lipoproteins [considered beneficial], and an improvement in the ratio of high-density to low-density lipoproteins."

Their finding? "Golf, which is a leisure-time activity that is associated with a high compliance rate when compared with other forms of exercise, is a sport *that should be encouraged* [emphasis added]." Thank you, gentlemen. There you have it, scientific proof. The next time anyone gives you any lip about golf, or walking, ask him how his high-density lipoproteins are doing.

## BRASSIE COME HOME

Nothing short of a miracle or a random act of kindness (take your pick) will ensure that a lost club will find its way home. Marking clubs with an address and phone number offers at least a fighting chance. One came back to me long after I'd given up hope. Someone found it, put it in his bag, and forgot about it. Six weeks later the Samaritan noticed it (he hadn't played since), saw the phone number, and called.

Personalized club labels seem unnecessarily pricey, $10 for eighteen labels, for example.

Two tightwad suggestions: Imprint Products sells 250 for $4.95, Artistic Greetings sells 250 for $6.95. Both offer up to four lines of print and several styles from gold to clear. They advertise regularly in *Parade* magazine.

Yup, they're mailing labels, not as fancy or as indelible as labels made especially for golf clubs, but they suffice. You get so many that replacing them is no big deal. And, of course, you can use extras on your envelopes.

## BIODEGRADABLE TEES . . .

An estimated forty thousand birch trees are used each year to produce 1.7 billion golf tees. Needless to say demand is up. Several tee designs using recycled materials or organic mixes provide an ecologically benign alternative. None, however, has as yet caught the public's fancy. The bottom line, of course, remains price. For most golfers the cost is still prohibitive.

Eco-Tee from Dennco in New Hampshire looks identical to a wood tee. Eco-Tees retail in packs of twenty for $1.95, one hundred for $7.95. Made of Novon 3001, a specialty polymer composed of potatoes and cornstarch, they have a plastic feel. Completely biodegradable, petroleum- and paint-free, they disintegrate at the rate of leaves or grass clippings.

In a series of random unscientific tests involving several free-swinging members of the River City Golf Association of Austin, Texas, the Eco-Tee got a thumbs-up with one proviso. It is definitely a one-shotter. No one was able to use a tee twice. They snap like twigs. Kmart and Target stock them. (For promotional purposes, Dennco will offer Eco-Tees to large tournaments.)

Terra Tees from TerraForm are another option. A carton of fifty boxes of fifteen tees sells for $47.75. TerraForm also has a "Quick Dissolve" tee in promotional four-pack matchbooks. Imprinted with a corporate logo or message, they include a fully compostable and biodegradable ball marker. After a day of watering, the tees start puffing up like a weary heavyweight. Ecco/Green Packaging sells one thousand for about $45, about five cents a tee.

Gary Player endorses The Green Tee, made of "non-toxic photodegradable and biodegradable compounds and filled with a fertilizer material." A box of 750 tees sells for only $25. Used exclusively in South African PGA events, The Green Tee is endorsed by the South African Nature Foundation. It's available from The Gary Player Golf Equipment Company.

And then there's the Tastee Tee. Harmon's Grain Products in McCook, Nebraska, for forty years a leader in toothpick manufacturing, now sells artificial-mint-flavored tees. Perfect for discreet dental hygienics or nervous Nellies, the tees pack flavor promised to "last to the 19th hole!" They're sure to help you "go for the greens" (between your teeth, anyway). Other flavors in the works: lemon, chocolate crème de menthe, black jelly bean, and cinnamon. Also biodegradable, they're made of a softer, yet high-fiber, wood to lock in flavor. At pro shops nationwide, ask for them by name. Available in a decorative tartan tin. Golden Golf can help you find them locally. Question: Can nutritionally supplemented, edible, or even the vodka-tonic tee be far off?

### . . . AND MORE TEES

Several conventional tee makers sell directly to the public. While they all require minimum orders, don't be deterred. With some teamwork, you can realize some significant savings, going in for bulk.

H. Arnold Wood Turning, Inc.
Minimum order 20,000 (2-1/8″)                    $14.00/M

Eastern Golf
Minimum order $50 (1-7/8″)                    $13.95/M

Atlas Pen & Pencil Corp.
Minimum order 10,000 (2-1/8″)                    $12.15/M

Great Lakes Golf Ball Co.
Minimum order 1,000 (1-7/8″)                    $12.22/M

See also Finding the Green in New Hampshire for an unbeatable price.

### MARKS OF DISTINCTION

Chi Chi Rodriguez apparently won't mark his ball tails-side-up. His caddie told *Golfweek* that he marks birdie putts with nickels and par putts with a quarter. No pennies.

Every coin shop keeps a box of common inexpensive foreign coins. Compared with those flimsy plastic discs (or worse, a tee, leaf, candy-bar wrapper, etc.—), they make classy markers (and an inexpensive gift idea from child to parent).

An old British twopence is a perfect size. Unusual coins, square or with a hole in the center, also work nicely. A little Never Dull or some steel wool or polish and they shine up nicely. Oversized coins like silver or half dollars are kind of cumbersome.

My favorite marker comes from my friend Dan Strait (800/725-8877). In the music business for years, Dan saved the ivory stripped from old or broken piano keys. He carves authentic scrimshaw ball markers ($10) on the pieces. These are the real thing, not the imitation stuff. Dan has a wonderful eye. He won't carve them forever, just as long as people keep bringing in old pianos to have the keys replaced with plastic. Dan's doing nothing illegal with respect to the international ban on ivory. He just recycles keys that would otherwise get tossed. His distinctive golf scenes are truly special. He'll also etch a name across the front if you'd like.

### BUZZ OFF

Avon's Skin So Soft apparently has the hunting world abuzz. Insects don't like it, and it makes hunters smell better, two sterling qualities. My own preference is Mos*quit*o, a blend of herbal repellents akin to those discussed in Janette Grainger and Connie Moore's book, *Natural Insect Repellents for Pets, People, & Plants.* Mos*quit*o ($6 for 1/2 ounce) was put to the test camping near Memphis and in two Louisiana state parks in July. The herbal blends of citronella, pennyroyal, and eucalyptus proved remarkably effective, better than any commercial product I've used in decades of camping in various states that can each lay legitimate claim to the mosquito as state bird. With Mos*quit*o, nobody laid a mandible on me.

These environmentally friendly alternatives are inexpensive and readily available. They also double as a terrific vinaigrette in a pinch. Just kidding.

Janette and Connie's book includes recipes and suggestions for a wide range of herbal applications in the home. The book is available from The Herb Bar for $8, but the authors have graciously permitted me the inclusion of the following tips for making your own bug dope.

### Skin Moisturizer and Repellent

Using a good quality vegetable-based oil such as safflower or corn, pour enough of it into the container (lidded glass jars or heavy duty plastics—amber or dark colored containers will preserve the mixture longer) until it is 3/4 full. Fill the remaining quarter of the jar with citronella, pennyroyal or any other repellent oil. . . .

There is no precise science to diluting oils. . . . A good starting point is to begin by using half a teaspoon of oil per pint of cool water. . . . If this formula provides little or only short-term protection, try one or more teaspoons of oil per pint of water. . . .

Alternatively, use a combination of repellent oils according to personal taste. After capping and shaking the mixture well, it will be ready for immediate use.

Daub the underside of a cap or visor's brim with repellent to enhance effectiveness around your face. (Be careful of staining expensive fabrics. Do not put it on silk.)

Since perfumed soaps are like honey to the bee (and gnat and fly), you might consider laying off smelling like a rose out on the course. North Country Soap sells a glycerine citronella soap in liquid ($3.95) or bar ($2.75). It also sells tick repellent ($6). Prices for the above are taken from The Boundary Waters Catalog.

Quantum's Buzz Away is a natural alternative to diethyl metatoluamide (deet), classified as a pesticide by the Environmental Protection Agency. Buzz Away comes in pump spray (2 ounces for $4.99) or lotion (4 ounces for $6.99 with SPF 15 sunscreen). It contains lemongrass, cedarwood, eucalyptus, citronella, and peppermint oils with a castor oil base. It's available in health food and outdoor stores.

## SAVING FACE . . .

No need to harp on the risks of skin cancer, the most common form of the disease. The American Cancer Society's prediction of 600,000 new cases each year is well known, as is the EPA's estimation of 200,000 U.S. deaths attributable to melanoma over the next fifty years. Everyone knows that a wide-brimmed hat, bandanna, long-sleeved shirt, and pants afford the best protection.

No, until someone invents a greaseless product, the best advice about sunscreen, other than using it, comes from my friend and *Golf Etiquette* coauthor Barbara Puett.

I was grousing one day about trying to grip a club with sunscreen on my fingers. Barbara told me that when she's got a game, she puts her sunscreen on first thing in the morning, along with her makeup. For me, it's right after shaving. End of problem. To keep the stuff off your fingers, there are several roll-stick applicators. Bullfrog has a half-ounce sunscreen on a stick for $4.49, SPF 18.

Kiss My Face combines sunscreen with herbal insect repellents. KISS OFF, with a 15 SPF sunscreen, retails for $6.29 for four ounces.

## . . . AND MAINTAINING A FLUID SWING

Playing in hot weather can pose other problems. Here are strategies on beating the heat from Vanderbilt University trainer Mike Shue.

"If you're going to play in the heat," Shue told Nashville's *The Tennessean,* "it's a good idea to start getting your body fluids up the evening before. If you wait until you're out there, it's too late. It takes a while for the fluid to leave the gut and be absorbed by the body."

Retaining fluids throughout the round is critical to keeping cool, Shue says. "Hydration is important before, during and after, especially in the humidity we have here. The humidity determines the amount of sweat that will be evaporated. If it's humid, there's nowhere for the perspiration to go, and so the sweat doesn't have the cooling effect."

Shue strongly advocates golfers avoid drinks with alcohol or caffeine. "Basically those drinks will just increase the dehydration. If you have a couple of beers or Cokes, now you're losing fluids in two ways, through sweat and urination."

Light-headedness, fiery skin, and nausea are the initial signs of heatstroke. When they occur, "You need to get the body cooled down as fast as possible."

To bear the heat of August in Houston, former Masters champion Jack Burke, Jr., once advised U.S. Amateur competitors, "After you hit your drive, man, don't just walk straight down the fairway. You'll burn up. Head for the woods, get some shade, then cut across to your ball."

## SAFETY FIRST

Our story takes place in Kansas City several years ago. I'm indebted to "Kitty from Kansas City" for bringing the incident to the attention of Ann Landers.

Tom Watson was hosting his annual celebrity golf tournament when, near the start of his round, disaster struck in the form of a broken zipper.

"Need I tell you he was mighty embarrassed," wrote Kitty. Wait. A five-time winner of the British Open, however, is nothing if not resourceful. Requesting a safety pin from the gallery, Watson procured same, swiftly made the repair, and went on about his business.

Got room in your bag for a safety pin?

## A TOWEL THAT STAYS ON YOUR BAG

Golf towels are far too easy to lose. The blame partly rests on an archaic fastening device, a wire clasp that bends too easily, pinches too often, and comes unhooked at the drop of a bag. Sealing tape over the clasp doesn't help. There has to be something better.

There is, but it's expensive. One of the golf catalogs has monogrammed towels that snap onto a standard bag for around $10. Snaps make sense. Rain hood ports around the top of the bag are at just the right height for a towel. Taking it with you to the green's a snap. And when it's in place it stays put. Hmmmm.

Lo and behold, there is an inexpensive method to add snaps to your golf towels. This will work for every bag with a snap-on rain hood. For the high-tech bags that don't provide snap-on hoods, you can add a snap onto any bag without much trouble.

Tandy Leather, with 275 stores nationwide, sells a package of ten dot snaps for $1.98. The other supplies needed are an anvil, $.98, and the setter, $1.79. For $4.75, you can do ten towels. The dot snaps— they're not grommets—are catalog #1264. The tiny anvil is #1804. The setter is the tool for punching the pieces together. The instructions are included in Tandy's catalog, which also advertises nifty kits to make an Indian headdress, moccasins, and lots of other neat stuff.

Sun Mountain bags use Velcro for their rain hoods. Velcro is nearly as cheap and easy to affix to a towel as a snap. Any sewing store will have it. Get the sew-on kind rather than the stick-on kind (which can come off the towel in the wash).

## REPLACING LOST GLOVE SNAPS

Wherever lost towels go there must be a pile of missing glove snaps alongside. It just so happens that Tandy Leather has those too. They're called garment snaps (#1248) and come in packs of twenty for $2.98. They're ostensibly for dudeing up Western-style shirts but are identical to golf glove and shoe snaps. In your choice of seven glow-pearl colors. To put them together you will need a garment snap setter (#1781) and a rubber anvil. Total cost: $4.98. Whether this is $4.98 you'd rather put toward the cost of a new glove is the kind of decision that separates the merely cost-conscious from the incurably cheap. (The discovery was so exciting, however, I just couldn't resist passing it on.)

## IN ONE'S CUPS

Along with a smattering of broken tees and dirt, the most common sight when I annually clean my bag are the crumpled remains of those paper-triangle drinking cups. They barely hold enough liquid to rinse and spit. Meager and wasteful, they often end up littering the course, dropped or easily blown from bins. And when you most need a drink, surprise! No cups! The dispenser's empty!

This may sound ridiculous, but an obvious solution is to carry your own cup. Even the toniest camping stores sell reasonably priced drinking cups. (Apparently no one calls them collapsible cups anymore.) It must be the cheapest thing at REI, but the store sells a rubber folding cup, with a quenching seven-fluid-ounce payload, for $2.

Don't misunderstand me. This is golf, not prospecting. One needn't set out provisioned like a 49er. There have been times that I've enviously eyed another man's water bottle, but even I have my limits. Water bottles, coolers, cans, etc., seem so much excess baggage (and good hiding places for intrepid hornets and yellow jackets). A one-ounce collapsible cup, however, will hardly weigh you down.

For those who can't play golf without a portable mini bar, Top It Can Caps from Chesal Industries (two for $1.95) will prevent insect invaders from sneaking inside. Chesal also stocks an impressive line of portable products designed to keep cans cold.

## DIY YARDAGE BOOK

Those who play well enough to benefit from a course guide will like Yardage Marker ($5.95) from Practicorp. No artistic skill is required to complete this do-it-yourself yardage book. You make it up as you go along over several rounds.

Handy instructions, a symbol guide, and a diagrammed sample hole make it fairly idiot-proof. You just fill in the blanks with artwork, arrows, and yardage. There's also room to pepper the illustrations with strategic or inspirational messages.

Those without the game to benefit from Cliffs Notes of this kind might still enjoy packing a copy of Yardage Marker. Confound friends and opponents by studiously consulting a blank copy.

## STAT SAVING

Someone at the PGA Tour must've put down the sports section one day in disgust, recognizing that professional golf was clearly statistically challenged. The game lacked the breadth and sophistication of numerical minutiae so beloved in other sports. No RBIs or first downs. No scoring leaders or first-serve percentages. The game was a stranger to scoreboard pages across America. Something had to be done. Why not come up with some golfing equivalents? Give the folks some gooey appetizers like sand saves, driving stats, and the percentage of downhill putts made by former Southeast Conference members wearing all-natural fibers after eating grilled chicken sandwiches. Announcers will love us for it, he must've figured (and so they do).

Which brings us to Logisoft, because compiling and mulling over your own GIRs and total driving is loads more fun than reading about someone else's. Its GolfWorks program will plot and print forty-nine separate reports: putting and green stats, up-and-downs, scores relative to par threes, fours, and fives, driving stats, all that good stuff. Easy to use, toll-free customer support is also available. Another option is *Golf Digest*'s Scorecard for Windows from Parsons Technology.

## A ROUND AND AROUND

A cordless alternative for stat gazers, Pin High's The Round File ($6.95) is a pocket-sized notebook that includes space to record the particulars for twenty-four rounds.

Fairways and greens in regulation, putts, par, handicap, scores for four players at a time, sand saves, up-and-downs, even room for immortalizing the infamous "other" is provided. A practice log is included on the back cover. The Round File is available at off-course retail chain stores.

## GETTING AND KEEPING A GRIP

When should grips be replaced? What about that business of "If you play once a week, regrip once a year"? What can the average player do to enhance or prolong the life of a grip? Here's some industry responses:

*Care and Feeding:*

Using warm water and soap with a scrub brush, rinsing [*sic*] away skin oils and dirt build-up. This should be done as often as needed . . . Washing the grip when cleaning the clubhead will maintain and

enhance the livelihood of the grip . . . Keep in mind that mild detergents should be used at all times for the sake of the rubber compound composition.
—"Answers to Your Gripping Questions," from Avon Golf Grips

Scrub them in warm water with a mild detergent and abrasive pad, rinse thoroughly, and towel dry.
—"Tips on Grips," Ken Venturi, from *Golf Pride Grips*

All you need is soapy water and a small scrubbing brush to clean the grips regularly, after every two or three rounds of golf.
—from *David Graham's Guide to Golf Equipment*
(See Reading the Green)

The first signs of deterioration are grips that are slick and hard or cracked and split from age and frequency of use. Grips in this condition should definitely be changed because you can rest assured that they are adding strokes to, instead of subtracting strokes from your golf game . . . For the average golfer, once a year should be about right . . .
—"Tips on Grips," Ken Venturi, from *Golf Pride Grips*

You need to replace the grips on your clubs every three years if you play more than 30 rounds of golf a year.
—from *David Graham's Guide to Golf Equipment*


### TAKE TWO PRACTICE SWINGS AND CALL ME IN THE MORNING

The idea of consulting a stranger, over the phone no less, on an intensely personal matter is not really appealing, especially when it's on the meter. I suppose, though, if there's room in this world for phone sex and the Internet, emergency golf road service is hardly far-fetched.

Golf-on-Call (800/8484-PRO) offers around-the-clock anonymous consultation with a PGA professional for $2.50 a minute. Another source is Primeline Golf Tips's "High Handicap Hotline," a recorded series of weekly updated tips (900/329-1630. Also $2.50 a minute).

At a considerable savings, of course, you may find it equally therapeutic to consult with the occupant of the next stool.

## LEAVING CLUBS IN THE TRUNK

They could get stolen first of all, but leaving clubs in the trunk never seemed a particularly good idea. An August drive through Yuma (108°F) and Palm Springs (110°F) sparked a genuine concern. Lit a fire, you might say.

Could it really get hot enough in the trunk to adversely affect a golf club?

This burning question was posed to the brains at GolfSmith International. Here's what they told me: The concern centers on two points, the epoxies that affix the head to the shaft and the tape that underpins the grip. For the epoxy to begin to break down, they estimated it would take temperatures of 250°F continuously for a duration of thirty days. Yuma was hot but not that hot. So far so good. The grip tape, however, is not nearly as resilient. Temperatures of 160° to 180° would be enough to soften the tape.

Until further studies on trunk temperatures (stay tuned), it seems best to play it cool, and safe, by taking your sticks inside.

## CLEANING CLUBS

Brookstone has sadly discontinued a brass wire brush recommended to me by Bob Kuntz, cofounder of the Golf Collectors Society and author of *Antique Golf Clubs, Their Restoration and Preservation* (available through GolfWorks). Bob's a man with a sustained belief in the positive influence of inexpensive household items like Elmer's glue and Murphy's Wood Oil Soap. He agrees that some of the brushes on the market specifically advertised for club cleaning are far too sharp and abrasive. He suggests a soft wire brush like those used by furniture strippers. This brush resembles a long toothbrush with bristles 9/16″ × 9/16″ × 9″ long, about 1/2″ tall. It took me two calls to locate one ($1.25). Look under Furniture Repairing & Refinishing—Suppliers in the Yellow Pages. With luck you'll find a three-brush pack that Bob found for $1.50. It includes one steel (good for cleaning shoe soles), one brass, and one nylon brush.

The Fuller Brush Company's hand and nail brush ($5.99) is soft and sturdy enough to scrub dirt from grooves without damaging anything. This brush is ideal for scrubbing grips.

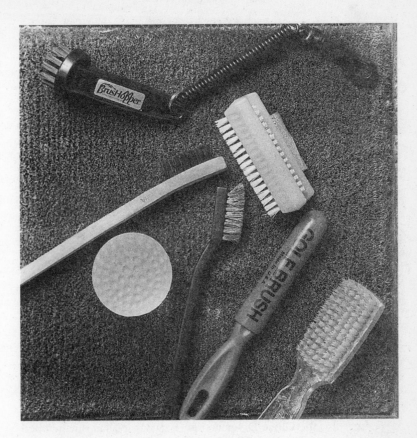

Two others: "Hang-Me-Up" by Brushtech has taut plastic bristles and a leather hanging strap; BrushHopper has nylon bristles and a retractable rubber coil that clips onto a bag.

## WRONG-HANDED AND CORINTHIAN LEATHER GLOVES

The best annual garage sale in town had a table full of new golf gloves. After trying one on, I nabbed several. It wasn't until later that I realized I'd bought two for the wrong hand. There must be something the gloves are good for, I thought, and of course there is. Wrong-handed gloves are great for cold-weather golf.

So many materials are used to make gloves one wonders that after cabretta, Abyssinian sheepskin, and various synthetic blends, whether Corinthian leather, that distinguished-sounding but meaningless material, can be far behind.

Cubic Balance, for instance, sells a glove made of Japanese sea snake (around $12). At the company's suggestion, I immersed a gloved hand completely in a bucket of water. (Don't try this with just any sea snake.) After it dried, darned if the thing wasn't as good as new.

With respect to wear, a glove manufacturer once confided to *Golf Pro* magazine: "We guardedly say a leather glove should last eight to twelve rounds and really don't think synthetic gloves will last much longer." Another responded with this analogy:

> How many miles do you get out of your car tires? It depends on the roads you drive, the alignment of your wheels and other factors. How you hold and swing the club and the makeup of the grips on your clubs also dictates how long a glove will last.

Pocketec sells the Lady Classic, a women's golf glove that accommodates long nails and a ring. It comes in several styles (from $10 to $15). Pocketec will sell one by mail, if you can't find one locally.

For a louder fashion statement, Tour Golf Company sells a glove made of 80 percent nylon and 20 percent Lycra in fluorescent colors and downright psychedelic patterns. The gloves are machine-washable and can be scrunched up without any adverse effects.

There's also the Glove Dryer Frame ($3.95), a plastic outstretched hand, to help prolong a glove's usefulness. Such is golf's popularity that gloves now routinely turn up on sale at budget stores, like Target, but I've pretty much given up. Having lost many more gloves than I've found, for the duration it's me and the sea snake.

## SOLE SEARCHING

There was a time when a new baseball glove or a pair of jeans required a certain commitment. The baseball glove needed softening balms and nights under the mattress. All manner of nonsense was used with jeans. Today gloves are ready to go from store shelf to outfield in the time it takes to remove the tag. Jeans are prewashed or broken in with buckshot.

Golf shoes still require some modest prep work. To make it easier to replace worn spikes later, before you wear them, take the spikes off. Grease the threads with Vaseline, then firmly screw the spikes back in place.

Connecticut Pro Golf Discount hands out an excellent set of guidelines, "SHOE DO'S," from which the following suggestions are excerpted. Nothing revelatory, the shoes you save may be your own.

- Replace all spikes as a group when most have worn down 1/8″.
- Lost spikes should be replaced as soon as possible after cleaning receptacle with a Q-tip.
- Always allow your shoes to air dry slowly at room temperature. And never leave them in the trunk of your car, especially when they're wet.
- Clean your shoes often; after every round if possible. Clean spikes with the bristle type spike cleaner found at most golf courses, and a damp towel is usually all that is required for the uppers.
- For longevity, if at all possible, do not wear the same pair of shoes two days in a row.
- The use of shoe trees helps to maintain the original shape of your shoes.

David Graham mentions a neat tip (see "Straight Dope on Equipment" in "Reading the Green"). Stuff soaked shoes with crumpled newspaper to absorb excess moisture. "This will put the shoe back in shape and avoid the problem of the shoe tree locking in moisture where it is in contact with the inside of the upper," he writes. *Do not* place them near a heater to dry out. And by all means, if you want to save money, avoid those blister packs with only a handful of replacement spikes. Several catalogs sell generic spikes by the box at a considerable savings. Just make sure they'll fit your brand.

## NO MORE BROKEN SPIKE WRENCHES

You can break a spike wrench trying to use it on holes encrusted with dirt. (At least I did.) A solution: First pour a little hydrogen peroxide into the holes. The dirt will start dislodging in seconds. Clean them out with a safety pin. Towel dry. Wrench away.


## GO FIGURE

If each member of a foursome wastes fifteen seconds per hole, that's one minute lost, or a total of eighteen minutes added to the length of the round without any other calamities. Here are ten effortless ways to speed play that require nothing more than good sense:

1. Carry an extra ball in your pocket.
2. When someone looks at you to hit, as long as it's safe—hit.
3. Leave your bag or cart off the green toward the next tee.
4. Closest in (to the hole) tends the pin. First in (to putt out) retrieves the pin.
5. Line up your putt while others are putting.
6. Step aside as soon as you tee off.
7. Buy your drink from the beverage cart after you play your shot.
8. Finish the story walking down the fairway.
9. Take one less practice swing.
10. Help someone else find his or her ball.

The following advice appears on the back of a booklet prepared by the Greens Committee at Bucknell Golf Club in Lewisburg, Pennsylvania.

A fresh ball mark repaired by a player takes only
FIVE SECONDS
A freshly repaired ball mark will completely heal in
24 HOURS
A fresh ball mark left unrepaired for only one hour requires
15 DAYS TIME
before the ugly scar has satisfactorily healed.
PLEASE REPAIR ALL BALL MARKS

## SHIPPING AND PACKING

UT Golf sells half a dozen club-shipping cartons, square- or triangle-shaped, for $7.75. GolfWorks will sell you one for $5, then apply a $2.50 credit to the cost of any club repairs. Unfortunately, 3 1/2″ × 5 3/4″ × 48″ corrugated carton is not a stock size. You might let your fingers do the walking, starting under Packaging Materials in the Yellow Pages. Several of the franchised packing stores do carry a similar box, albeit a little longer, 52″. Prices vary from $1.59 to $2.95 a box. Be sure to wrap clubs well. Collectors use bubble wrap, old socks, and sealing tape to protect club heads during shipping and stuff in plenty of padding to prevent the clubs from sliding.

Several off-course golf stores said they'd be happy to find a good home for the pile of old boxes taking up space in the back. Try them first.

When traveling, unless you've got a hardened plastic case, turn your clubs head side down into the bag before you slip the cover on. Put head covers or a sweater over the grips for some extra padding.

Several airlines now sell golf bag covers. When mine was ripped apart in transit, USAir made good on the spot with a replacement. It didn't have as much padding as mine, but the zipper was much, much stronger. I even had a choice of colors. USAir ticket counters also sell a sturdy canvas-type cover in navy blue for $30. It comes with a small lock. United will wrap a bag with heavy plastic for free. It also sells a nylon cover for $26 and a "pro size" cover for $10 more.

Worried about my bag's tripod stand getting damaged en route, I sent queries to several manufacturers asking for advice. None responded, but it seems sensible to secure the tripod in some way. I used a sleeping-bag strap and fastened it tightly to keep the tripod from opening and then getting clipped. It's worked so far.

## A POTASSIUM PICK-ME-UP

Bruce Lietzke's caddie, Al Hansen, in an inspired act of sleuthing, once slipped a banana under the head cover of his boss's driver. PGA Tour veteran Lietzke is renowned among his peers for his relaxed work ethic. He'd told his caddie that he would not be practicing during an upcoming sabbatical. Hansen didn't believe it; hence the ploy. Six weeks later when they reunited, the proof was in the pudding. The banana was untouched.

Let alone under a head cover, a banana in a golf bag would seem to tempt the Fates. Nonetheless the fruit is justly hailed as a nutritional dynamo. Tour pros often munch on them at the turn. And after four hours in the hot sun, nothing energizes the body quite like a frozen banana on a stick, a culinary feat even a bachelor can manage. Before freezing, peel and wrap in wax paper.

What's so great about bananas? They're very high in natural sugars, full of magnesium (needed to convert blood sugar into energy and vital in preventing heart attacks). They taste a heck of a lot better than those peat-mossy energy bars, and they're also a monster source of potassium.

So?

According to the *Nutrition Almanac:* "Early symptoms of potas-

sium deficiency include general weakness and impairment of neuromuscular function, poor reflexes, and soft, sagging muscles." Not
exactly the stuff of a furious charge on the back side. (But it does
make for a novel excuse. "What can I say, my neuromuscular function's impaired from a prolonged potassium deficiency. I hate it
when that happens.")

Of course, nothing resuscitates the spirits quite like the humble
banana in consort with the equally restorative properties of a
postround frozen daiquiri. In his seminal work, *Old Mr. Boston De
Luxe Official Bartender's Guide* (1946 edition), Mr. B details the path
to higher consciousness through the following elixir, the West Indies
Frosted Cocktail:

> Juice 1 lime
> 1 teaspoon powdered sugar
> 2 oz. Old Mr. Boston Imported Rum (to this, I take the liberty
> of adding frozen banana chunks, cut before frozen).
> Agitate in electric mixer filled with shaved ice for about 2 min-
> utes. Strain through coarse meshed strainer into 6 oz.
> Champagne glass.
> (The strainer can be dispensed with, and any glass will do.
> Consume very slowly. Repeat as needed.)

Better natural foods stores sell sweetened or unsweetened dried
banana chips that will fit in your bag without spawning fruit flies, if
you forget them. They are, however, murder on your fillings.

## PROPOSED: A NATIONAL DAY OF AMNESTY

Millions of golf pencils are MIA, desk-drawered, glove-compart-
mented, and golf-bagged in obscurity. This unplanned obsolescence
has got to end. Golfers, sharpen your old pencils! Return them to
active service! Clear out the deadwood! Recycle those pencils!

What municipally owned course would not appreciate the savings?
Then let us set aside a day to honor this national effort for pencil
renewal and liberation, National Golf Pencil Amnesty Day.

As a matter of fact, there are golf pencil collectors, folks whose
holdings near Ripley's proportions. Should a course turn you down,
you can always reuse them yourself. Thanks, but don't send them to

me. Send them instead to Brother Bill McCarthy. Brother Bill, who wistfully recalls the days when courses had "clergy card" discounts, has started a golf museum at Central Catholic Marianist High School in San Antonio, Texas. He'd be glad to add them to the fledgling collection. Send your donation, the farther-flung the better, to:

Brother Bill McCarthy
Central Catholic
Marianist High School
1403 North St. Mary's
San Antonio, TX 78215-1785

## ODDS AND ENDS

Along with a wholly entertaining catalog of lifesize miniature golf props like circus animals, and other range and supply equipment, Eastern Golf Corporation will sell you one flag, one flagstaff, and one cup for your backyard, if that's all you want—or a step-on spike cleaner.

As Harvey Penick suggests, you may very well have one in your garage, but if you don't, his favorite practice aid, a weed cutter, is about $14 at local hardware stores. Remember to pretend you're being paid by the hour and take your time.

CHO-PAT offers a wide variety of products aimed at supporting or reducing pain with respect to knees, lower backs, shins, wrists, and Achilles tendons.

# THROUGH THE GREEN

COPE'S

J. H. TAYLOR.
TOP OF SWING FOR A DRIVE.

"Kenilworth"
CIGARETTES.

*Personal expressions of golf devotion dot—one might even say litter—the landscape. There are innumerable avenues to take: clubs, balls, autographs, photographs, ice trays, trading cards, cocktail napkins, goofy signs, goofier mailboxes; there are even golf credit cards and checks. Not to put too fine a point on it, golf gifts can have a cringing effect.*

*The following pages are hereby entered as evidence, lest there be any doubt that there is considerably more to life than exploding golf balls and the works of LeRoy Neiman. Company addresses and phone numbers for products in this section are listed in the Appendix.*

## GOLF-AHOLIC ANONYMOUS

Marilyn Clark's Imaginating series includes the accurately titled "Golf-Aholic" #99 ($6). Instructions are provided for creating needlepoint visor fronts, bag towels, sweatshirts, drink holders, and a suitable-for-framing relief of Santa holding a golf bag with the inscription "All I want for Christmas is a Hole in One."

## KNIT WITS

There are those who frown on needlepoint golfing Santas and such, but if you or someone you know is looking for homemade golf gift ideas, yes, Virginia, there are patterns for knitted head covers.

Ann Norling has several, rated "very easy" to "experienced." Golf Club Cover Mitts, Pattern #4 by Betsy Tempy ($4), features Argyle and Irish designs. Directions are also included to make those lovable little beanies that go on top. Local yarn shops will have, or can order, the pattern.

## SEND THE PRESIDENT VEERING
## TO THE RIGHT

Several companies imprint photos on golf balls. My favorite is GolfShots, which does a very spiffy Clinton, Bush, or Quayle.

A dozen are expensive ($29.95), but you can mix and match to make a sleeve of three balls for $10. Choose from the above or take

a whack at Ted Kennedy, Ross Perot, Hillary Clinton, Saddam Hussein, Pat Buchanan, or David Duke. GolfShots will also immortalize your mother-in-law or ex-husband. Top-Flites are standard, but you can save yourself $6 by providing your own balls, an option that most of GolfShot's competitors do not offer.

## SIFTING THROUGH THE STUFF OF LEGENDS

Fred Raphael pounded Madison Avenue for years trying to drum up support for his idea of putting senior golfers on television. He knew the idea was sound, but he could hardly have anticipated the success the Senior PGA Tour would enjoy. He could also have never anticipated Howard Smith.

An entirely sound and engaging individual, "Smitty" attended the first Legends and got so caught up in the bonhomie, so taken with the outpouring of fellowship and camaraderie, that he had no hesitation in dropping $2,000 on as many commemorative Legends of Golf plates and souvenirs as he could carry.

Still, something was missing. As he started back to his car for the last time, Smitty wondered if there wasn't some other, better way of hanging on to those special feelings. As it happened he paused beside the Dempsey Dumpster. "They were throwing all this neat stuff away. I couldn't understand it," he recalls. "I saw them dumping it and thought, 'That's where all the history is, that's where all the neat stuff is.' " On a whim Smitty consulted with various bewildered tournament officials. He then purchased the contents of the tournament Dumpster, lock, stock, and banana peel. "Oh jeez, did it stink!"

Discarding the less-attractive matter from his now own personal dustbin of history, Smitty culled a wealth of paper ephemera from the tournament that started the Senior Tour: personal letters, parking badges, media badges, programs, daily tournament ribbons. "I didn't do it for commercial reasons," Smitty emphasizes. "This was all a labor of love. Come on, this is great stuff!"

Smitty's put together a package of early Legends memorabilia, which he sells for $15, programs are $7 (no, they don't smell). They're in great shape and yessir, as he is wont to say, "It's pretty neat stuff." Smitty is also one of the few people you'll meet in the collectibles racket who'd just as soon talk with someone genuinely interested as make a sale.

Another curious bit of PGA ephemera is sold by Chuck Furjanic, a dealer in antique clubs and such. He has a stack of actual scorecards from the 1982 and 1983 Atlanta Golf Classic. They're in the $10 to $20 range and include a smattering of familiar names, from Wally Armstrong to Roger Maltbie to Nick Price and Chip Beck.

## GOLF CREATEEVITY

There are tees in the shapes of missiles, fishhooks, molars, daisies, peanuts, and naked women. One has a set of praying hands clasped reverently beneath the ball. Such ingenuity may come as a surprise to those accustomed to more standard fare. But not to I. R. Valenta, a scholar in the fertile yet underappreciated study of the humble tee.

Irv has catalogued the fruits of his research in an as-yet-unpublished work, "Evolution of the Golf Tee." Fortunately, his efforts are reproduced in a series of decorative and informative color posters.

Golf Tee Explosion 1920–1950 and Golf Tee Creativity 1950–1992 (there's also I.R.'s Golf Tee Hall of Fame 1500–1921) are part of a larger and more expensive collage. Each of the individual posters, however, is available for $7, signed and numbered.

They are an unusual size, 11″ × 17″, but that's the perfect size for— brace yourself—place mats. Laminated for a few dollars at a local copy store, these colorful and informative additions to the breakfast table never fail to enliven a bowl of corn flakes. The creative advances from the first tee, Dr. William Lowell's wooden peg, "The Reddy Tee" (1921) are all here: leaners, swivels, decoratives, illegals, even a tee made of gold. Irv has also put this tee collection on a colorful series of T-shirts ($19.95).

Irv offers a bounty "to the first person who can capture a full complement of original tees displayed on any of these tableaus." Good luck.

## POSTCARDS

Appealing collectibles, entertaining and inexpensive to display (under a glass desktop, in frames, scrapbooks), postcards also score high with respect to the pedestrian but important question of storage.

With most collectibles, the wealth is accumulated among an ardent core of enthusiasts. Postcards, however, are not a lost cause. Without really looking I bumped into a colorful 1940s souvenir folder of "*Beautiful and Historic*" Augusta, Georgia, for seventy-five cents. Along with shots of other landmarks (the Richmond Hotel, Broad Street at night), sure enough, there was a card of the Augusta National clubhouse. In some circles, this is a $5 card.

The Golf Collectors Society has an active group of postcard aficionados. One recommended reference is *Golf—On Old Postcards* by Tom Serpell, available from Grant Books in England. Many cities have postcard clubs that hold regular events. Stamp stores may help you find them. Barr's Postcard News certainly will. It features extensive club, show, and mail-auction listings as well as historical background. A free issue is yours for $2 postage. The British publication *Picture Postcard Monthly* also has several back issues with articles related to golf cards. *PostCard Collector* magazine in Wisconsin is another recommended resource.

Longtime collectors Garry and Lee Hauk suggest going to postcard shows or poking around antique stores and flea markets. Most golf course postcards should sell for $1 to $5. Some will be higher depending on content and age. Less common are cards that are actual photographs. These are usually $3 and up. Subjects can run the gamut from golf-playing animals to famous courses, women, comics, etc. Cards signed by the artist are very desirable. You might concentrate on certain eras or themes. Garry likes to visit a course he's found a card for and, if possible, play it. Don't overlook their historical content. Many postcards document an event or even a course that time has passed by.

In their encyclopedic *Golf Antiques: and Other Treasures of the Game* ($19.95), Morton and John Olman recommend contacting the International Golf Philatelic Society in Virginia.

## BRINGING YOU THE JOYS OF THE SEASON

With respect to personal preference, let's just say there are golf-themed greeting cards to suit nearly every occasion and taste.

Sportcards stocks a representative sample from the understated to the fanciful. The USGA offers a similar assortment. Golf Gifts and Gallery has a complete line featuring the "lovable, blue-eyed golf ball Ernie Dimples."

One of my favorite cards is only slightly larger than a golf ball, which is what it depicts. Paper House Productions of Woodstock, New York, has reproduced a DT Titleist, complete with script, numeral, and shape. GOLF BALL (ESP07-90) opens to a small blank card and retails for ninety cents.

In addition to its more traditional stock, that is, if you can call Santa undergoing video swing analysis from the reindeer traditional, Sportcards also sells reasonably priced golf-themed note cards, pads, and boxed stationery. A 625-sheet note "cube" with illustrated golfers and slogans on all four sides is $7.50 (two for $14). Golf Gifts and Gallery also has several designs of notepads and cubes in addition to an impressive array of related products, from four lines of golf bathroom tissue ($5.95) to tee-shaped pens ($2.95) and golf-themed cocktail napkins ($1.80).

Those with an aversion to nearly everything mentioned above should consider two final suggestions. Golf Specialtees of Scotland sells several famous golf paintings reproduced as cards ($2.75), along with a wide selection of postcards of early golf at St. Andrews

*Infuriated foozler (after his first experience of a steel shaft). "G-r-r-r-r-h! The cursed thing won't even break."*

and women players from the turn of the century ($1). It also offers an excellent array of historic prints in the $12 to $30 range.

B.J.S. Turner Golf Art has a nice selection of pen-and-ink British golf cartoons from the twenties and thirties. The subjects of the Vintage Golf Notes series ($10 for eight boxed blank cards and envelopes) take some predictably droll turns, but they're handsome, classy cards.

## THEY'RE ONLY CARDBOARD

Never meant but destined to become investments, golf cards—small, rectangular bits of cardboard, if we clinically reduce them to their essential element—produce a strong emotive pull. These (mostly) British antecedents to baseball cards are colorful, informative, sometimes humorous, easy to display and store. Many bygone-era sets are now being proficiently and affordably reproduced. Original sets that fetch several thousand dollars are being faithfully reprinted for under $30.

Desirability is determined by the potentially lethal mix of supply and demand, nostalgia, emotion, and greed. Already long gone, I sought more seasoned and rational expertise. Mike and Mike graciously offer their help on getting started.

Mike Baier is coauthor of *A Century of Golf Cards,* recognized as the hobby's definitive reference. It's available from the author for $23 postpaid or at TPC pro shops. Mike Daniels sells an ever-widening selection of original and reproduced card sets through his business, Gifts Fore the Golfer. First, Mike Baier:

A good way to get started is with the newer cards. The 1990 PRO SET set can be found for $5 or less; the 1991 and 1992 sets for $10—$15. Reprint sets are also gaining in popularity . . . It is also great fun to find cards with golf themes in non-golf sets.

PROLINE football sets show a number of football players in golf settings, SKYBOX basketball, Disney sets, James Bond, "The

Addams Family," "I Love Lucy" and many more. Most of these cards can be found in opened stock at card shops and card shows for 25 cents or so.

Mike Daniels:

There are several sets that I am particularly fond of . . . Copes Golfers 50 card set has been reprinted (about $25). Some of the photo card sets from the 20s & 30s are real nice. A couple (of reproduced) sets that come to mind are The Churchman Famous Golfer sets, both the 50 small card set ($25) and the larger 12 card series ($20).

New issues keep popping up. There are collegiate sets, Ryder Cup team sets, and international sets. Mike Daniels also mentions that the PRO SET PGA Tour cards make a great backdrop for autographs.

## TAKING NAMES

The professional tours will provide player addresses for those interested in collecting autographs. All LPGA Tour members can be contacted by writing directly to the LPGA office. Each day mail is forwarded to the next tournament site or sent directly to the player's home.

Here's a few to get you started:

Tom Kite
c/o Pro's Inc.
P.O. Box 673
Richmond, VA 23206

Phil Mickelson
c/o Cornerstone Sports
2515 McKinney Ave.
Lock Box 10
Dallas, TX 75201

Fred Couples
c/o Players Group Inc.
8521 Greensboro Dr., Ste. 1150
McLean, VA 22102

Paul Azinger/Payne Stewart
Leader Enterprises Inc.
390 N. Orange Ave., Ste. 2600
Orlando, FL 32801

In writing for an autograph, enclosing a self-addressed, stamped envelope is never a bad idea. Your correspondence will of course be personalized. Asking for more than one autograph has come to be seen as unabashedly mercenary and bad form, which it is. If you don't see *The Official Media Guide of the PGA Tour* in bookstores, it is available for $12.95 from 800/335-5323.

Those who remember fan clubs will be heartened by Mochrie's Maniacs, a tribute to LPGA star Dottie Mochrie. The mascot is the pugnacious chow "Shank," who achieved some notoriety for mistaking Dottie for a prowler and taking an ill-planned "bite out of crime."

"The objective of the fan club is to promote Dottie as the premier player that we think she is," reads the form. "Second is to help promote the LPGA Tour on which Dottie participates. Third, and far from last, is to send a healthy donation to one or two charities each year." Basic membership is $20. This being the nineties, however, there is a gold card membership available for $500.

Basic members get an official registered membership card, a tee gift pack, bag towel, 8″ × 10″ personally autographed photo plus a choice of cap, visor, or T-shirt. There's an astonishing range of merchandise, from shirts, key chains, tumblers, and umbrellas up to a set of Dottie Mochrie graphite shaft irons by Joe Powell.

## A WHOLE NEW MEANING TO A
## JACK NICKLAUS CHARGE

Affinity cards have taken hold. Everyone from the Sierra Club to Mothers Against Drunk Driving offers them. Every time you make a purchase with your affinity Visa or MasterCard, a donation trickles down to the assigned charity. (Just how much is certainly a question you should ask.)

So what's this got to do with golf? Well, it just so happens that Marine Midland Bank, in conjunction with the champion once nicknamed "Snow White" but better known as the "Golden Bear," issues the Golden Bear Visa Card.

Annual membership fee on the regular card is $20, $36 on the Visa Gold (first six months free). The APR (annual percentage rate) is variable 16.95 percent on the regular card, variable 14.95 on the Visa Gold. Benefits? How about:

- 10 percent off items in The Jack Nicklaus Collection Catalog.
- Discounts on Hartmarx Jack blazers and slacks.

- Complimentary green fees to registered hotel guests at half a dozen Marriotts and The Boulders and Grand Cypress resorts.
- 100 percent of transaction fees going to The Jack and Barbara Nicklaus Endowment Fund to benefit junior golf, including summer golf camps and programs for minorities and underprivileged children.
- Exclusive tips from Jack with your monthly statement (on golf presumably, not finance).
- Participation in the annual Golden Bear Golf Tournament.

*And* a complimentary copy of *The Jack Nicklaus Golf Handbook* (800/446-5336).

## BUTTONING THE STIFF UPPER LIP

Vestiges of bygone days, antique golf buttons are—surprise!—collectible. Tender Buttons in Manhattan has an astonishing selection, including some splendid golf buttons. These are new buttons, perfect for cardigan or blazer. Ordinarily mail order is not offered. The golf issues are specific enough that they are available by mail. There are scrimshaw golfers ($4 and $5), enormous brass buttons with the crests of Royal Blackheath and Royal St. George's ($4.50 and $5.50), inlaid golfers on gold-plated buttons ($14.50! and $19.50!), but my favorite is a gorgeous blue-luster enamel button with crossed silver clubs ($5 and $6). It also comes in black. The funny thing is, I'm told, these are known in the trade as "shank" buttons because of the attachment on the back. Seems to fit. Tender Buttons also has a store in Chicago.

## A FEW MINUTES TO LEARN, A LIFETIME TO MASTER

Long ago, before miniature golf moved outdoors for good (it was once very much a parlor game), there were numerous tabletop golf games. Some were little more than hybrid tiddlywinks; others had clubs that fit around your finger and were played over "courses" with hazards and doglegs.

These evolved into metal banks and other mechanical toys, many of which are no doubt today ruinously collectible. The popular

Arnold Palmer at the end of a stick game owes its origins to a patented 1920s design.

Nason Richmond has made a study of these ingenious and obscure games in his entertaining book, *Patented Golf Games Gimmicks and Gadgets* ($4.50). What's more, he went ahead and invented his own tabletop game, Flickmaster ($13).

"Computer golf is essentially a matter of timing, when to push a button," writes the father of the sport and founder of the DGA (Desktop Golf Association). "Flickmaster calls for timing, tempo and the patience to develop dexterity." With the above forces in harmony (and a lot of practice), The Flickmaster Super Wedge Flick Stick can produce hooks, slices, and backspin. It would make an ideal gift for a golfer laid up in bed in need of diversion. His book and humorous commentary on unusual, and sometimes downright torturous, early golf aids will also lift spirits. The game makes an agreeable activity for sitting on hold or for those moments when the boss is otherwise engaged. Recommended for teens and up.

Another pleasant rainy-day diversion is Golf Joker, a card game from Switzerland ($9.95). The cards allow a match over the links of St. Andrews, Pebble Beach, or Biarritz. The caricatures seem to have stepped from the pages of *Through the Looking Glass*. A vexed king snaps a wedge across his knee on the "Sliced to Rough" card. You play niblicks, spoons, brassies, lost balls, even a stymie. Look for it at upscale pro shops.

## ROLL WITH IT

The truly astonishing variety of golf balls presents an equal number of gift and collecting avenues. Ten dollars will still buy something worthwhile.

Ed Granados has an impressive and rationally priced assortment of new and older balls. Professional signature models from Sir Walter (Hagen) to Lloyd Mangrum and Patty Berg (the first woman professional to be so honored) to the enigmatic "Les Strokes," playful monikers, and numerous designs abound. For instance, you could fill several egg cartons (the preferred storage method) with balls decorated with generations of airplanes. The trick is calling your shots and being able to say no occasionally. As a collector warned: "It gets nuts after a while if you don't have some direction."

Thrift-shop golf-bag pockets can also turn up interesting oddities. The atomic energy symbol appears on one ball, an unqualified "rare buy" at ten cents. Wonder if it's radioactive? And who knows how much a Liquid Center ball with Gary Player's signature on one side and Shakespeare's (?) on the other will be worth someday?

A photo or endorsement of a famous player on a sleeve or box of balls will certainly enhance its value. As it is elsewhere, packaging is coveted. Seventy years from now, someone will thank me for saving contemporary boxes. Sleeves of balls from the fifties, spotted in one of the most expensive golfiana catalogs, were still eminently affordable (about $15). Worn examples of rubber-core balls from the twenties and thirties won't break the bank either. Golf's Golden Years, with several locations in antique malls around Chicago, routinely has mesh balls like the Silvertown Silver Prince or the PGA Teemee in the $15 to $25 range.

Finally, if you must: Golf Gifts and Gallery sells not only exploding balls but The Jetstreamer ($3.50), which emits fifteen feet of spiraling red ribbon on impact. It's also got the Wobbler, a havoc wreaker on the green (ho-ho!), and the water-filled Phantom, both $3.35 (800/552-4430).

## MY VICTORY AT OAKMONT

On a swing through Pittsburgh, the opportunity presented itself for a visit to neighboring Oakmont and its famous club. I called first, of course, and then nearly missed the entrance, unobtrusive, as one might expect, at the top of Pill Hill (so named for the doctors who make their homes in the area). After admiring the venerable clubhouse included in *The National Register of Historic Places* and the eighteenth green, I wandered into the pro shop to secure a few scorecards and pencils for friends.

There was plenty of moderately priced booty. As the Open returns to Oakmont at regular intervals, I couldn't resist purchasing several yardage books. Sure to enhance the couch-potato experience the next time round, they make a very classy souvenir for $6. There is an embossed logo on the front, and the inside pages include a color print of the clubhouse and several wire service photos of past champions.

Naturally, the shop had an inexhaustible supply of logoed balls and ball markers. Change came back from a five. The staff bore no apparent reluctance to transact a sale from a commoner.

Walking into the nation's top-echelon clubs unannounced is not recommended. Augusta National will also not send out scorecards or pencils. At many, however, a polite written request will probably receive a satisfactory result. The courtesy of a phone call will quickly determine a club's willingness to admit deferential out-of-town visitors.

## LOOKING FOR A GREEN JACKET?

The Augusta National Golf Shop sends out a price list of Masters merchandise. It will even fax it to you. For under $30: bag towel, ball markers, socks, hat, cap, visor, and umbrella. Visa, MasterCard, American Express accepted (706/667-6200).

## ACHIEVING THE PERFECT SLICE

The idea of golfers packing blades does not seem entirely sound given the spate of disturbing on-course incidents. For those who feel

positively naked without their Swiss Army knives, however, the Golf
Pro model is welcome news. Several catalogs stock it, including Golf
Day and Austad's, for $29.95. A ball-mark repair tool, spike wrench,
and, most important, a bottle opener, are included.

## DISCOUNT CLUB RACKS

Here's an exceptional value for displaying clubs, a homemade inven-
tion that's not only cheaper and classier but just plain works better
than its competitors.

John Gates has designed a three-club wall rack from red oak,
which he sells for $20. His racks include a terrific innovation that
allows clubs to be hung vertically. A hidden hinge locks clubs in
place, providing an additional security feature that saves display
space to boot.

## "TEE TO GREEN PROTECTION"

Those seeking golf-related gifts of a more "adult" nature may not be
aware that there is now a golf ball that explodes to reveal a condom
($2.95).

Hole-N-One Condoms ("Designed to Keep Your Balls Safely in
Play"), in "three putt" packs for $3.95, may not be for everyone—the
copy is clearly written with an eye on the bachelor party set—but
there's a method to the madness. A note on the packaging reads:

> The humorous approach we use in presenting our products is an
> attempt on our part to create a lighter and easier entree into poten-
> tially lifesaving conversation about the benefits of proper protec-
> tion.

Available at those kinds of shops everywhere.

## FAIRWAY GINGER ALE: FIVE CENTS

Many households once revolved around a room commonly known
as "the den," where the male of the species typically sought refuge

from the rigors of his daily existence. Den walls were often decorated with nostalgic advertising signs for reasons best left to cultural anthropologists.

Those looking for high-quality reproduction tin signs should give Tin Pan Annie a call. She offers several colorful turn-of-the-century golf advertisements. At $12 apiece or two for $20, this is a certified blue-light special. I've seen them elsewhere for much more, and Annie's signs are no phonies. They are accurate reproductions of real ads.

The poetic abuse notwithstanding, my favorite remains one of a series of Campbell Kids ads, circa 1904. The kid swings wildly, and the accompanying verse reads:

My game of golf is something classy
I wield a fearsome, wicked brassy
And when I've laid them all a stymie
Straight home to Campbell's Soup I hie me!

Okay, it's not Yeats, but it's fit for kitchen or bar. There's also Fairway Ginger Ale ("Always Up to Par") and a green and white miniature golf sign with clubs crossed.


## HOT CHECKS

The Styles Company offers three vivid golf scenes available on personalized checks. Suitable for cashing, two hundred checks are $13.95, deposit slips, book cover, and register included.

Less dramatic and less expensive is the "woodcut" ball on a tee available from Current Checks. It shows an iron behind a ball and fits in the check's upper-left-hand corner. The motif costs an additional $2.95, but two hundred checks are only $4.95. Please note, however, the golf design is not available on the special-edition Cathy or Elvis series.


## NOT ANOTHER BAG TAG

For those who welcome another tournament entry-bag tag about as much as a three putt, here's a premium, or gift, that's cheap and so childishly simple to make the services of a child are not even required. It also will help those who show a genetic predisposition to losing keys.

You need:

One golf ball (old, new, logoed, meaningful—from a hole in one or not)
One key ring (available at Tandy Leather or party supply stores. Approximate cost: twelve to fifteen cents)
One other small key loop (also at Tandy)
One 3/16" thread-length screw eye (about fifty-four cents for twelve)
A vice or C-clamp
Hammer or, preferably, a drill and small bit

Directions:

By whatever means, put a hole in the ball sufficient to allow the screw eye to be screwed in place.
Twist the screw in place. Add loop and key ring. Attach keys.
Congratulations. You've just made a golf-ball key chain.

## T-SHIRTS A CUT ABOVE AND BELOW

A pioneer in the study of motion, Harold Edgerton captured the artistry of golf in a multiple-exposure photograph using strobe lights to capture the path of the swing on film.

His photo makes for a very classy T-shirt. The Center Shop, the museum store of the Pittsburgh Center for the Arts, has it in black with the superimposed swing of, I believe, either Byron Nelson or Jug McSpaden. At $18.95, it's not cheap, but it is very cool.

Paintings by Tom Lynch, widely known for his work at several U.S. Opens, are reproduced on a series of T-shirts. These really have to be seen to be believed. The four-color printing process produces wonderfully vivid colors and shades, light-years ahead of what you're used to seeing on a T-shirt. I was assured that the shirt will wear out before the colors do. Available from Links Graphics, Inc., for $16.95.

BJDesigns sells shirts bearing reproductions of magazine covers featuring women golfers. It also has designs of nattily dressed golfing cats. My favorite is a reprint of a *Liberty* magazine cover. An apron-clad woman is holding a golf bag in one hand while stoically pointing out the vacuum cleaner to a quizzical male. In 100 percent heavy cotton, the shirts sell for $13.95. BJDesigns also has an extensive line of golf-themed handbags, scarves, luggage, and other gifts.

That knuckleheaded triumvirate, Moe, Larry, and Curly, looking their undistinguished best with clubs in hand, pose stoically (for a stooge) on a shirt from The Lighter Side. Golf With Your Friends is $20. A Polyester Stooges Golf Tie is $17.50. Competitive Edge Golf also has the shirts and a Stooges coffee mug ($10).

*Caddyshack* fans may find the color T-shirt with the Bushwood Country Club logo on one side and the memorable phrase "Be the Ball!" on the other to their liking ($15.95) (800/753-0171).

## AVOIDING BLEACHER BURN

Let's assume you're not in the market for a tent, backpack, or even packets of freeze-dried chicken cacciatore. Camping stores and out-doors catalogs are still worth checking into, and not only for durable clothes.

Case in point. If you watch any golf at all—from anywhere other than in front of the tube—you soon realize the importance of procuring a comfortable seat. Bleachers, although often set at key vantage points, are not comfortable. Neither is propping up a tree. Look around the next time you attend a tournament, which is certainly an entertaining thing to do. Hardened vets recline in relative comfort in stools and chairs. Rookies get bleacher burn.

Campmor has a great selection of lightweight folding chairs and camp stools ideal for tournament viewing. Many are under $30. The Boundary Waters Catalog sells the Northwoods Company Canoe Chair, two pounds of aluminum and Dacron-backed comfort, for $20. Variety International sells the Triangle Chair, which weighs just over a pound and folds up to an amazing two inches in diameter ($16.95). Shooting sticks are another possibility, although one would hardly call them comfortable.

None of the above offer the enhanced comfort of a La-Z-Boy, but they sure beat pulling splinters out of your butt or baking in the hot sun.

## ODDS AND ENDS

Perhaps there's nothing—not one damn thing—that appeals to you on the preceding pages. To you receiving gifts must be a burden. You never get anything you really want. Boxes of balls you would-n't put in play at miniature golf have been cheerfully, if in secret disdainfully, received. No doubt there were other well-intentioned golf gifts that for one reason or another came up a little short.

May I make a suggestion? Do everyone a favor. Should someone near to you ask for ideas, suggest the one gift very nearly foolproof. It is also recommended for difficult golfers on your own list. A driving-range gift certificate is the gift that keeps on giving, or slicing, as the case may be.

Finally, although somewhat deficient in the coaster-appreciation department, I did notice a very attractive set made by Pimpernel International in England. The accompanying place mats are expensive, but the coasters, featuring attractive color scenes of famous British courses, come six for a very sporty $15. I spotted them at a fancy coffee store. They're entitled, oddly enough, the Famous Course Series. The Jack Nicklaus Collection also has them for $14, #8106.

# READING THE GREEN

*Away from the course, golf becomes easier to appreciate and enjoy, unsullied by personal tragedy. Whether solace, companionship, or inspiration comes from a book, video, audiocassette, newsletter, or catalog, any effort to understand the game beyond the stark confines of the scorecard is rewarded in kind. The journey is made all the more pleasant by the best writers in sport, the famous and sometimes the infamous.*

*Information on titles discussed in this section can be found in the Appendix.*

## TAKING THE HIGH ROAD

The rare guidebook conveys a sense of permanence. David Hamilton's *Good Golf Guide to Scotland* ($12.95, Pelican Press) is one such guide, serving up dollops of insight impervious to the inevitable upward spiral of green fees. Anyone contemplating golf in Scotland should make the effort to find it. With primers on history, customs, appropriate dress, the popularity of two-ball matches, and more than a word on the weather, it would also make a thoughtful gift to anyone making the pilgrimage or even toying with the idea.

Also recommended is the informative "Scotland, Home of Golf," produced by the Scottish Tourist Board. It's free with a call to the British Tourist Authority in New York (212/986-2266) or Los Angeles (310/477-3322). The oversized and detailed road map is backed with directions, general price guidelines, and delightfully terse and descriptive capsules. "One hundred years old, unchanged and designed by God," reads one enticing note. Order it for fun.

Likewise, the "Official Guide to Golf Courses in Switzerland" is delicious food for thought and provides information to contact foreign golf associations throughout Europe. It's free from the Swiss National Tourist Office (212/757-5944, 310/335-5980).

## SLAINTEMHATH!

Doesn't it seem curious that the advent of distillation in Scotland roughly parallels a quantifiable surge in golf's popularity during the 1400s? Pondering such mysteries, or those peculiarly inherent to golf, requires a drink no less fortifying than single malt Scotch. For those seeking true enlightenment, *Michael Jackson's Complete Guide to Single Malt Scotch* ($24.95, Running Press), a handsome hardcover, is required reading and also a lot of fun.

"When I leave the bottle," he writes affectionately, "I like to be whistling the tune."

Most of us would assuredly rather drink Scotch than read about it. From his book, one learns the relative merits of bourbon wood in aging, that the Lowlands tend to produce whiskeys untempered by Highland peatiness, that most single malts average 40 percent alcohol.

You may not need to know these things. With this book at the very least you will be able to pronounce the malts and impress your friends. (Glenmorangie rhymes with "orangey," Glen Garioch is pronounced "geery.")

Each brand's label is artfully reproduced. Maps and concise histories provide the necessary background. Information on touring distilleries is also thoughtfully provided.

For drinking the stuff, $30 will put you in the middle to low average for malts. Several recommended for under $30 are Abelour, which scores very well with Mr. Jackson and Old Fettercairn.

Both Glenfiddich and Glenlivet, the latter the biggest-selling single malt in America (named for the river Livet), and a personal favorite, The Dalmore, are still under $30.

Incidentally, "Slaintemhath!" is Gaelic for "Good Health!"

## RICK TEES OFF

The Oklahoma Library for the Blind and Physically Handicapped, in conjunction with the PGA of America, offers an audiocassette of David G. Walker's juvenile page-turner, *Rick Tees Off*.

The story follows Rick, a considerate and inquisitive lad, as he makes his way along in the game. Two cassettes.

## STRAIGHT DOPE ON EQUIPMENT

The future is certain. No matter how much you like your current set of sticks, the time will come. You'll want, then need, then lust for this year's model. When the inevitable day arrives, you will need ammunition. Choices are certain to be maddening, advertising ever more alluring, and sticker shock a given.

*David Graham's Guide to Golf Equipment* ($16.95, Charles E. Tuttle) cuts through the accumulating drifts of technical mumbo jumbo on clubs, shafts, frequency matching, torque, etc., like a snowblower. Even I understood it.

Graham shares his experience as a top player (he is a former PGA champion and U.S. Open winner). Better still, he conveys his formidable insight as a club designer with an obvious enthusiasm for the game. These assets are directed to finding the proper fit for the reader, whether the reader is just starting out or ready to quit (again).

He works his way through the bag and beyond with tips on enhancing equipment performance. A pleasant surprise, he toes no company line and has no ax to grind. An expensive though modestly produced paperback, the book is still considerably cheaper than an inappropriate set of clubs. *David Graham's Guide to Golf Equipment* is a recipient of The Golden Apfel Award for Meritorious Service to Apfordable Golf.

## VIDEO AND MORE VIDEO

The USGA Catalog from Golf House continues to chronicle U.S. Open Championships from 1956 to the present for $19.95 (discounted $5 to USGA members). The oldest title chronicles Dr. Cary Middlecoff's win at Oak Hill in Rochester, New York. Panning the driving range, the camera pauses to watch Mr. Ben Hogan. (Put that footage on a loop, suggested a friend.) Great fun, if all too brief.

PGA of America Home Video presents official highlight films from recent Ryder Cup matches, also for $19.95, and several PGA Championships for $24.98 (800/323-0442).

GolfSmart offers a terrific selection of current books and videos. It also seems to have the new stuff before anyone else. Masters highlights are $19.95. Digitally mastered tapes of "Shell's Wonderful World of Golf" are $24.95.

Doak Ewing of Rare Sportsfilms has made it his quest to restore as much sports footage as he can find. He's got several esoteric golf titles and promises more to come.

An hour of the 1960 Masters, the first year shot in color, is $29.95. It's loads of fun, from the ride up Magnolia Lane in a Cadillac that would choke the Panama Canal to a tour of the trophy room. Then it's out to the Par 3 Tournament (the inaugural year, won by "The Slammer," Sam Snead) and the main event. Claude Harmon's ball nestles up against a purse; Ben Hogan spends several lifetimes over putts and plays shoeless from the watery grave at the twelfth that was to deny him a chance at victory. No less dramatic are Arnold Palmer's . . . I won't spoil it.

Several episodes of "Challenge Golf," a 1963 made-for-TV team event that aired on ABC, have also been resurrected. Byron Nelson and Ken Venturi battle the hosts (and miked) Arnold Palmer and Gary Player at Pebble Beach (fifty minutes for $24.95). The other shows feature the hosts against Bob Rosburg and Mike Souchak and, also at Riviera, Dave Ragan and Joe Campbell. The team of Snead and Sanders challenges at Torrey Pines. Save $10 by ordering any two.

Gifts Fore the Golfer has an astonishing array of golf on video, representing nearly every decade in this century. There's Harry Vardon and James Braid in 1904 (two and a half minutes for $20), "never before seen" Bobby Jones footage, instructional films with Archie Compston, Sam Snead, Tommy Armour, Johnny Farrell, even episodes of *The Jimmy Demaret Show.* If you're dying for footage of the 1956 Canadian Open, look no further. Most titles are $20. The list goes on and on. (See also "Finding the Green in New York").

## "AKZEPTIEREN SIE BALLABSCHLAGEZEITEN?"

*Do You Speak Golf?* by Gregg Cox ($4.95, Pandemic International) is written for the golf traveler who never got past the first Berlitz tape. Whether traveler's checks are accepted to the always useful "Does anyone here speak English?" (very) basic points of reference are covered in French, Spanish, Swedish, German, Danish, Italian, Norwegian, Portuguese, and Dutch. Pocket-size, the book also includes handy conversion tables from meters into yards and feet.

Phonetic pronunciations in English follow each phrase. This is guaranteed to heighten the amusement for any foreigner with whom you attempt to converse. Pity an effort to include more colorful expressions wasn't made. There's no "worm burner," "froghair," "kitty litter," not even "bite," "run," or "come back." I do know *"la plage"* ("the beach") can mean the bunker in French, and "Ah, Dieu" will serve well on several continents. Incidentally, the heading is German for "Do you accept tee-off times?"

## UNSINKABLE

Civilization can be thankful it was dealt only one Titanic Thompson. Golf, on the other hand, can afford a more rounded view of its scoundrels. After all, as early Scottish club records unequivocally attest, golf has been a fluid gambling device for centuries.

It seems fitting that the story of the game's most notorious hustler now rests with one equally skilled in sleight of hand. Palmer Magic now markets *The Unsinkable Titanic Thompson* by Carlton Stowers ($18.95). If reading about instruction leaves you bleary-eyed and the top players seem self-righteous to the point of infinite boredom, curl up with tales of such unadulterated skulduggery that one wonders how Hollywood could have possibly overlooked the exploits of Alvin Clarence Thomas.

Here was a man as enterprising in leaving as little to chance as he was in creating schemes to part the arrogant and egotistical from their money. (Not that Ti wouldn't take it from anybody; the cocky ones were just that much easier to fleece.)

How formidable a golfer was he? Ed Dudley, who taught Titanic out in California in the early days and later served as head pro at Augusta National, once answered this way:

> . . . for my money, that skinny fella out there is one stroke better than anybody else in the whole goddamn world.

## SHERLOCK HOLMES, THE GOLFER

Oh yes, Mycroft's more industrious brother found the Royal and Ancient Game sufficiently stimulating to his powerful intellect and less renowned but equally refined physical prowess.

Dr. Watson was otherwise ensconced in his practice. It is to one Bob Jones that we are indebted for revealing Holmes's early devotion to golf. The providential discovery of the great detective's betting book, golf journal, and private correspondence provides the basis for the stories in *Sherlock Holmes, the Golfer* ($8.85) and *Sherlock Holmes Saved Golf* ($9.25). Both paperbacks are available from the author to members of the Golf Collectors Society and "keen Sherlockians only."

## GOLF SECRETS FROM THE VAULT

Harvey Penick fans will recognize the name Bill Melhorn. "Wild Bill," so called for his penchant to go on scoring binges (rather than for any aberrant behavioral tendencies), was leading money winner several times in the fledgling years of the professional tour.

No less authorities than Tommy Armour and Ben Hogan believed that from tee to green no one was better. Putting betrayed Bill cruelly, and he left the vagaries of the nascent seasonal tour for the security of teaching.

Onetime PGA Tour player and collegiate coach Bobby Shave sat down with Bill and a tape recorder. The transcripts are sometimes ponderous reading, but Bill's recollections, from Harry Vardon to the rough-and-tumble of the early tour to his insight on the intricacies of the swing, are fascinating. Take his observations on course management, for instance:

> Everybody knows when they don't take a long swing they're more accurate. That goes too, when you're 50 yards away or 100 yards away. I don't see anybody doing that today. They'll say, "Oh, you have to pitch to every green, the green is soft." All right the green is soft. Well, pitch it just a little further than the front of the green and let it run the rest of the way. I know this, in all my golf, I don't believe I hit over 50 shots full with an iron. Only when I had to. Because I've got another club to hit it that distance and be comfortable.
> —From: *Golf Secrets Exposed,* M&S Publishing ($9.98).

## BUYING BOOKS

Many book collectors have doubles or even triples of popular titles acquired as throw-ins or presents. They're often glad to find a good home for a beloved title (and clear some shelf space). The friendships that can result from these transactions, aside from whatever savings are realized, make the quest all the more worthwhile.

Reading copies, worn to the point of perhaps negligible interest to the collector, are also an option to those who simply want to read a book, not retire on its perceived investment value. Several collectors/dealers send out their own lists of sale books from first editions to reprints. You might make inquiries of the Golf Collectors Society or, better yet, join and put out some feelers.

The nice thing about books: The bigger sellers they are, the sooner they turn up in used bookstores and thrift shops. While still on the way up the best-seller charts, duking it out with *Cooking with Regis and Kathie Lee* and *How to Satisfy a Woman Every Time,* a new copy of *Harvey Penick's Little Red Book* turned up at a local Goodwill.

Interlibrary loan can open the door to pleasant surprises. Better university libraries can also yield exciting finds. Golf museums house extensive, sometimes irreplaceable holdings, available to read on-site, if not for checkout.

Several specialty golf book dealers publish catalogs. George Lewis Golfiana has an eclectic range of titles and prices from $10 for a 1939 *U.S. Seniors' Golf Association Handbook* to $1,250 for a first edition of Tulloch's *The Life of Tom Morris*. Several others are Maxwell's Bookmark, GolfSmart, and Richard E. Donovan Enterprises, The Golf Bookshopper, offers free shipping and gift wrap. Even if you're not in the market, the better catalogs make for informative reading.

The Classics of Golf offers a Book-of-the-Month Club approach, reprising some of the game's most famous writing in attractive reprints.

Finally, it hardly needs to be said, but you can't walk into a book-store these days without bumping into a stack of lavishly produced coffee-table volumes of the *World's Most Exclusive Golf Courses That You Couldn't Get on with an Executive Order,* etc., consigned to dis-count racks.

## LOOKING FOR THE DESIGNER LABEL

A certain myopia about golf course architecture is understandable. Golfers have more immediate concerns. Maintaining one's dignity, pace of play, and eye on the ball (though not necessarily in that order) can blind players to a fuller appreciation of the effort under-taken on their behalf. Golfers spend their time trespassing, schem-ing, and negotiating their way around, over or through the designer's handiwork. They strive to put as much of it out of their minds as pos-sible. Whether the "trouble" was ruinously expensive to build and maintain never enters his mind.

If it is true, as the maxim goes, "The course is there. The architect's job is to find it," beyond budget, time, environmental, and other con-straints, there is still room to move. (And some courses are easier to find than others.)

An understanding of course design becomes all the more enchanting when one recognizes that the yeoman's work on the Old Course at St. Andrews was performed by burrowing rabbits.

A fascinating primer on the subject is available from the Golf Course Superintendents Association of America. The attractively produced and informative twenty-page booklet, *Golf Course Design . . . An Introduction,* is written by Geoffrey Cornish and William Robinson. It explores the artistic and pragmatic questions that must balance an architect's hand. It's available from the GCSAA for $8 (913/841-2240). Mr. Cornish, with Ron Whitten, has written the definitive books on the subject, readily found in most libraries. They are *The Golf Course* and *The Architects of Golf.*

*A Directory of Golf Courses Designed by Donald J. Ross* by W. Pete Jones lists Ross courses across the nation, though without any inkling whether they are public or private, substantially altered or intact. A copy makes for intriguing possibilities nevertheless, many of which are included in the individual state sections. Ross courses are definitely worth the effort to find. For a copy, contact Martini Print Media in Raleigh, North Carolina, 919/872-6601.

Although his name is synonymous with the best of his craft, Ross himself left very little behind by way of explanation. Here is one of his rare statements of purpose:

Make each hole present a different problem; so arrange it that every stroke must be made with a full concentration and attention necessary to good golf: build a hole in such a manner that all wastes none of the ground at your disposal and takes advantage of every possibility you can see.

One must take into account prevailing wind conditions for laying out a course altering hole routings accordingly. One of the main things which may influence the design is that of getting away from parallel fairways. There must be short holes and long holes and medium holes. Each must present its own problems. It must not be simply a case of teeing a ball up and driving it into space.

The traps must lie in such a position that the player must think on every shot, must figure how he is going to play it for the fewest possible strokes. Putting greens must not be flat and regular. They, too, must present their puzzles. The putt must be just as much a reason for study as the drive or the pitch.

. . . A golf course should contain these points: It must be a sporty one, not an easy drive, pitch and putt affair . . . It must be as scenic as possible . . . the hazards must be real, not merely holes cut in the

*Donald J. Ross*
COURTESY OF THE TUFTS ARCHIVES OF GIVEN MEMORIAL LIBRARY, PINEHURST, N.C.

ground here and there and banked or ditches dug or streams deflected . . . Trees must be removed where they interfere, but so many must not be taken away as to spoil the beauty of the course . . . above all, it must be a test of the best golf a player is capable of. The course must be a pleasure to the player rather than a monotony.

## ALL THE NEWS

Independent newsletters cover golf as they do life elsewhere, with opinion and candor. Their authors may live by their wits and operate on a fraying shoestring budget, but they can face the day without subservience to the sensibilities of advertisers. Many will send a complimentary issue or sell a single copy as an inducement to subscribe. The category runs the gamut from resort-travel scuttlebutt to instruction to history to the financial analysis of golf stocks. A favorite is *Golf Links,* awarded a Golden Apfel for its historical, literary, and entertaining diligence. Some others are:

*Al Barkow's Golf Report* $40/12 issues
460 Bloomfield Ave.
Montclair, NJ 07042
201/746-2191
   "The Game's Most Comprehensive Newsletter." Skinny from author, broadcaster, former editor on courses, equipment, the Tour, travel.

*Bottom Dollar Golf* $14/6 issues
P. O. Box 402101
Austin, TX 78704
800/473-0142
   "The consumer value golf guide. Bargains and straight dope."

*Bradley's Golf Insider* $175/12 issues
416 Wilson Pike Circle
Brentwood, TN 37027
615/370-0064
   "The Golf Newsletter for Investors and Observers." Updates, stock tracking, impending IPOs. "You can't buy a golf game, but you can buy a golf company."

*Gary Galyean's Golf Letter* $78/12 issues
Box 3899
Vero Beach, FL 32964
407/231-1688

"The Inside Report on World Golf." Pays its own freight to review and rank the crème de la crème. Somebody's got to do it.

*Global Golfer* $25/4 issues
275 Madison Ave.
New York, NY 10016
800/833-1389

A publication from Golf International, Inc. "The Leader in Customized Golfing Vacations." How's $10,000 for a trip to Scotland?

*Golf Links* $16/4 issues
5486 Georgetown Rd.
Frankfort, KY 40601
502/695-1035

Short stories by A. W. Tillinghast, the travails of Porky Oliver. Great reading, professional production.

*GolfPsyche Update* $32/4 issues
P.O. Box 1976
Boerne, TX 78006
210/537-5044

Fascinating research and findings from the files of clinical psychologist Dr. Deborah Graham, who counsels over 130 Senior and PGA Tour pros. Back issues are $8. Order through your PGA pro and get a year's subscription for $28 (back issues $7).

*Golf Travel* $79/12 issues
P.O. Box 3485
Charlottesville, VA 22903-0485
804/295-1200

"The Guide for Discriminating Golfers." In-depth rating system, Sherlockian eye for flaws, insider guide to the finest resorts.

*Harvey Penick's Little Red Golf Letter* $29/12 issues
Bellvoir Publications

75 Holly Hill Lane
Greenwich, CT 06830-2910
800/424-7887

>More instructional parables from the self-effacing grown caddie and from those closest to him who teach just what you need to know.

*The Pelz Report* $38.50/4 issues
1200 Lakeway Dr., Ste. 21
Austin, TX 78734
800/833-7370

>"A scientific look at golf." Sporadic but incisive reports on the research trail. Often the basis for *Golf* magazine articles.

*Traveling Golfer* $13/12 issues
1469 Bellevue #804
Burlingame, CA 94010
415/342-6192

>"A monthly newsletter about pleasure golf travel." Personable spin on bargains and deals from freelance travel writer Lee Tyler. News you can use from an old hand.

For an informative look behind the scenes at the business of golf, ask a course for a back issue of one of the golf trade publications. *Golf Shop Operations, Golf Pro,* and others cover a lot of ground. Sometimes investigative, sometimes chatty, occasionally even funny, the writing is often lively, the reporting commendable. They decipher advertising, analyze trends, keep up with new products, and make sense of the technobabble. You'll read about it first here long before it makes the general interest magazines.

## CATALOGS

The Direct Marketing Association estimates you receive on the order of eighty catalogs a year. Image may be everything in mail order, but in the golf biz some manage very well with just a typed sheet of prices, many so juicy, apparently, you have to call to find out just how juicy they are. The magazines are filled with such ads. Are we to assume this is just a precautionary measure aimed at preventing otherwise sound but price-conscious golfers from busting their charge-card limits for some discounted Ping Zings?

At any rate, whether you're looking for clothes, ball retrievers, duck-head paperweights, gopher head covers, or even clubs, if the catalogs haven't found you yet, here's some suggested bedside reading.

### Austad's Golf

Lots of clubs and tchotchkes and drivers with funny names. Don't get their catalog? And you call yourself a golfer.

### Cambridge Golf Antiquities Ltd.

What do they have for under $30? "Advice." And a few sleeves of 1950s balls for $15.

### Catalog from Golf House/USGA

Suitably eclectic mix of upcoming Open apparel, photos, books, art. Nice coasters from Pimpernel in England, featuring four famous courses, six for $15.

### Chesal Industries

Know someone who can't bend over to tee up a ball? "Tee up" will do it ($29.95) and pick a ball out of the hole. Incredible accessories catalog including camouflage collapsible Sunday bags and a dazzling array of retrievers.

### Competitive Edge Golf

No messing around. Warm up your balls with the Hot Shot Ball Warmer. Introductory club trials. Clothes, clubs, etc. (See also "Finding the Green in New York.")

### Edwin Watts Golf Shops

Complements mostly southeastern store chain. Operates its own course in Mobile, Alabama.

### Golf Day

Mind candy for long winters with pages of name-brand goodies. Those gopher head covers have been closeout specials for a while, however.

### The Golf Shop Collection

History for sale at New Age prices.

### Golf Haus

No-frills club price list. Minimum order $50. Free postage/handling within U.S. Better know exactly what you want. Store is open to the public.

### GolfSmith International

Soup-to-nuts from a golf supermarket. (See also "Finding the Green in Texas.") Employees do the modeling. Jack Whitaker reads Harvey Penick while you wait on hold. If they don't have it, you can pretty well get along without it.

### Golf Specialtees of Scotland

Marvelous selection of historic reproduced prints, postcards, greeting cards, odds & ends. Much under $30.

### The GolfWorks

A Sears catalog of golf. A *Life* magazine–sized page filled with forty-two putter heads. Zowie! Does anyone really buy the Stars & Stripes driver?

### Grant Books

Publishes two antiquarian book catalogs a year together with one new book and many updates during the year. Also stocks clubs, prints, and pictures.

*House of Bruce*

You either laugh or cringe at those signs like GOLF IS NOT A MATTER OF LIFE OR DEATH. IT IS MUCH MORE IMPORTANT THAN THAT. And SHOW ME A GOOD LOSER AND I'LL SHOW YOU A MAN PLAYING GOLF WITH HIS BOSS. House of Bruce has got more of them, page after page, and sells them for quite a bit less than anyone else.

*LPGA Merchandise Center*

Small but rationally priced selection of official LPGA products. Under $30: logoed T-shirts ($12.95) and sweatshirts ($21.95), Velcro golf towel ($10), key chain ($4), and lapel pin ($2). *Annual Media Guide* is $10.

*The Leadbetter Collection*

In case you missed him. Practice aids, books, etc.

*Lefties Only*

Astonishing range of equipment for southpaws. No returns. National Association of Left-handed Golfers (800/844-NALG) (after 6:00 P.M. Mountain Standard Time).

*Phil Mason's Golf Shopper*

Includes "The Catalog of Catalogs" with ways to receive even more catalogs.

*The Jack Nicklaus Collection*

Some froofy stuff, some froofy prices. Still sore the Collection discontinued my favorite socks, featuring the famed triumvirate of Braid, Vardon, and Taylor. Then there's also The Jack Nicklaus Collection in Carmel (800/841-7766). Bronzes for $1,500, reproduction golf bags for $635, a $42 letter opener. Yikes.

*Newark Golf Company*

Geared to the club maker. Some accessories on the cheap.

*Pro Shop World of Golf*

Price lists of special purchases and closeouts, ladies' clubs, name brands. Says there's also hundreds of other items for sale not listed. Ten percent "restocking" fee on returns.

*Telepro Golf Shop*

Discount price list on bags, balls, accessories, single clubs and sets, part of a small chain of stores in Southern California. Filling in a do-it-yourself fitting chart is recommended.

*Up 2 Par*
*Golf Shop for Women*
　　Unique demo program. For $20, Up 2 Par will ship three woods and three irons from three different sets. Buy them and apply the $20 to the purchase.

*Warner Bros. Catalog*
　　Now playing at a mall near you, polo shirts with the Tasmanian Devil, logoed balls, hats, divot repair tools, towels, and ball markers.

### AND MORE CATALOGS

*Maryco Products*
*Old Chicago Golf Shop*
*Sporting Designs*

### . . . OF SPECIAL INTEREST TO WOMEN

*GolfHer Inc.*
*La Golfeur*
*SandBagger Enterprises*

### GOING GOING GONE

Hard-pressed as one might be to find anything in their pages for under $30, auction catalogs make interesting reading nonetheless. Often filled with lavish photos of the pristine and unique, they are appealing in and of themselves.

　　With the prices realized list (obtainable after the sale), one can marvel at the mysteries of supply and demand. The gaveled price is not an accurate barometer of worth. It attests to what one person was willing to pay for one particular item on one particular day. A veteran explains it as a test of wills and egos. Who walks away with the goods may come down to a simple demonstration of "My dog is bigger than your dog, my pocket is deeper than yours."

　　Attending the preview or the auction itself, of course, doesn't cost a dime. More sales are taking place in this country, although the bigger shows are held in Great Britain. Any sports memorabilia sale conceivably may include some golf items. While supplies of their catalogs are limited, several houses offer old catalogs for half price at year's end.

Christie's
502 Park Ave.
New York, NY 10022
212/546-1000

Oliver's
Box 337
Kennebunk, ME 04043
207/985-3600

Phillips
406 E. 79th St.
New York, NY 10021
212/570-4830

Sotheby's
1334 York Ave.
New York, NY 10021
212/606-7000

Sporting Antiquities
47 Leonard Rd.
Melrose, MA 02176
617/662-6588

## ADVICE FOR THE PAR-LORN

Golfers incur a ceaseless instructional bombardment. Courses are strewn, as one pro observed, with "David Leadbetter's take-away, Lee Trevino's grip, Hank Haney's stance, and a Fred Couples follow-through." Shell shock and a fatal resignation pervade many of the walking (and riding) wounded.

Instruction often travels along an informal network that only compounds the problem, golf tips are no more effective than the haphazard exchange of sexual hearsay among teenagers. The one thing about advice, the price is right (still, you likely get what you pay for).

Then there's cloak-and-dagger appeals like the one from former PGA player Jerry Heard. His letter arrived with a "Recorded Dispatch Number" *and* a "Restricted and Registered Correspondence Number." The security clearance precedes an explosive offer to receive "the very exclusive secrets we pros keep amongst ourselves." These are apparently divulged in his book, *The Golf Secrets of the Big-Money Pros*.

While mulling over Mr. Heard's terms, it seemed wise to check in with some of those who have spent the better part of their adult lives on the front lines of golf's fiercest battlefields. Maybe they'd share some of those exclusive secrets. At the very least, their advice has to be better than the driving range rumor mill. The question posed was simply, What was the best golf advice *you* ever got? Here's what a handful of PGA and Senior Tour regulars had to say. (Just to be on the safe side, better keep it under your visor.)

Practice your bunker play because if you are not a good bunker player you can't win tournaments. The guy who wins is the guy who recovers.

—Lee Trevino

The best advice I ever received in golf was to *swing within myself* and *play within my abilities*. I heard this early in my development, and it helped me to focus on balance and timing in the "swing." And the other . . . *play* within my abilities taught me to carefully examine my game (frequently) so as to be a good manager of my abilities on a given day.

—Mike Reid

When I was thirteen or fourteen years old, I slipped into a habit of sliding my right thumb off the grip portion of the club into a baseball fist wrapped around the club. This gave me a slight flip at the top of my swing and sometimes allowed me to "buggy-whip" the club through impact to produce more distance (but less accuracy). My dad noticed this new adjustment to my swing. (I played so much at that age—I didn't realize what I was doing.) He asked me what my goals were for golf. I answered that I wanted to be the best player that I could be! Based on that answer—he instructed me that I was not allowed to play another round of golf until I corrected my grip by hitting practice balls. I was crippled for four or five days improving my grip! He checked me out after a week! Thanks to Dad I was back on the course with a better game!

—D. A. Weibring

The best advice I heard came from Nancy Lopez's dad. He said, "Just play happy."

—Johnny Miller

The best advice I ever got about golf has to have come from my father [William C. Hulbert]. At the age of eight or nine years old he told me I had to change my grip. At the time it was cross-handed, and I changed to today's overlap grip. Thank you, Dad.

**—Mike Hulbert**

The best advice I ever got in golf was that golf is a gentleman's game, and you always play it in an honorable way.

**—Chi Chi Rodriguez**

I suppose the piece of advice I have felt most valuable is that a mistake made on your downswing is the result of a mistake on your backswing. It seems quite simple, but kept in mind can help to alleviate major problems. A good backswing is preparation for a good downswing.

**—Hal Sutton**

The best advice I ever got was from a golf professional who was retired but had been the pro at Rivercrest Country Club in Fort Worth, Texas. The advice he gave me was that when you are attempting to play a shot during a round, imagine that you have a third eye in your left temple. Through this eye, you can visualize the terrain and direction of the hole, etc., that you are trying to play a particular shot to; and while playing the shot, you are picturing all of these different things in your mind visualizing the ball flying in the manner you have pictured. In order to hit the shot the way that you have planned at that point, it then becomes, basically, muscle reflex. I feel that the bottom line of this lesson is that it provides you a positive mental result of what you are trying to do rather than a negative one, thus increasing your percentage of success.

**—Charles Coody**

My father, who was only a medium handicap player, advised me to keep the swing simple and to do it the way that was natural for me.

**—Hale Irwin**

Pssst. Jerry Heard's number is 216/494-4282. His book is $20.

# FINDING THE GREEN

*A state highway map, free with a call to tourism offices or for the asking at visitor centers, is still the best travel deal going. Despite the burden of lugging my clubs along, I prefer to have my own when I travel. Having them forfeits an ironclad alibi and increases the risk of misfortune, but, knowing as I do what most courses offer in the way of rentals, experience suggests you'll be much happier with your own sticks. Undoubtedly an asset, a sense of direction is not mandatory to making the best use of this section. Do one thing though, wherever you intend to play, call the course before starting out. You'll save yourself some driving time, and increase the odds of avoiding unpleasant surprises.*

## DEFINING DECENT

The search for a "good" course can take on tragic, even mythic, qualities; consensus remains the exception rather than the rule. One golfer's masochistic hell is another's pastoral heaven. In time, every golfer develops and refines his or her own personal checklist. In the quest for courses that teach everything one needs to know about golf, those courses under $30 that I've found fulfill one or more of the following criteria:

- An old course with some history
- A course designed by a famous architect
- A former country club or military course, now public
- Past or present involvement with a pro event
- Participation in the USGA Amateur Public Links Championship
- Host to a top state association tournament
- A city championship site
- A course in a state park
- A university- or college-owned course
- An especially scenic course

In addition to the above-stated bias (for which I make no apologies), you have pearls of wisdom from golf writers across the country. They've graciously recommended "decent" affordable courses on their beat, unbeatable local knowledge. The landscape is dotted with diamonds in the rough. If you've ever put down a golf magazine and wondered why no one ever writes about enjoyable, affordable, and well-managed courses anyone can play, *Willkommen.*

Many of the reporters who cover golf in their communities have written guidebooks or authored special sections for magazines or newspapers. Make an effort to find these resources. Their insight will bring you up to date, as will the largely homespun provincial golf press that, on the whole, does an excellent if unheralded job of covering golf in the hinterlands. Take my word on this: It's largely a labor of love. Trust me.

Each course listing includes yardage, slope, and course ratings from the middle tees—where, needless to say, most of us belong. The prices listed are the highest walking green fees for 18 holes on weekdays and weekends, unless otherwise noted as twilight or off-season. The good news is that twilight fees are increasingly common, the bad news is that Friday is increasingly considered the weekend. Remember to call ahead. Save yourself the aggravation.

## DRAMAMINE FOR LAYOVERS

After a thorough reading of three newspapers, a prolonged debate deciding between the frozen yogurt or the "soft" pretzel, and a careful consideration of the merits of flight insurance, what else is there to do at the airport? Not much.

To the rescue come Paradies PGA Tour Shops. Oases, if sometimes very crowded oases, these upscale pro shops are stuffed with pleasant and absorbing, not to mention time-consuming, diversions. Scan posted copies of the *Inside the PGA Tour* newsletter. Watch a video. Peruse posters and prints. Try out a putter. Or delve into the extensive bookshelf.

The Pittsburgh International Airport store (past the Calder mobile, behind the escalator, dead ahead) has a diorama detailing the history of the PGA Tour with replica clubs, photos, old programs, and front pages along the outside wall. The stores are also a good place to get close to the newest equipment you may have only read about. Bargains are not unheard of; my favorite display is the smattering of shirts, hats, and towels from various PGA Tour stops. Just don't miss your flight.

The Paradies PGA Tour Shops

Burbank/Glendale/Pasadena
(Terminal A)
Dallas/Fort Worth International
(Terminal 2E, near Gate 19)
(Terminal 4E)
Denver International
(Terminal B)
Detroit Metropolitan
(Smith Terminal)
Indianapolis International
(Main Terminal)
Jacksonville International
(Main Terminal)
Nashville International

(Concourse A)
Pittsburgh International
(Retail Court)
St. Louis International
(Main Terminal)
Sarasota/Bradenton
(Main Terminal)
Savannah International
(Main Terminal)

## TALKING GOLF ON THE RADIO

Granted it's not always easy to find, and it doesn't get the attention devoted to, say, college football, but golf comes up with increasing frequency on the sports-talk circuit. Several radio shows are noted in the individual state listings. Some feature renowned teaching professionals. Be advised, these shows can be especially dangerous when driving. When the talk turns to swing mechanics, the steering wheel makes a poor substitute for a club. Experimenting with a grip change, for instance, can produce a more fateful result (like a sideswipe) than even a snap hook.

"Tee2Green" is the only nationally syndicated golf radio show, carried approximately coast to coast on the Business Radio Network. Like most syndicated programming, some stations air it live, while others put it on tape delay and air it whenever. The show's an entertaining discourse on travel, the pro tours, and the game in general and features interviews and call-ins.

What's unusual about it, and you know this if you listen to the garden-variety sports-talk shows at all, these guys are actually knowledgeable and conversant about golf. What a concept! For more specific programming info, as they say, check your local listings, or call the Golf Radio Network, which isn't a bad idea, as it is generous with promotional goodies during tapings (800/697-8625). Stations airing "Tee2Green" include:

| | |
|---|---|
| Atlanta | WLAQ-AM |
| Baton Rouge | WIBR-AM |
| Boston | WVEI-AM |
| Cincinnati | WCVG-AM |

| | |
|---|---|
| Colorado Springs | KTWK-AM |
| Dallas | KUII-AM |
| Denver | KNUS-AM |
| Houston | KSEV-AM |
| Kalamazoo | WKMI-AM |
| Kansas City | KSIS-AM |
| Los Angeles | KMPC-AM |
| Miami | WQAM-AM |
| New York/Greenwich | WGCH-AM |
| Philadelphia | WQGL-AM |
| Sacramento | KWWN-FM |
| Washington | WPGC-AM |

For more information: 205/424-4653.

## EMILY'S LIST GOES GOLFING

Golf is hard enough, but women have never had it easy, from finding a game to finding their place in it. The National Golf Foundation has even quantified the unmistakable feeling of those who know when they're not particularly welcome. It's known as the "intimidation factor," and while it is borne to a large extent by all newcomers, it is surely a testament to golf that so many women are willing to weather the initiation that often boils down simply to sink or swim. Even more surprising are the indices that show women are flexing their strength as a demographic powerhouse in golf.

The game's attraction touches many levels. The perception that it helps in business is certainly strong. Health and Human Services head Donna Shalala once said she took up golf "Because I want to be able to ride around in a golf cart and hit people up for fifty thousand bucks."

Several organizations are making up for lost time, stealing a page from the old boys' network. The Executive Women's Golf League is a national organization of professional women eager to mix business with golf. There are sponsors, an annual meeting, and a flourishing network of local chapters. Headquarters is 407/471-1477. Two other regional organizations of interest to professional women who play golf are listed in Virginia and the District of Columbia.

## STALKING THE ELUSIVE DEEP DISCOUNT

Do golf discount cards save money? They can. That's the idea any-way. Without an abacus or a General Accounting Office study, let's just say it depends. How many courses you have to play, or can play, to defray expenses is key. That will necessarily depend not just on dollars and cents but the feeling that the card was worth it, even if you didn't play every course. (And who does?)

The premise is certainly sound. Courses open their doors at a reduced rate during traditional down periods. As discount cards pro-liferate, it is not at all unusual to see several cards: charity-affiliated and for-profit programs, even two different charity cards, working the same beat. This demonstration of the free enterprise system at work only betters the savings opportunities.

Look over the terms closely. Don't be buffaloed by the advertised number of participating courses or by a few plums. These change on a daily basis. Courses drop in and out. Be realistic. Ask yourself how many courses you will probably play. Discounts on the other side of the county, let alone the state—or even the country—might as well be on the dark side of the moon unless you have some definite travel plans or at least the intention to do so. Obviously, the personal ben-efit is negated if you never play the course. You do the math.

Any doubts about the veracity of a program's claims (and sending money to post office boxes can induce a certain healthy skepticism) can be assuaged by calling a couple of the courses listed on the brochure for confirmation. If the brochure doesn't get specific about what courses are included, pass, no matter how enticing the offer.

Prices vary considerably, and so do the benefits. Some offer one round, others offer unlimited play, still others two-for-one green fees. Some are spiced with ancillary discounts from rental cars to restaurants. Most have member publications. Golf Card International, for instance, puts out an excellent quarterly magazine, *Golf Traveler,* which covers the game at large with details on making the most of membership. Something else to think about, the charity cards beg the interesting question of how much of the membership fees actu-ally filter down to the stated beneficiary. This is a question worth asking.

Another consideration, regardless of the potential savings or phil-anthropic impulse, is time. Make darn sure you're aware of when the card takes effect and when it expires. Some follow the calendar year.

Some run twelve months from the date of purchase. This is assuredly not the same thing. *There is always fine print.* Some programs are in force during the off season, some the off-off season. This makes for an interesting proposition in places like Tucson or Palm Springs, where summer afternoons are fit only for Gila monsters. That's not to say you won't get your money's worth—by playing nine, or teeing off at dawn. But even if you do have the skin of a scorpion, you will want to understand the terms in advance.

As the clock ticks down on a card with, say, several months left before it expires, some card companies slash their fees. Around the holidays the statewide charity cards, which typically kick in January 1, also roll out discounts to take advantage of the gift-giving season. They also discount in late summer and fall. Hale Irwin's Golfers Passport even offers a six-month trial membership for $29.

Contact information and brief capsules on available discounts are included in the state listings. Many of the courses in these programs are a step up to, for instance, resorts or better public courses, sometimes even private clubs. The allure of playing a course on the cheap that you might not otherwise even consider is strong. Many programs also offer driving-range discounts, equipment, travel, or other related tie-ins.

Restrictions of some sort almost always apply. Many place restrictions on top of the restrictions. How severe depends. Most but not all require cart rental and varying degrees of advance notice. That's pretty much a given. The card may only reduce, not waive, the green fee; this misunderstanding is common. Whether that constitutes enough of a bargain depends on the desirability of the course, the size of the discount, the cart fee, and so on.

Increasingly, some courses are bending the playing field slightly by employing a sliding scale for discount-card-carrying golfers. Those paying the regular green fee will pay one price for a cart. Those on the card will have another, higher cart fee. An executive for one of the national cards told me this tiered pricing is a serious concern. You could rent a car for what some courses are apparently charging for a golf cart. I heard of one course, it happens to be in south Florida, where carts are $65 for eighteen holes! Some deal. Such shenanigans are something to be aware of.

Money aside, there is one other concern. The number one reason courses drop out of these programs is discourteous golfers. Play it straight. Call ahead. Follow the procedures for attire. Treat the place with respect. I know golfers, discount card in hand, who drove a considerable distance to play a country club participating in a charity-affiliated discount program. They were dressed, as they would be for their muny, in T-shirts and cutoffs. The club's dress requirement caught them completely off guard. After being invited to purchase a shirt with a collar in the pro shop, they declined. They were not allowed on the course, needless to say, and no doubt shared a long and unpleasant ride home. A card entitles you to enjoy the course. It does not make you a limited partner. You're still a guest and are expected to act accordingly.

Most state cards are $30 or less, with the notable exception of the PGA-sponsored programs. The national cards, which have a considerably wider scope, are higher. Even where the initial fee exceeds $30, these programs are included in deference to the presumption of savings. How much you save, again, is anybody's guess. Here are several national and regional discount card programs.

### National Golf Card Programs

WHO: Golf Access
WHAT: 50 percent off green fees at over two thousand courses nationwide. One year from time of purchase.
   **$49.95**
WHAT ELSE: Four rounds at each course; rental car, driving range, resort, cruise, golf school discounts. Addendum subscriptions to receive new course updates. $8.
   **Golf Access**
   **P.O. Box 27965**
   **Salt Lake City, UT 84127-0965**
   **800/359-4653**

WHO: Golf Card International
WHAT: "Play as many as 2,400 complimentary rounds at top golf courses in the U.S. and [*sic*] internationally . . . Members pay only for the rental of a powered golf cart."
   **$95.**
WHAT ELSE: "Save hundreds of dollars on your golfing vacations at 400 renowned resorts in the U.S., The Bahamas, Dominican Republic, Puerto Rico, Jamaica, and Canada."

Golf Card International
64 Inverness Dr. East
Englewood, CO 80112
800/321-8269

WHO: golf fore less club
WHAT: ". . . a thick confidential warehouse catalog of the latest golf
equipment from the leading firms . . . The Member Prices shown
are, in many cases, the same price a discount store would pay
when purchasing directly from the manufacturer or distributor."
$50.
WHAT ELSE: ". . . you automatically become a member of 'Golf
International' and receive the exclusive state-by-state, town-by-
town listing of over 2,000 golf courses where you can play golf for
1/2 price and save on fine resort packages."
**golf fore less club**
**2 Ridgedale Ave.**
**P.O. Box 533**
**Cedar Knolls, NJ 07927-9972**

WHO: Hale Irwin's Golfers Passport
WHAT: Over two thousand golf courses and resorts in forty-eight
states and twelve foreign countries. The largest pass on the market. Most courses offer two free rounds.
$59.
WHAT ELSE: That $59 is for a two-person membership. Six-months:
$29. Extensive listing of package discounts. Thirty-day money-
back guarantee. Free course updates.
**Hale Irwin's Golfers Passport**
**1415 E. Apache Blvd. Suite 313**
**Tempe, AZ 85281**
**800/775-GOLF**
**800/421-7469 (From Michigan, Indiana, and Ohio)**

WHO: National Golfer's Club
WHAT: ". . . we want to promote the sport of golf in a way that allows
golfers to:
1) play more golf,
2) on more local courses,

3) more often, and
4) for less money."
$49.

WHAT ELSE: ". . . you also receive all the benefits from any other clubs within your state for no additional charge."
**National Golfer's Club**
**544 Wilmore Ct.**
**Smyrna, TN 37167**

## Get Just the Fax

With Caddy Fax, a national golf travel assistance program, you can dial up tour results and/or receive course listings from cities nationwide. It's $4.95 per listing and includes par, slope, fees, and amenities. With a $9.95 annual membership, individual city information is available for less, $1.95 per listing. You can also dial up pro tour information or even submit scores for a calculated handicap (800/MY-CADDY).

## Regional Golf Card Programs

WHO: Club Key Enterprises
WHAT: ". . . receive two complimentary greens fees for an entire year on over 200 quality golf courses located in Ohio, West Virginia, Kentucky, Virginia, Pennsylvania, Georgia, Florida, North Carolina and South Carolina." (Most, however, are in Ohio.)
$55.
WHAT ELSE: Restaurant discounts in Hilton Head and Myrtle Beach. Starts from the date you join.
**Club Key**
**P.O. Box 7625**
**Hilton Head Island, SC 29938**
**800/221-7443**

WHO: *Fairways* Golf Sampler Card
WHAT: Four discounted rounds at thirty-two courses along the Alabama, Mississippi, and Florida Gulf Coast.
$40.

WHAT ELSE: Grand prize drawing. Valid one year from date of purchase.

**Bayside Publishing Group**
*Fairways* **Magazine**
**11 Midtown Park East**
**Mobile, AL 36606**
**800/647-2447**

WHO: American Lung Association Golf Privilege Card
WHAT: Over five hundred courses in Florida, Georgia, Alabama, and Mississippi.
$25.
WHAT ELSE: Newsletter, discounts on a variety of items.

**Golf Privilege Card**
**6160 Central Ave.**
**St. Petersburg, FL 33707**

WHO: American Lung Association Golf Privilege Card
WHAT: One hundred courses in Iowa and Minnesota, fifty in Nebraska, and seventy in South Dakota.
$30.
WHAT ELSE: Alamo car rental and some resort discounts.

**Golf Privilege Card**
**1025 Ashworth Rd. Suite 410**
**West Des Moines, IA 50265**
**515/224-0800**

WHO: Club 19
WHAT: "Save up to $5,800 in Green Fees at over 400 Courses" in California, Nevada, Oregon, Arizona, Washington, and British Columbia.
$49.
WHAT ELSE: Travel and miscellaneous discounts, newsletter.

**Club 19**
**Box 222594**
**Carmel, CA 93922**
**800/347-6119**

*Jim Apfelbaum*

WHO: American Lung Association Western Region
WHAT: "Free or reduced rates at 400 courses, from Ukiah to San Diego in Calif; 30 courses in Palm Springs area alone."
$35.
WHAT ELSE: Oregon (11 courses), Idaho (23 courses), Montana (28 courses), South Dakota (51 courses), Arizona (9 courses), also Utah, Nevada, and Washington. November to November.
**American Lung Association**
**800/LUNG-USA**


WHO: American Cancer Society of South Carolina Golf Pass
WHAT: 150+ courses in South Carolina, North Carolina, and Virginia.
$40.
WHAT ELSE: Twenty-one in North Carolina, 6 in Virginia. Price drops $10 as the year rolls on.
**American Cancer Society**
**803/448-2562**
**800/ACS-2345**


WHO: ALA Mid-Atlantic Region Golf Privilege Card
WHAT: Over two hundred courses in Maryland, Pennsylvania, Delaware, and Virginia.
$35.
WHAT ELSE: Drawing for a set of Head Golf "Big Head" irons.
**GPC**
**ALA of Maryland**
**1840 York Rd., Ste. M**
**Timonium, MD 21093**
**410/560-2120**

# ALABAMA

## Local Knowledge

Public golf's great monument, its Great Pyramid of Cheops, is up and running. The Robert Trent Jones Trail is in the ground. All eighteen courses are being played, nurtured by $100 million and the prayers of pensioners from Ardmore to Gulf Shores.

Oxmoor in Birmingham was the first course to open, in April of 1992. Silver Lakes is the final piece of the puzzle. It opened in December of the following year. All are within fifteen minutes of an interstate. All allow walking (but no pull carts). All are prodigally destined to become premiere public courses, a phrase that, let's face it, has been given a measure of recognition and respectability it did not have before the trail's conception. As many as seven separate tee boxes per hole can allow one hundred yards' difference from front tees to back. Clearly no golfer has been excluded.

They've built it, now will they come? Fees in the neighborhood of $30 may not raise hackles in your corner of these united fairways, but they apparently do in the Heart of Dixie.

"Thirty dollars here is outrageous," a restless native told me. "This state's not gonna pay it." The central question remains, Will visitors?

Alabama produces exceptional travel brochures and services to attract prospective golfers. An 800 number will connect you to any pro shop on the trail. There are three-, five-, and seven-day passes, trail samplers, early bird specials, a passel of "short courses," even AAA discounts (800/949-4444).

The state open has been held at Bent Brook in Bessemer, which has also hosted Monday qualifying for the Senior Tour. There are three nines, all with bent-grass greens and four sets of tees. Jimmy Bryan at *The Birmingham News* also recommends Eagle Point in Birmingham, on a par with Bent Brook, both, he said, "real fine golf courses."

Sectional public links qualifying has been held at Lagoon Park in Montgomery, which also hosts the city championship, and Grand National in Auburn/Opelika (on the RTJ Trail).

Mike Cason at *The Montgomery Advertiser* also suggested River Run, "much easier, much more forgiving than Lagoon," and Oak

Hills, a former country club, designed by Byron Nelson. "They've let it run down a bit," Mike says, "but it's still a nice course." *The Advertiser* runs an annual golf guide in early April ($1.50 for back issues, 205/262-1611).

Don't overlook the Alabama State Park courses. Oak Mountain, about fifteen minutes south of the Birmingham city limits, has also hosted publinx qualifying. It's very highly regarded. Other resort state park courses: Joe Wheeler in Rogersville and Lakepoint Resort in Eufaula, both with marinas and resort lodges, Gulf State Park in Gulf Shores, Roland Cooper in Camden, and Lake Guntersville in Guntersville (800/ALA-PARK).

Those traveling I-10 should pick up a copy of "Fairways: THE Gulf Coast Golfing Guide." It's at welcome centers, chambers of commerce, or free from 800/647-CHIP. An unabashed promotional piece that appears twice a year, it does offer a measure of candor one normally doesn't expect from advertorials. For instance, one description mentions a course "known as the fastest draining course on the coast." Even the course photographs are large enough to get a sense of the layout, a rarity.

Two college courses in Mobile, Gulf Pines (run by the University of South Alabama) and Spring Hill, are reviewed in *Fairways* magazine. Spring Hill got a new, totally automated sprinkler system in 1987, and the course is said to feature "small, elevated greens and very hilly terrain . . . much of the design . . . is just as it was when it opened in 1928." Gulf Pines, they say, has "beautiful scenery and a good test of golfing skills." It's short (just 5,661 yards from the whites), with tiny greens, susceptible to gusts blowing off Mobile Bay.

Finally, if you don't know already, as Jim Shepherd of the "Golf Tee2Green" radio show and a Birmingham resident likes to say: "Nothing breaks left in Alabama." Roll Tide.

### Discount Cards

American Heart Association Alabama Golf Card. One free round at eighty-nine courses throughout Alabama and west Florida. Calendar year. 205/592-7100. $30.

American Lung Association Golf Privilege Card. Free green fees at 100 courses in Alabama and Mississippi (all but five in Alabama). 205/933-8821. $25.

P.S. All Robert Trent Jones Trail courses offer 15 percent off "full posted green fees" and all nonsale merchandise with a valid AAA membership card.

### Shopping

By all means, in Selma drop by and visit the Otey Crisman Golf Company at 201 Faulk. Otey III intends to write some of the family's more famous customers and put together a display. Crisman putters have been a fixture on the PGA Tour for decades. The company offers a short factory tour. There's also a practice putting area to take an Otey out for a test drive. You might just find something you like. There aren't a whole lot of family operations like this left in golf—or elsewhere in American business, for that matter. Definitely worth a stop (205/872-8486).

And, heck, if the road ever takes you to Scottsboro, the Unclaimed Baggage Center is where airline luggage lost and given up for dead goes up for sale. The center does get clubs from time to time. When I called, there were some odd clubs and a full set of Northwestern sticks for $210. Do they get many clubs? "We don't ever know," said a kindly southern voice. "Just what comes through with the luggage." Anything that anyone might travel with also turns up here. After three months, if no one puts in a claim with the airline, the object gets shipped to Scottsboro (205/259-5753).

Riviera Centre Factory Stores in Foley has over eighty stores, J Crew, Duck Head, Aureus, Ruff Hewn, and Reebok for starters (800/5-CENTRE). Boaz Shopper's Paradise has over 140 stores (205/593-8154).

## FINDING THE GREEN IN ALABAMA

**Bent Brook Golf Course ($19/$29) 27 holes**
**Windmill/Brook: 6,500 yds. (70.1/116)**
**Graveyard/Windmill: 6,400 yds. (70.0/118)**
**Brook/Graveyard: 6,600 yds. (70.6/119)**
**7900 Dickey Springs Rd.**
**Bessemer 205/424-2368**

Cambrian Ridge/RTJ Trail ($22/$29) 27 holes
Canyon/Loblolly: 6,136 yds. (70.5/131)
Sherling/Canyon: 6,086 yds. (70.7/132)
Sherling/Loblolly: 6,106 yds. (69.4/123)
1591 Braggs Rd.
Greenville 205/382-9787

Eagle Point Golf Club ($19/$28) 6,200 yds. (67.4/121)
4500 Eagle Point Dr.
Birmingham 205/991-2076

Grand National/RTJ Trail ($22/$29) 36 holes
Links Course: 6,070 yds. (69.9/131)
Lakes Course: 5,948 yds. (70.2/129)
3000 Sunbelt Pkwy.
Opelika 205/749-9042

Gulf Pines Golf Course ($8/$10) 5,661 yds. (66.6/109)
University of South Alabama
167 Old Bay Front Rd.
Mobile 205/431-6413

Gulf State Park Golf Course ($19/$19) 6,171 yds. (70.4/na)
20115 State Hwy. 135
Gulf Shores 205/948-4653

Hampton Cove/RTJ Trail ($20/$27) 36 holes
River Course: 6,027 yds. (69.8/124)
Highlands Course: 6,066 yds. (68.9/124)
450 Old Hwy. 431 South
Owens Cross Roads 205/551-1818

Highland Oaks/RTJ Trail ($22/$28) 27 holes
Highlands/Magnolia: 6,386 yds. (na/124)
Highland/Marshwood: 6,454 yds. (na/126)
Magnolia/Marshwood: 6,248 yds. (na/121)
904 Royal Pkwy.
Dothan 205/712-2820

Joe Wheeler State Park Golf Course ($12/$12) 6,054 yds. (70.0/114)
Rte. 4
Rogersville 205/247-9308

Lagoon Park Golf Course ($14/$18) 6,413 yds. (69.3/121)
2855 Lagoon Park Dr.
Montgomery 205/271-7000

Lake Guntersville State Park ($12/$12) 6,258 yds. (68.8/123)
7966 Alabama Hwy. 227
Guntersville 205/571-5458

Lakepoint Resort State Park Course ($12/$12) 6,500 yds. (71.4/121)
Hwy. 431
Eufaula 800/544-LAKE or 205/687-6676

Magnolia Grove/RTJ Trail ($20/$27) 36 holes
Crossings Course: 7,150 yds. (na/na)
Falls Course: 7,240 yds. (na/na)
7000 Lamplighter Dr.
Semmes 205/645-0075

Oak Hills Country Club ($10/$15) 6,394 yds. (71.2/122)
7160 Byron Nelson Blvd.
Montgomery 205/281-3344

Oak Mountain State Park Golf Course ($13/$18) 6,374 yds.
(69.8/124)
John Finley Dr.
Pelham 205/620-2522

Oxmoor Valley/RTJ Trail ($22/$29) 36 holes
Ridge Course: 6,165 yds. (70.1/133)
Valley Course: 6,088 yds. (68.1/123)
100 Sunbelt Pkwy.
Birmingham 205/942-1177

River Run Golf Course ($13/$16) 6,147 yds. (67.9/111)
Rte. 5 Dozier Rd.
Montgomery 205/271-2811

Roland Cooper State Park Golf Course ($10/$10) 3,215 yds. (na/na)
City Hwy. 41
Camden 205/682-4838

Silver Lakes/RTJ Trail ($21/$28) 27 holes
Heartbreaker/Mindbreaker: 5,954 yds. (na/na)

Heartbreaker/Backbreaker: 5,894 yds. (na/na)
Mindbreaker/Backbreaker: 5,914 yds. (na/na)
730 Lake Dr.
Gadsden 205/892-3268

Spring Hill College Golf Course ($8/$12) 6,375 yds. (na/na)
4000 Dauphin St.
Mobile 205/343-2356

University of Alabama Golf Course ($12/$14) 18 holes/3,173 yds.
(na/121)
Loop Rd.
Tuscaloosa 205/348-7041

# ALASKA

*Local Knowledge*

I'll go out on a limb here—but chances are you've never played golf
up an Alaskan mountainside, amidst brush, spruce, snow, and sev-
enty-mile-per-hour winds. Not bloody likely, you may say. But
should you find yourself on Kodiak Island in March, the Pillar
Mountain Golf Classic will quell even the worst case of golfing cabin
fever. This going-to-extremes fundraiser for local charities is, well,
different. Think of it as golf's Iditarod.

The two-day one-hole tournament has, as its objective, the summit
of Pillar Mountain, elevation approximately four thousand feet above
sea level. Qualifying is held from the very bottom to the top. The second day the event begins from halfway up the mountain. Ax, pruning
shears, and no doubt other implements similarly and undeniably dis-
approved for USGA-sanctioned events are permitted to those industrious enough to clear a path to their ball and then to play it.

Tim Murray at the *Anchorage Daily News* has covered the event.
He told me that it took one winner, given the above-stated conditions over a distance of about half a mile, only nine strokes. And you
think you've got a golf story?

Tim says that public golf in Alaska is "much better than you might
expect." When the season does arrive, it's long in the sense that day-

light through June and most of July allows tee times almost until midnight. That's the good news. The bad news is that the courses are jammed. "Demand is very intense," says Tim.

Alaska has twelve courses. Military courses are open to the public. Twenty-five years ago there weren't any public courses, hence the open-door policy. Eagleglen at Elmendorf AFB was designed by Robert Trent Jones. It's hosted sectional qualifying for the publinks (why not Pillar Mountain?) and is one of four courses used for the state amateur. The others under $30 are Moose Run and Palmer.

Of Eagleglen, Tim says, "If there's a championship course here, that's it." Palmer, about forty-five miles north of Anchorage, is generally the first course in the state to open, as the melt-off there is quicker. It may be the longest course in Alaska, relatively straight, "a lot of fun to play." Settler's Bay in Wasilla, warmer and sunnier than Anchorage, has a beautiful nine-hole course that passed for a time as something of an "undiscovered little gem." No longer. It's about a seventy-five-mile drive northwest of Anchorage.

The Anchorage Golf Association has a directory to help visiting golfers find their way. It includes descriptions, ratings, and phone numbers. It's free with a large SASE (big enough to hold five or six sheets 8 1/2″ × 11″) from AGA Inc., P.O. Box 112210, Anchorage, AK 99511 (907/349-4653). General travel information from Fairbanks lists a couple of courses (800/327-5774).

## FINDING THE GREEN IN ALASKA

**Eagleglen Golf Course ($28/$28) 6,024 yds. (68.5/119)**
**Elmendorf AFB**
**Elmendorf 907/552-3821**

**Moose Run Golf Course ($24/$24) 6,499 yds. (69.8/119)**
**27000 Arctic Valley Rd.**
**Fort Richardson 907/428-0056**

**Palmer Municipal Golf Course ($22/$22) 6,585 yds. (72.1/124)**
**231 W. Evergreen Ave.**
**Palmer 907/745-4653**

**Settler's Bay Golf Course ($20/$20) 9 holes/6,240 yds. (68.8/113)**
**8.2 Kinik Goosebay Rd.**
**Wasilla 907/376-5466**

# ARIZONA

## Local Knowledge

TeeBox's *Arizona Golf Guide* ($16.95) cuts to the quick with incisive bullets. Fairway width, annual number of rounds, whether a course favors a fade, and a word on when annual maintenance is scheduled make this a better-than-average companion. Maps and assorted lists (including most and least expensive courses) round it out.

It features a welcome sense of humor. Favorite listing: "Don't forget your . . . ," which in turn can be: "Bring everything you can carry" from ball retriever to rock iron. Updates are promised every two to three years. In stores or available by calling 602/919-2980.

Author Steve Harper singles out Fuzzy Zoeller–designed Pueblo El Mirage in El Mirage as an especially good value. "One of the best rounds of golf for the money," he says, a course that gets neither the recognition nor the play it deserves.

Steve also likes Papago in Phoenix, past host to the national publinx, and a *Golf Digest* Top 100 Best Public Course. The TPC at Starpass is the sister course to the famed Stadium course that hosts the Phoenix Open. Steve calls it "just as good a layout for at least half the money." Twilight fee offseason is under $30. Also in Phoenix, Maryvale has hosted sectional public links qualifying.

Another source is Mike Armfield's *Valley of the Sun Golf Guide,* which reviews fifty courses in Phoenix, Scottsdale, and what's known as the East Valley ($11.65 from Golf Guys).

"For those high handicappers who desire a challenge without being overwhelmed," the Golf Guys recommend Rolling Hills in Tempe and Continental, an eighteen-hole executive course in Scottsdale. They also think highly of Ahwatukee Lakes, another executive course in Phoenix. It has water in play on twelve holes. Jack Rickard, who writes about golf for the *Tucson Citizen,* seconds the motion. He calls Ahwatukee "one of the state's most challenging executive courses." Painted Mountain (formerly Camelot) in Mesa and Chuparosa (formerly Rancho del Rey) in Queen Creek are two other courses the Golf Guys ranked among their Top 10 "Most Playable Layouts."

The *Citizen's* supplement, "Tucson Golf," includes a handy map and directory, with prices. It comes out the first Tuesday of each month and lists courses throughout southeast Arizona. Back issues can be ordered for $1.50 (602/573-4551).

On a pleasant road trip to northern Arizona, Jack Rickard found Prescott Country Club, in Dewey, "most enjoyable," without a bad hole.

"The Tucson & Southern Arizona Golf Guide" is a glossy annual freebie, available from visitors' bureaus, courses, and golf shops. It's got a good map, and the text doesn't shaft the public player. There's a similar fulfillment publication for Phoenix golf (602/998-7025).

*Arizona Golfer* is the state's monthly golf tabloid. A roundhouse of reporting and coupons, it also has a back-page directory that includes green fees. Publisher/editor Tom Draper will send out sample copies gratis (602/575-0025).

For out-of-the-way courses, Tom likes Pueblo del Sol, outside Tucson, which he says may have the "best greens in the state of Arizona, a really super little course." He also recommends Arthur Pack, "well laid out," if bearing the wear and tear of a popular public course. Harper notes it hosts qualifying for the PGA Tour's Northern Telecom Open.

Another freebie guide, though geared to the high end, *Golf Arizona* is available from Golf-Mkt (800/942-5444). Mapmakers Fore Better Golf have revised a 1991 state golf map, in pro shops for $3.95 or by calling 708/893-8672.

Tucson has exceptional munys, good enough to entertain the best. The pro tours have played Randolph North, and the PGA Tour played the Tucson Open for years at El Rio. In season, I was told, six-hour rounds are not unheard of at Fred Enke, the desert course out past Davis Monthan AFB. If you want the desert golf experience without spending a small fortune, here it is. Locals resign themselves to the wait, enjoying the scenery, chasing roadrunners, or hunting for balls amongst the saguaro, ocotillo, and creosote bushes. Enke also has a great practice facility. Be advised, Randolph North does ninety thousand to one hundred thousand rounds a year. Pete Dye did the redesign in 1980.

Desert golf must be an acquired taste. Those interested in a better appreciation of the Sonoran landscape should visit the Living Desert Museum. The natural beauty can then be enjoyed unencumbered by bag, cart, stray shots on blind holes, or chance encounters with desert flora and fauna. P.S. Only a bedouin would walk Fred Enke. El Rio and Silverbell are, however, negotiable. Flooding at Randolph North precipitated major reconstructive surgery, but a new irrigation system is in the ground.

The Scottsdale Chamber of Commerce puts out a glossy destination guide with public and private course listings, shops, and other golf-related info (800/877-1117). To my surprise, there were some courses included for under $30; okay, three: Cypress, Coronado (nine holes), and Continental (executive).

Oh, by the way, remember, it's a dry heat.

### Discount Cards

Samaritan Tour Pass Club. Eighty-four courses discounted 20 to 60 percent, including some of the best in the state. Samaritan Foundation, 602/495-4498. $70.

Tucson's Resort Golf Card. "Golf at discount prices All Year Long" at fewer than a dozen swanky courses, May 15–September 30. 602/886-8800. $69.95.

### Shopping

Casa Grande has Reebok, Izod, and Crazy Horse (800/727-6885). Page has Polo/Ralph Lauren, and there's a VF Factory Outlet in Tucson (800/772-VFFO).

## FINDING THE GREEN IN ARIZONA

**Ahwatukee Lakes Golf Club ($20/$25) 18 holes/3,660 yds. (57.4/93)**
13431 S. 44th St.
Phoenix 602/893-3004

**Arthur Pack Desert Golf Course ($20/$20) 6,384 yds. (69.2/113)**
9101 N. Thornydale Rd.
Tucson 602/744-3322

**Chuparosa Golf Course ($22/$22) 5,840 yds. (67.5/110)**
21515 Rancho del Rey Blvd.
Queen Creek 602/987-3633

Continental Golf Course ($10/$15*) 18 holes/3,766 yds. (57.4/86)
7920 E. Osborn Rd.
Scottsdale 602/941-1585

Coronado Golf Course ($22/$22) 1,850 yds. (56.7/92)
2829 N. Miller Rd.
Scottsdale 602/947-8364

Cypress Golf Course ($16/$16) 18 holes/4,946 yds. (na/na)
10801 E. McDowell
Scottsdale 602/946-5155

El Rio Golf Course ($20/$20) 6,013 yds. (68.6/108)
1400 W. Speedway Blvd.
Tucson 602/791-4336

Fred Enke Golf Course ($20/$20) 6,363 yds. (70.4/129)
8251 E. Irvington
Tucson 602/296-8607

Maryvale Municipal Golf Course ($25/$25) 6,200 yds. (68.3/111)
5902 W. Indian School Rd.
Phoenix 602/846-4022

Painted Mountain Golf Course ($30/$30) 5,490 yds. (64.6/92)
6210 E. McKellips Rd.
Mesa 602/832-0156

Papago Golf Course ($25.50/$25.50) 6,590 yds. (70.7/123)
5595 E. Moreland
Phoenix 602/275-8428

Prescott Country Club ($22/$28) 6,783 yds. (71.4/123)
1030 Prescott Country Club Blvd.
Dewey 602/772-8984

Pueblo del Sol Golf Course ($25/$25) 6,599 yds. (70.8/122)
2770 S. St. Andrews Dr.
Sierra Vista 602/378-6444

Pueblo El Mirage Country Club ($18/$20) 6,125 yds. (68.1/114)
11201 N. El Mirage Rd.
El Mirage 602/583-0425

*Off season

Randolph Park Golf Course 36 holes
North Course: ($22/$22) 6,436 yds. (70.0/121)
South Course: ($20/$20) 5,939 yds. (66.5/99)
600 S. Alvernon Way
Tucson 602/791-4336

Rolling Hills Golf Course ($16/$16) 18 holes/3,509 yds. (56.3/72)
1415 N. Mill Ave.
Tempe 602/350-5275

Silverbell Golf Course ($20/$20) 6,284 yds. (68.8/110)
3600 N. Silverbell Rd.
Tucson 602/791-4336

TPC at Starpass ($28/$28*) 6,383 yds. (71.3/127)
3645 W. 22nd St.
Tucson 602/622-6060

# ARKANSAS

*Local Knowledge*

With change back from a ten on green fees and beautiful natural
backdrops, golf in Arkansas certainly has its upside. Play has nearly
doubled in the last decade, but four-hour rounds are still the norm.
Tee times are routinely a civilized ten minutes apart. That's the good
news. The downside is condition. Without any higher-niche public
courses (Quapaw, a British-style open course in North Little Rock,
may help), munys take a pounding.

Beck Cross covers golf for the *Arkansas Democrat-Gazette*. She
likes Burns Park in North Little Rock, where an innovative check-
point system maintains pace of play. It's hosted publinks qualifying
and is slated for another nine holes.

Down the road in Benton, Longhills has also hosted sectional publinx qualifying. Its reputation is for as-good-as-you'll-find public

*Off season

greens. The staff is conscientious and friendly, and the course rolls and turns through thick glades. Unfortunately, the county's dry. Console yourself with one of the club's logoed T-shirts ($10). This is a terrific course for the buck, a personal favorite.

The venerable War Memorial course near the Little Rock Zoo has its charm. Stopping traffic on University Avenue or scalding one onto the Wilbur B. Mills Memorial Freeway ("The Fanne Foxe" to locals) is entertaining—and not all that hard to do—but even that can't alleviate the neglect. Several fairways double for parking when the Razorbacks are playing at the nearby stadium, which can't help matters.

Rebsamen gets the most play. Flat, right next to the river, it does get a thankful breeze, but unfortunately the river overflows now and then, drowning the course. Easily walked, it's popular with seniors. There's also a short nine of 2,557 yards, with one par three and one par five.

DeGray Lake Resort State Park is Arkansas's only state park course. The front side is undistinguished, but the back winds through gorgeous forest and the holes are in better shape. The nearby lake, marina, and hotel (camping's also available) make this a terrific vacation spot on the cheap. In the fall, the area must be spectacular.

The *Democrat-Gazette*'s annual golf section, including a state course directory, is available from the Arkansas Golf Association soon after May 1 (501/227-8555). Tourism information is available by calling 800/NATURAL. The free *Arkansas Golfer*, with a few coupons, can be found at most courses.

Other suggestions: Western Hills Country Club and Hindman Park in Little Rock and Diamondhead near Hot Springs, right outside Lake St. Catherine State Park.

The course of young John Daly's matriculation is Bay Ridge Boat & Golf Club in Dardanelle. I asked. "A dump," I was told. Public play is restricted to weekdays only. If you do pass through Hot Springs, have the good sense to eat at McClard's Bar-B-Q, many times voted the best restaurant in the state. Ray Floyd can surely be counted on to know a good BBQ joint when he finds one. His picture's on the wall. The Cokes come in bottles.

Traveling on I-40 west from Little Rock toward Fort Smith in northwest Arkansas, don't miss the Arkansas Golf Museum and Craft Center in Ozark (Exit 37). Hundreds of clubs, trophies, artwork, ephemera, memorabilia, and, perhaps, one day soon, a nine-hole "antique" course (800/951-2525).

Fort Smith also has a country club, built in 1904, that's open to the public. They say it's the second-oldest course, still on the original plot, west of the Mississippi.

### Discount Card

American Lung Association Golf Card. 70 courses, fourteen driving ranges, nine miniature golf courses (carts not required at many), March 1–November 30. 800/880-5864 or 501/224-5864. $30.

## FINDING THE GREEN IN ARKANSAS

Bay Ridge Boat & Golf Club ($15/—) 6,036 yds. (69.0/na)
Hwy. 22
Dardanelle 501/229-4162

Burns Park Golf Course ($8/$10) 6,003 yds. (66.8/102)
Military Rd.
North Little Rock 501/758-5800

DeGray Lake Resort State Park Golf Course ($10/$11) 6,417 yds.
(69.7/130)
Hwy. 7
Bismarck 501/865-2807

Diamondhead Country Club ($26.25/$26.25) 6,172 yds. (70.2/118)
Hot Springs 501/262-3734

Fort Smith Country Club ($7.75/$7.75) 2,476 yds. (na/na)
5500 Midland Blvd.
Fort Smith 501/783-9308

Hindman Park Golf Course ($7.50/$9.75) 6,400 yds. (68.9/109)
60 Brookview
Little Rock 501/565-6450

Longhills Golf Course ($9/$13) 6,143 yds. (68.2/105)
327 Hwy. 5 North
Benton 501/794-9907

Quapaw Golf Links ($12/$25) 6,699 yds. (71.2/117)
110 State Hwy. 391 North
North Little Rock 501/945-0945

Rebsamen Park Golf Course ($7.50/$9.75) 6,271 yds. (67.9/100)
Rebsamen Park Rd.
Little Rock 501/666-7965

War Memorial Park Golf Course ($7.50/$9.75) 4,432 yds. (na/na)
5511 W. Markham
Little Rock 501/663-0854

Western Hills Country Club ($10/$15) 5,939 yds. (67.4/105)
5207 Western Hills Ave.
Little Rock 501/565-5830

# CALIFORNIA

## Local Knowledge

The California State Automobile Association publishes two regional golf guides each year. Free to AAA members, anyone belonging to an affiliated state AAA can also get one for free by mail or by stopping in at any CSAA office in California or Nevada. These are handy guides, with terse charts crammed with particulars for 450 courses (Auto Club of SoCal, P.O. Box 2890, Los Angeles, CA 90051-0890, or CSAA 150 Van Ness Ave., San Francisco, CA 94102-5279).

The Southern California Golf Association sells its annual *Directory of Member Clubs*. It's $15 but unfortunately makes no distinction between private and public (818/980-3630 or (213/877-0901). Somewhat fancier, the *Bluebook Edition* ($17.50) is the Northern California Golf Association equivalent. Some of it will be useless to visitors, but the listings are concise and comprehensive with great maps, directions, and updated prices (408/625-4653). Highly recommended despite the price.

Foghorn Press publishes the two definitive statewide guides: *California Golf* ($17.95) and *The Ultimate California Golf Guide* ($15.95). Although now dated, *Golfing Northern California* ($29.95, Pelican Publishing) by Tim Keyser is a hardcover hybrid of guide and coffee-table book. Clinical insight is matched with crisp color photos: a beautiful book, thoroughly researched and well thought out.

*Golfer's Guide to Southern California* is another significant achievement but more up to date. A yardage book with narrative, everything, and I mean everything, from the availability of adequate rest rooms to the ratio of grasses blended on the greens, is surveyed and appraised with a consumerist zeal. An example:

ROUGHS: Difficult; one cut at 1 1/2″ of dense fine fescue with some creeping red fescue and Bermuda grasses that slow down club speed. Play safe and deliberate, laying to an opportunistic location for next shot.

Six courses are typically dissected in each pocket-size issue. Pick one up at any Southern California Audi dealer. No guide—and there are some good ones—comes more highly recommended. Best of all, it's free. Subscribers do qualify for some great discounts. Course detective and author Dave Mills also shares his insights on XTRA Sports 690 and 670-AM in L.A. A two-year subscription to *Golfer's Guide to Southern California* (eight issues) is $29.95 (310/841-4866). For its remarkable attention to detail, it is awarded the Golden Apfel Award for Meritorious Service to Apfordable Golf.

"The best value in golf in Southern California," Dave says, "is Industry Hills at Twilight." (Certain times of the year, twilight rates kick in as early as 11 A.M., one of the few bright spots in a state where Friday is routinely considered the weekend and green fees are jacked accordingly.)

"This is a course that understands the concept of downtime," he explains. "That it's better to have people on the course at $20 or $25 than to have the course empty." There are two courses here, the (Ike) Eisenhower and (Babe) Zaharias, and you will be hard-pressed to find more bang for the buck. Leave time at Industry Hills to visit the Ralph W. Miller Library/Museum at the resort and convention center. Its extensive collection includes some of golf's most famous books, magazines from around the world, videos, memorabilia, artwork, and much more. Open Tuesday through Friday 9 A.M.–6 P.M., weekends from noon to 4 P.M. Closed Mondays (818/854-2354).

Dave also recommends Simi Hills in Simi Valley ("eminently walkable . . . breathtaking vistas . . . fair—yet challenging"). He gives it a par rating, meaning simply: "Good is good." Other suggestions: Los Robles in Thousand Oaks, River Ridge in Oxnard—both host to their respective city championships—and Knollwood, a former country club in Granada Hills.

The Ventura Freeway is literally an L wedge from the opening holes at Los Robles, but the course is attractive and venerable, with mature oaks, poplars, and willows. The wind and the hills make it challenging enough. There are three par threes a side, and it's easy to find and walk.

Rancho Park in West Los Angeles is a phenomenon: Nearly 150,000 rounds of golf are recorded each year; the marvel is that it runs as smoothly as it does. Yes, it is plagued by slow play (would you believe six-minute tee times?). Yes, you best keep an eye on your clubs. But service is dispensed with the aplomb and efficiency of a crowded New York delicatessen. And, not unlike a deli, numbers are called out over a loudspeaker. Originally a private club built in the 1930s, Rancho has hosted several dozen professional tournaments, including eighteen L.A. Opens. The course winds through appealing narrow tree-lined fairways, home to coyotes, hawks, and owls. Predators of a different sort lurk across the street at Twentieth Century–Fox.

Past the tributes to former L.A. Open champions there is a convivial luncheonette (with a bag rack inside). The food's good too. There's the Trevino Burger (guacamole and cheese), the Aoki (with the house teriyaki sauce), and even the Daly (on a long French roll); the peach pie is exceptional.

Despite the congestion, Rancho is worth the effort. Whatever transpires on the first seventeen holes, the plaque on the eighteenth tee is sure to inspire a contemplative respect for the golf gods. It reads:

> The first day of the 35th L.A. Open, Arnold Palmer, voted Golfer of the Year, took a 12 on this hole. As an inspiration to all golfers, the L.A. Jr. Chamber of Commerce dedicates this monument. Palmer hit a fine drive. He sliced his next 2 shots into the driving range, then hooked two more onto Patricia Ave. Hit the green with his sixth shot, and two putted. Eight strokes plus four penalties add up to 12.

The lines are no shorter at Griffith Park, past the zoo, the joggers, the cyclists, and those involved in more furtive activities. The stone fortress of a clubhouse, built by the WPA, is a great place to kick back and reflect on some marvelous holes. The eighth on the Harding course, adorned with a stately willow and tiered reflecting pool, has the sculptured look of a Japanese garden. Passing the zoo on the way up the eighteenth fairway, depending on one's partners, can seem somehow appropriate. There's also the FDR short course, near the Greek Theater (three par threes, longest par four is 392).

Drugs have been blamed for many ills, but I never thought them responsible for high green fees. That is, nevertheless, the explanation I got at Brookside, next to the Rose Bowl in Pasadena, when I asked about the steep fees. Anywhere else these courses, stately and pleasant as they are, would be $10 to $15. Nonresidents pay an outrageous $30 and up on the weekend.

"Cocaine," an old-timer explained. "Dulls their brains. Otherwise [golfers] would be out here picketing." Both courses are used for parking during Rose Bowl events. Brookside One is longer and more demanding. Course number two is tight, considerably shorter, with small and well-protected greens. Although it's easy to walk, you will need every club in the bag and all the guile you can muster.

South from L.A., tucked behind the sprawl on El Camino Real, San Clemente is one primo muny. Everything is right where it should be: a bench, a shoe scraper, a water fountain. There are some gorgeous holes that nicely integrate with the canyons and the changes in elevation. Fifteen is a scenic par three played over a giant sculpted bowl backed by palms. Rationally priced range balls make the "Pride of the Pacific" assuredly in the top percentile of affordable golf.

When the dust settles from the restructuring at Balboa Park in San Diego, it will be another upscale muny. Wait till it does. Tecolote Canyon in San Diego is an eighteen-hole executive course designed by Robert Trent Jones that's a lot of fun.

If you can find Hesperia on the map, play the Hesperia Golf and Country Club, a onetime PGA Tour stop that pushes all the right buttons. Gene Littler holds the course record with a sixty-two. The Mojave Water Agency's Morongo Basin Pipeline has undercut the course, but if the construction's complete, you'll find narrow fairways leading to narrow greens guarded by narrowly defined hazards. I heard the magic words from members: "You can play it every day, and it's never the same from morning to afternoon."

Whispering Lakes in Ontario, described in *California Golf* as "among the least crowded courses in Southern California," hosted sectional publinks qualifying in 1994.

The ferry across is more than $30, but golf on Catalina Island is a blast. Tee off from a bluff over a street and a restaurant. Marvel at the wild boar traps (you get relief from any boar diggings). Smell the sea air. Admire the swaying palms. The oldest course in Southern California (1892) still retains something from its days as a playground for the rich. The museum has some interesting Bobby Jones memorabilia. William Wrigley sponsored an amateur tournament that lasted into the fifties. The course is walking distance from the ferry. Equipment can be rented.

North from L.A. on the Ventura Freeway, Camarillo Springs offers wonderful scenery—once you get past the ticky-tacky. The fourth through eighth holes play toward the Santa Monica Mountains under slopes covered with cacti. Dave Mills calls this stretch "a genuine joy to walk and play." A nice golf experience if a tad overpriced, I found it an efficient operation and a shortish but entertaining course.

En route up the coast, two fine public courses are Avila Beach

*Bobby Jones teeing off on Catalina Island. The tournament that bore his name was played every spring from 1931 to 1955.*
COURTESY OF THE CATALINA ISLAND MUSEUM

Golf Resort near San Luis Obispo and De Laveaga in Santa Cruz. I've
played courses as nice as these, two, even three times as expensive.
Avila Beach features an inspired design and spectacular scenery. The
front side winds up and around crags of gnarled oaks and sycamores
and is not without some quirkiness. The back side is flat, closer to
the ocean, but nestles up along the hillsides. Wind certainly compli-
cates matters. Locals say it's less crowded than other area courses, a
resort masquerading as a terrific and affordable facility. Chalk
Mountain in Atascadero and Black Lake in Nipomo also come highly
recommended. Soule Park in Ojai is a beautiful course, next door to
Ojai Valley, where the Senior Tour stops. A near six-hour round on
a Monday, however, has a way of clouding the brain.

Magnets seem to attract stray shots into the ravines at De Laveaga.
Thankfully, most of the hazards are lateral. Put the driver in the bag;
better yet, leave it in the trunk. Give it away if you have to.
Intimidating carries and a devilish design insist you keep the ball in
play. It's hard to imagine a course any shorter being any harder.
Follow the signs past the "Stroke Center" (no joke). Tim Keyser's
exhaustive checklist produced a rating of "very good." Worth the
trip.

A pang of envy is understandable to those of modest means
headed through the Monterey peninsula. Don't despair. Head for
Pacific Grove, a muny with a lighthouse and some fabulous links
holes. After a pedestrian front side, the course parallels the ocean
with the same views considerably more expensive up the street. The
price keeps rising at the poor man's Pebble Beach, but it's still worth
it. Shame on you if you ride. The lighthouse raises funds by collecting and selling balls for a quarter.

To play Pebble Beach for $3.50—and get the scenic seventeen-
mile drive thrown in for free (it's regularly $6.50)—here's the deal:
Tell the gatehouse guard you'd like to play the Peter Hay course.
Give him $6.50. Save the receipt. Take the receipt to the course,
which is walking distance from the Lodge.

You can play the Hay Course all day for $3.50 with the receipt.
Afterward, walk around the Lodge, commune with the Lone Cypress,
enjoy the drive, and see if anyone's actually playing the notoriously
empty Cypress Point. (Sorry to disappoint those still hoping to get on
at *The* Pebble Beach golf links, but hey, a lot of folks never even
realize this delightful short course exists.)

Peter Hay was the pro at Pebble, and he left as his legacy an immaculately maintained par three course. This must be the finest pitch and putt in America, and it's a real treat.

Morro Bay is just as much fun, a state park course with holes framed by enormous Monterey pines that make it nearly impossible to hit into adjoining fairways. The wind can be brutal, but the Pacific makes an invigorating backdrop. Stay in the park and sneak over to the course near sunset with a wedge and putter and it doesn't get any better. A heron rookery off the twelfth hole attracts fans in May.

A somewhat clannish nature prevails here among the seniors who consume the lion's share of the tee sheet, but the staff makes a concerted effort to please. There's a cool giant photo in the clubhouse of a match between Jimmy Thomson and Lawson Little.

There are no towels on the ball washers at Harding Park in San Francisco and one measly water fountain. They're indicative of the scant amenities (there's also some funky bunkers), but the course is in otherwise good shape, if mobbed. The finishing holes, bordered by majestic junipers, are terrific. There's also a great yardage guide ($2).

Mission Bay Golf Center, downtown under the freeway, past the boathouses, trailers, and warehouses, is your typical big-city range (fifty-nine balls for $6, and they hit you $5 to fool around in the bunker).

Boundary Oak, a decidedly upscale conditioned muny in Walnut Creek, is ranked as one of the Top 10 Best Public Courses in Northern California by the *San Francisco Examiner*. Don't let the rattlesnake signs scare you; someone wandered up into the hills and got bit, hence the liability jitters. The course is operated by Senior Tour player Bob Boldt; pick up his chatty newsletter, *Thunderboldts*.

A few Northern California designer labels:

*Robert Trent Jones*
  Forest Meadows, Murphys
*Alister Mackenzie*
  Haggin Oaks, Sacramento
  Northwood, Monte Rio
  Sharp Park, Pacifica
  Wawona, Yosemite National Park

## More Local Knowledge

The state is dotted with free golf publications. *Golf Today* includes plenty of coupons and course reviews and a better-than-average mix of commentary, history, humor, and instruction. Former USGA executive director Sandy Tatum often contributes, joined by Snobby Golfbum and "Ask the Shrink!" (415/802-8165). Where else but California?

Pat Sullivan's "On Golf" column appears in Saturday's *San Francisco Chronicle*.

In Los Angeles and points south, there's *Golf Southern California*, "Your link with the local golf scene" (six times a year, 800/669-6595). *The Desert Sun* in Palm Springs provides terrific daily golf coverage, not surprising given the mother lode of courses. Favorite Features: "Road Trip of the Week" and "Hole of the Week." There's also a monthly supplement, "Desert Golf," with a valley course map. The visitor center also hands out a course list.

The College of the Desert in Palm Desert houses artifacts from longtime collector Jude Poynter (619/346-2190).

*The Golf Guide & Coupon Book* ($19.95) promises over $400 in coupons, most of the buy-one-get-one-free variety. There are also slim but serviceable listings for over two hundred courses around Southern California. Make sure to check the expiration date on the coupons before you buy (909/397-5711).

*Golf Courses of California* magazine ($5.95) is part of a growing chain of glossy state-by-state golf publications. Slanted in favor of resorts, there is a meaty alphabetical state course listing and some instructional articles (713/623-4613).

B&M Maps produces a map and directory of San Diego County courses ($3.25). Available at some visitor centers, it is dated (619/729-4408). Premier Publications puts out an excellent annual series of golf maps for Riverside and San Bernardino counties, Los Angeles and Ventura counties, and San Diego and Orange counties. Two dollars in area golf stores. Fore Better Golf has course maps for San Francisco, Los Angeles, and the Sacramento Valley ($3.95, 708/893-8672). Golf Reservations of America, Inc., books tee reservations at over fifty courses throughout Southern California as far in advance as sixty days. For $3 to $5 (fine print: per golfer, per game), it will do the spadework (800/TEE-TIME).

More local free golf info is available from Carlsbad (800/CARLS-BAD), Long Beach (800/4LB-STAY), Newport Beach (800/94-COAST), Palm Springs (800/34-SPRINGS), and Ventura (805/648-2875).

Finally, you might say a prayer for Fort Ord, Presidio, and some of the other choice military courses to open their doors. Golfers are monitoring the situation closely. The army was not shy about co-opting some magnificent beachfront.

### Discount Card

Desert Discount Golf Pass. Discounted green fees at fifty tonier courses in and around Palm Springs, including PGA West, Indian Wells, and Mission Hills. Free two-day admission to the Dinah Shore. June–September. 619/324-4546. $39.

### Shopping

For starters, there are outlets in Anderson, Barstow, and Cabazon. Gilroy has two factory-outlet centers, one with 150 stores, including Eddie Bauer, Nike, and Fila. Lake Elsinore has Bass, Cape Isle, North Face, Cole Haan, and more. Ashworth Warehouse has outlet stores with overstocks and last season's apparel, mostly first quality, some seconds, at discounts up to 50 percent off. They don't make a big deal about it but there are four stores in California: Carlsbad (619/438-6610), San Ysidro (619/690-5900), Anderson (916/365-8090), and Vacaville (707/447-0237).

While soaking up the vibes in Pebble Beach, do visit Cambridge Golf Antiquities and ogle the antique and classic clubs—and the prices. The Jack Nicklaus Collection also has a store, in nearby Carmel.

## FINDING THE GREEN IN CALIFORNIA

**Avila Beach Golf Resort ($23/$30) 6,048 yds. (69.0/116)**
**Avila Beach Rd.**
**Avila Beach 805/595-2307**

Balboa Park Golf Course ($20/$25) na yds. (na/na)
Golf Course Dr.
San Diego 619/235-1184

Black Lake Golf Resort ($16/$19*) 6,068 yds. (68.6/114)
1490 Golf Course Ln.
Nipomo 805/481-4204 or 805/343-1214

Boundary Oak Golf Course ($17/$22) 6,406 yds. (70.2/120)
3800 Valley Vista Rd.
Walnut Creek 510/934-6211

Brookside Golf Course ($25/$30) 36 holes
Course One: 6,661 yds. (71.6/117)
Course Two: 6,060 yds. (68.4/112)
1133 Rosemont Ave.
Pasadena 818/796-8151

Camarillo Springs Golf Club ($13/$17*) 5,931 yds. (67.9/108)
791 Camarillo Springs Rd.
Camarillo 805/484-1075

Chalk Mountain Golf Course ($20/$25) 6,026 yds. (68.6/118)
10000 El Bordo Rd.
Atascadero 805/466-8848

De Laveaga Golf Course ($15/$19.75*) 6,010 yds. (70.4/133)
401 Upper Park Rd.
Santa Cruz 408/423-7212

Forest Meadows Golf Course ($16/$22) 18 holes/3,886 yds.
(58.3/95)
633 Forest Meadows Dr.
Murphys 209/728-3439

Griffith Park Golf Course ($16/$20.50) 36 holes
Harding Course: 6,450 yds. (69.1/108)
Wilson Course: 6,720 yds. (70.9/109)
4730 Crystal Spgs. Dr.
Los Angeles 213/664-2255

*Twilight

Haggin Oaks Golf Course ($13.50/$16) 36 holes
North Course: 6,660 yds. (69.9/112)
South Course: 6,296 yds. (69.3/110)
3645 Fulton Ave.
Sacramento 916/481-4507

Harding Park Golf Course ($24/$29) 6,586 yds. (71.3/119)
Harding Rd. and Skyline Blvd.
San Francisco 415/664-4690

Hesperia Golf and Country Club ($15/$20) 6,695 yds. (72.4/127)
17970 Bangor Ave.
Hesperia 619/244-9301

Industry Hills Sheraton Resort ($25/$30*) 36 holes
Eisenhower Course: 6,262 yds. (70.9/130)
Zaharias Course: 6,124 yds. (70.3/130)
One Industry Hills Pkwy.
City of Industry 818/810-4653

Knollwood Golf Course ($17/$21) 6,170 yds. (68.1/112)
12040 Balboa Blvd.
Granada Hills 818/363-8161

Los Robles Golf Course ($15/$20) 5,868 yds. (67.0/110)
299 S. Moorpark Rd.
Thousand Oaks 805/495-6421

Mission Bay Golf Center
Sixth St. near Channel at China Basin
San Francisco 415/431-PUTT

Morro Bay Golf Course ($20/$25) 6,113 yds. (69.1/116)
201 State Park Rd.
Morro Bay 805/772-4560

Northwood Golf Course ($20/$28) 9 holes/5,746 yds. (68.8/115)
19400 Hwy. 116
Monte Rio 707/865-1116

Pacific Grove Municipal ($24/$28) 5,533 yds. (66.3/115)
77 Asilomar Ave.
Pacific Grove 408/648-3177

*Twilight

Peter Hay Golf Course ($10 all day) 1,570 yds. (na/na)
17 Mile Dr.
Pebble Beach 408/625-8518

Pismo State Beach Golf Course ($12.50/$14) 1,465 yds. (na/na)
25 Grand Beach Ave.
Grover Beach 805/481-5215

Pointe Catalina Island Golf Club ($30/$30) 9 holes/4,203 yds. (60.0/98)
One Country Club Rd.
Avalon 310/510-0530

Rancho Park Golf Course ($16/$20.50) 6,216 yds. (69.0/108)
10460 West Pico Blvd.
Los Angeles 310/838-7373

River Ridge Golf Club ($17/$22) 6,111 yds. (68.7/109)
2401 W. Vineyard Ave.
Oxnard 805/983-4653

San Clemente Municipal ($17/$24) 6,104 yds. (68.4/112)
150 E. Magdalena Ave.
San Clemente 714/492-1997

Sharp Park Golf Course ($17/$25) 6,273 yds. (70.0/115)
Sharp Park Rd. and Hwy. 1
Pacifica 415/359-3380

Simi Hills Golf Club ($16/$23) 6,133 yds. (68.7/110)
5031 Alamo St.
Simi Valley 805/522-0813

Soule Park Golf Club ($18/$22) 6,398 yds. (69.1/107)
1033 E. Ojai Ave.
Ojai 805/646-5633

Tecolote Canyon Golf Course ($12/$16) 18 holes/3,166 yds. (56.0/94)
2755 Snead Ave.
San Diego 619/279-1600

Wawona Hotel Golf Course ($17.50/$17.50) 9 holes/6,015 yds.
(69.1/117)
Yosemite National Park
Hwy. 41
Yosemite 209/375-6572

Whispering Lakes Golf Course ($15/$18) 6,288 yds. (68.8/114)
2525 Riverside Dr.
Ontario 909/923-3673

# COLORADO

## Local Knowledge

The Colorado Golf Association's annual "Shag Book" comes out each March. Ostensibly for members, it provides useful course listings, including maps and a word on the Colorado Golf Hall of Fame (located at the association's offices in Englewood). The guide's a steal for a dollar (303/779-GOLF).

*Colorado Golfer, The State Golf Newspaper,* ($6 for 7 issues) puts out a handy annual guide in April with extensive course listings and updated green fees (303/699-GOLF).

Each issue of the handsome quarterly *Colorado Golf* magazine has a state course guide and map. Pick up a copy at Safeway, King Soopers, and most grocery stores (or call 303/688-5853).

A recent *Colorado Golf* annual Top 10 poll included eight courses under $30, at least during the week:

1. Fox Hollow, Lakewood
2. Walking Stick, Pueblo
3. Riverdale Dunes, Brighton
4. Pine Creek, Colorado Springs
6. Mariana Butte, Loveland
8. Hyland Hills, Westminster
9. Meadow Hills, Aurora
10. Ptarmigan, Fort Collins

Riverdale Dunes, designed by Perry Dye, hosted the Amateur Public Links Championship in 1993. The "links-style" course gets thirty thousand rounds a year and has bent-grass greens, fairways, and tees. Hyland Hills hosted the Women's Amateur Publinx Championship in 1990. Ptarmigan was designed by Jack Nicklaus, Walking Stick by Arthur Hills.

For your viewing pleasure, the Colorado Golf Resort Association offers a fifty-five-minute video travelogue produced by Rand McNally. *Golf Colorado* is $25, but $20 is refunded when you return the tape. The association also puts out a splashy free brochure, Colorado Golf Vacations, 2110 S. Ash, Denver, CO 80222.

The annual golf supplement in the *Colorado Springs Gazette Telegraph* also covers a lot of ground. It comes out each spring (719/632-5511).

The state's oldest course is Patty Jewett in Colorado Springs. Built in 1896, it is another of those courses staking claim to the first golf course west of the Mississippi. Harry Vardon was said to have pronounced the course "the sportiest club in America" in 1900. Steve Trivett, who anchors the *Gazette Telegraph*'s golf section, says it's one of the most heavily played courses in the state.

Wellshire, in Denver, was a country club in the early thirties. It's listed as having been designed by Donald Ross in 1924.

Other courses that have either hosted the state public links championship or sectional qualifying for the national publinx:

Collindale, Fort Collins
Indian Tree, Arvada
The Meadows, Littleton
South Suburban, Littleton
Tiara Rado, Grand Junction
Twin Peaks, Longmont

There are no state park courses in Colorado, but Rifle Creek Golf Course is adjacent to Rifle Gap State Park in northwest Colorado. *The Colorado Official State Vacation Guide* lists golf vacations among its spring and summer activities (800-COLORADO). Fore Better Golf does Denver with its '94 edition golf map (708/893-8672).

### Discount Card

Mesa State College Golf Pass. Twenty-six courses, most free, some two-for-one green fees. 303/248-1278. $25.

### Shopping

There are outlets in Durango (Polo/Ralph Lauren), Silverthorne (J Crew), and Castle Rock (Brooks Brothers). But if your travels take you to Colorado Springs in June, see if a company called ECM is holding its annual fire sale. It handles fulfillment for the USGA Catalog from Golf House. A past ad for the sale, held on consecutive weekends, promised "Everything at Least 50 percent Off." Clothes, prints, books, jewelry, the works (719/590-1300). Worth looking into.

Golf for Her, "The Complete Golf Shop for Women," is in Englewood at 7475 E. Arapahoe in Heritage Place Shopping Center (303/770-0406).

## FINDING THE GREEN IN COLORADO

Collindale Golf Course ($13/$14) 6,432 yds. (69.3/120)
1441 E. Horsetooth Rd.
Fort Collins 303/221-6651

Fox Hollow Golf Club ($27/$27) 27 holes
Links/Meadows: 6,295 yds. (69.0/122)
Links/Canyon: 6,347 yds. (69.0/124)
Canyon/Meadows 6,154 yds. (68.0/128)
13410 W. Morrison Rd.
Lakewood 303/986-7888

Hyland Hills Golf Course ($19/$19) 6,227 yds. (68.1/120)
9650 N. Sheridan Blvd.
Westminster 303/428-6526

Indian Tree Golf Course ($18/$18) 6,256 yds. (67.9/108)
7555 Wadsworth Blvd.
Arvada 303/423-3450

Mariana Butte Golf Course ($18/$25) 5,956 yds. (67.1/116)
701 Clubhouse Dr.
Loveland 303/667-8308

Meadow Hills Golf Course ($22/$24) 6,242 yds. (69.3/130)
3609 S. Dawson St.
Aurora 303/690-2500

The Meadows Golf Club ($21.50/$21.50) 6,131 yds. (67.6/118)
6937 S. Simms
Littleton 303/972-8831

Patty Jewett Golf Course ($13/$13) 6,463 yds. (69.9/120)
900 E. Espanola
Colorado Springs 719/578-6825

Pine Creek Golf Club ($20/$24) 6,040 yds. (68.1/121)
9850 Divot Tr.
Colorado Springs 719/594-9999

Ptarmigan Golf & Country Club ($20/$25*) 6,586 yds. (70.0/128)
5412 Vardon Way
Fort Collins 303/226-6600

Rifle Creek Golf Club ($22/$22) 5,747 yds. (67.0/117)
3004 State Hwy. 325
Rifle 303/625-1093

Riverdale Golf Course 36 holes
Dunes Course: ($26/$26) 6,364 yds. (68.8/120)
Knolls Course: ($16/$16) 6,418 yds. (68.8/114)
13300 Riverdale Rd.
Brighton 303/659-6700

South Suburban Golf Course ($22.50/$22.50) 6,359 yds. (68.2/117)
7900 S. Colorado Blvd.
Englewood 303/770-5508

Tiara Rado Golf Course ($16/$16) 5,907 yds. (67.1/112)
2063 S. Broadway
Grand Junction 303/245-8085

Twin Peaks Golf Course ($16/$16) 6,237 yds. (68.8/115)
1200 Cornell St.
Longmont 303/772-1722

Walking Stick Golf Course ($15/$17) 5,996 yds. (67.1/117)
4301 Walking Stick Blvd.
Pueblo 719/584-3400

Wellshire Golf Course ($18.75/$19.75) 6,542 yds. (69.3/121)
3333 S. Colorado Blvd.
Denver 303/757-1352

*Off season

# CONNECTICUT

### Local Knowledge

*Golf in Connecticut* is simply superlative. The breadth of detail and the clever layout and packaging make this an indispensable resource for anyone interested in playing here.

The guide features two booklets: a course directory and a separate course locator. There's also a foldout color state map. It all fits snugly into a two-pouch plastic cover small enough to fit comfortably into a golf bag's top pocket. Wait, there's more. Buy the guide for the ridiculously low price of $9.95 and author Brian Harvey promises a free updated fee sheet every spring for the next three years. Brian's book represents the best of the genre, and for his reporting, organization, and imaginative presentation hereby receives the Golden Apfel Award for Meritorious Service to Apfordable Golf. Exceptional. (203/674-8866).

Courses that have hosted recent Connecticut State Golf Association Public Links Championships:

Bel Compo, Avon
Elmridge, Pawcatuck
Pine Valley, Southington
Shennecossett, Groton (designed by Donald Ross)
Tashua Knolls, Trumbull
Timberlin, Kensington
Tunxis Plantation, Farmington

Sectional qualifying for the national publinks has been held at H. Smith-Richardson in Fairfield and Simsbury Farms in West Simsbury. The CSGA sends out a directory of member clubs that simply lists course names and addresses. The state vacation guide includes a public course directory with notes on par, yardage, warnings about league play, and a list of restrictions. (You will have to dig a bit to find a course in a particular city or town as the list is alphabetical by course name.) It's free from 800/CT-BOUND. While supplies last, the Connecticut Association of Privately Owned Public Golf Courses offers a handy guide to twenty-two courses throughout the state. Write for it c/o Gene Williams, Lisbon Country Club, Kendall Rd., Lisbon, CT 06351.

The quarterly *Northeast Golfer* is an attractive mix of regional news, national features, and guidebook. Some of the fraternity's best writers are involved. Each issue also includes an extensive directory (with prices!) of New England courses. (203/747-4404).

Fore Better Golf has a '94 edition state golf map (708/893-8672, $3.95 at pro shops, $4 by mail). *Powers Northeast Region Golf Guide* ($14.95) by Bill Anderson profiles seventy-seven courses in its current edition, with coupons (800/446-8884).

Around Stamford, they sing the praises of Tracey Holliday. Offers from private clubs have as yet been unavailing, and she continues to serve the public trust as superintendent of greens at Sterling Farms Golf Course. Her superbly tended greens are one facet that make Sterling Farms another one of those very special courses that might best be thought of as private munys. Everything here gives the appearance of a country club. Geoffrey Cornish's design makes wonderful use of the terrain. The maintenance, the service, the amenities, from Tom Lupinacci's shop to the bar at the Fairway Inn, are all tremendous. That's the good news. The bad news is that residents have the upper hand. And as nice as Sterling Farms is, it's hardly a secret. Out-of-towners will find it nearly impossible to get on during summer weekends. (No foreigners tee off before noon.) Nevertheless, this has to be one of the best munys in America. After 4 P.M., rates drop to $19.

Closer to New Haven, Orange Hills Country Club, a friendly family operation that was also designed by Cornish, is scenic, well tended, and hard enough. That leaves the tough decision: burgers at Paul's, a Milford landmark (on the Post Road), or pizza at Sally's on Wooster Street in New Haven.

Some other Connecticut designer labels:

*Geoffrey Cornish*

Blackledge, Hebron
Candlewood Valley, New Milford
Cedar Knob, Somers
Crestbrook Park, Watertown
Millbrook, Windsor
Portland, Portland

*Tom Fazio*

Ridgefield, Ridgefield

*Robert Trent Jones*

Lyman Orchard, Middlefield
Pilgrim's Harbor, Wallingford

## Discount Card

American Lung Association Golf Privilege Card. One free round at twenty courses/range discounts. 203/289-5401 or 800/992-2263. $30.

## Shopping

Not far from the aquarium, Mystic has Factory Outlets I and II (203/443-4788). Smaller outlet centers are in Milford, Norwalk, and Branford.

## FINDING THE GREEN IN CONNECTICUT

Bel Compo Golf Club ($21/$25) 6,304 yds. (70.1/125)
65 Nod Rd.
Avon 203/678-1358

Blackledge Country Club ($22/$24) 6,173 yds. (69.6/116)
180 West St.
Hebron 203/228-0250

Candlewood Valley Country Club ($22/$27) 6,295 yds. (67.0/113)
401 Danbury Rd. (Rte. 7)
New Milford 203/354-9359

Cedar Knob Golf Course ($17/$19) 6,298 yds. (69.9/115)
Billings Rd.
Somers 203/749-3550

Crestbrook Park Golf Course ($20/$22) 6,376 yds. (71.1/125)
834 Northfield Rd.
Watertown 203/945-5249

Elmridge Country Club ($24/$28) 6,082 yds. (69.5/117)
24 Elmridge Rd.
Pawcatuck 203/599-2248

H. Smith-Richardson Golf Course ($22/$26.50) 6,323 yds. (70.2/124)
2425 Moorehouse Hwy.
Fairfield 203/255-6094

Lyman Orchard Golf Club ($25.50/$29*) 6,200 yds. (70.0/124)
Rte. 157
Middlefield 203/349-8055

Millbrook Golf Course ($20/$23) 6,074 yds. (69.5/121)
147 Pigeon Hill Rd.
Windsor 203/688-2575

Orange Hills Country Club ($20/$28) 6,084 yds. (69.7/119)
489 Racebrook Rd.
Orange 203/795-4161

Pilgrim's Harbor Golf Club ($20/$27) 3,337 yds. (72.6/127)
Harrison Rd.
Wallingford 203/269-6023

Pine Valley Golf Course ($20.25/$24.50) 6,039 yds. (69.8/121)
300 Welch Rd.
Southington 203/628-0879

Portland Golf Club ($21.25/$24.50) 5,802 yds. (68.9/121)
169 Bartlett St.
Portland 203/342-6107

Ridgefield Golf Club ($27/$27) 5,919 yds. (68.1/119)
545 Ridgebury Rd.
Ridgefield 203/748-7008

Shennecossett Golf Course ($22/$26) 6,142 yds. (69.6/119)
95 Plant St.
Groton 203/445-0262

Simsbury Farms Golf Course ($21/$25) 6,075 yds. (69.7/121)
100 Old Farms Rd.
West Simsbury 203/658-6246

Sterling Farms Golf Course ($19/$21*) 6,082 yds. (69.7/123)
1349 Newfield Ave.
Stamford 203/461-9090

*Twilight

Tashua Knolls Golf Club ($19/$24) 6,119 yds. (69.3/122)
40 Tashua Knolls Ln.
Trumbull 203/261-5989

Timberlin Golf Club ($19.50/$24) 6,342 yds. (70.5/123)
330 Southington Rd.
Kensington 203/828-3228

Tunxis Plantation Country Club ($22/$25) 36 holes
White Course: 6,241 yds. (70.4/125)
Red & Green Course: 6,101 yds. (70.1/117)
87 Town Farm Rd.
Farmington 203/677-1367

# DELAWARE

*Local Knowledge*

A private club until 1982, Three Little Bakers has hosted the state amateur championship and qualifying for USGA events. A high-placed source recommends it as a "terrific course." *Tee Time* magazine calls it one of the best public courses in Delaware or Maryland. It also has the highest slope rating in the state. Two holes on the back side, numbers fifteen and sixteen, turned up on a recent list of Delaware's most difficult holes as selected by club pros.

*Delaware Today*'s "Golf Guide," where the aforementioned rating appears, is a handy annual reference. The supplement comes out in either the April or May issue, a primer for the LPGA McDonald's Championship. Look for it at golf courses or visitor centers. To purchase a back issue call 302/656-1809.

Delcastle is gracious and wide open. On the site of an old state prison farm, it has some ruins that are still visible, but you make your own jail here. The scenery's pleasant, and the course is eminently walkable and in good condition. It was positively mobbed the day I played, but there were rangers and the starter was hustling and accommodating.

Garrison's Lake is featured in *The 479 Best Public Golf Courses in the United States, Canada, the Caribbean and Mexico* by Robert McCord. The public can play anytime during the week, but not until after 11 A.M. on weekends.

Hole number five at Porky Oliver, a par three of 210 yards, was included on a companion list of difficult holes in the "Golf Guide." Porky's US Open disqualification is a sad affair. Tied after the completion of four rounds, he was disqualified for teeing off too early. The Wilmington native played top golf for many years, particularly in the majors and in the Ryder Cup. The course named for him is short but requires some precision.

T-Time Maps offers a *Maryland & Delaware Golf Course Map and Directory* for $3.95 (410/667-6738). *Golf Greens* includes listings for twenty-four Delaware courses. The coupon book is $12.95 (800/394-GOLF or 609/547-4747). Both regional golf publications, *Tee Time* (301/913-0081) and *Metro Golf* (202/663-9015), are great sources of the ever illusive LK (Local Knowledge.) Call for directory, back issues, and subscription information. General tourism info is available from 800/441-8846.

### Discount Card

See "Stalking the Elusive Deep Discount" in Finding the Green introduction.

### Shopping

Yup, no sales tax. In Newark, Gore (makers of the best waterproof material since fins) has a retail store. From Valentine's Day until it's gone, it holds an annual sale with 20 to 50 percent off hats, gloves, etc.: Gore Apparel Center, 316 Suburban Plaza (302/454-7555). More shopping info is included in *Greater Wilmington's Guide to the Brandywine Valley* (800/422-1181).

## FINDING THE GREEN IN DELAWARE

**Delcastle Golf Club ($17/$21) 6,335 yds. (69.0/113)**
**801 McKennans Church Rd.**
**Wilmington 302/995-1990**

Ed "Porky" Oliver Golf Club ($19/$22) 5,864 yds. (67.9/120)
800 N. Dupont Rd.
Wilmington 302/571-9041

Garrison's Lake Golf Club ($20/$30) 6,595 yds. (70.9/126)
101 Fairways Cir.
Smyrna 302/653-9847

Three Little Bakers Golf Club ($21/$25) 6,165 yds. (69.8/126)
3542 Foxcroft Dr.
Wilmington 302/737-1877

# DISTRICT OF COLUMBIA

*Local Knowledge*

It's hard to imagine, but once upon a time there was a golf course on Wisconsin Avenue. Bitten by the golf bug, Edward McLean, owner of *The Washington Post,* had a course built on the grounds of his D.C. estate. Sportswriter Shirley Povich remembers the course as "eighteen great holes, with the only concession, seventeen greens; a big one served two holes, à la St. Andrews." PGA champion Leo Diegel was McLean's pro at one time. Not bad.

One day in 1922, young Shirley was asked to caddy for McLean's buddy, President Warren Harding. A waiter served a tray of drinks on the first tee, right outside McLean's back door, and a gay old time was had by all.

"He was a lousy golfer," Povich remembers of the twenty-ninth president, "in terms of par, etcetera. He tried to flirt with one hundred. But no question of his passion for the game. On many an occasion he played the West Potomac Park public course just south of the White House."

The muny-playing president used the South Lawn for a driving range and tried to teach his airedale, Laddie Boy, to retrieve the balls, apparently without success.

From *Washingtonian* magazine:

Best and Worst Time to . . .
 Get a tee time at D.C.'s East Potomac Park Golf Course.
 Best: 7 A.M. Weekdays
 5:30 P.M. Weekends
 Worst: 5 P.M. Weekdays
 9 A.M. Weekends

In the metro D.C. area, BusinessWomen's Golf*Link is an organization for professional women who play golf at all skill levels. (202/342-8631).

Incidentally, the handmade six iron that astronaut Alan Shepard chili-dipped on the moon is on display at Golf House, the USGA's museum in New Jersey. That's a replica at the Air and Space Museum. The Smithsonian had argued, unsuccessfully, that the club was the property of the U.S. government. The USGA, a higher authority, disagreed.

## Shopping

On the Hill, don't overlook the divot-repair tool on sale at the Senate Gift Shop (Room 180, Senate Russell Building). Affixed with the official seal, this weighty capitalist tool (ideal for cover-ups) sells for $7.

An additional $5 is levied on those ordering by mail. This obvious outrage calls for the appointment of a special prosecutor or, at the very least, an investigation by the General Accounting Office. Maybe hearings. Write your senator (or call 202/224-7308 to order; plastic accepted). If you look closely at the photograph, you'll notice that on mine the seal is set slightly off center, a fact to which the more cynical might find an ironic significance.

## FINDING THE GREEN IN D.C.

**East Potomac Public Golf Course** ($13.50/$17) 6,300 yds. (69.0/109)
E. Potomac Park SW.
Washington, D.C. 202/554-7660

**Langston Golf Course** ($13.50/$18) 6,340 yds. (69.0/115)
26th and Benning Rd. NE.
Washington, D.C. 202/397-8638

**Rock Creek Public Golf Course** ($13.50/$17) 4,715 yds. (62.5/112)
1600 Rittenhouse St. NW.
Washington, D.C. 202/882-7332

# FLORIDA

*Local Knowledge*

May 1 is a red-letter day in the state that arguably entertains more of the best and worst golfers than anywhere in the world. Tourist season ended, the snowbirds gone, residents take back their courses. Green fees drop 20 to 50 percent. Discount cards kick in; as temperatures rise fees melt. In the summer, business recedes to the point that courses will waive green fees entirely for the cost of a cart. "Everyone has to drop their prices to survive," sniffed a local course official to *The Tampa Tribune*. Darn.

*Best Guide to Florida Golf* ($14.95) by Richard and Marilyn Myers divvies up the state into twenty sections with graphs, maps, and good directions. It handily passed the lap test (ease at reading at high speeds on unfamiliar roads, before coffee). With a copy and a state highway map, you're set. Available in bookstores or from 904/795-7126.

The Myerses live in Central Florida. Here's where they say they like to play "as often as possible":

Citrus Springs, Citrus Springs
Seville, Brooksville
Twisted Oaks, Beverly Hills

Some "memorable sleepers":

Bella Vista, Howey-in-the-Hills
Coral Oaks, Cape Coral
Foxfire, Sarasota
Golf Club of Jacksonville
Lake City, Lake City
Marion Oaks, Ocala
Myakka Pines, Englewood

They also like Robert Trent Jones's par three course, King's Point, in Delray Beach. If you've still got some energy after Disney World, you can play the par three course at Million Dollar Mulligan on Highway 192 in Kissimmee. It's one of several par threes in the area. Tee off as late as 11:15 P.M.; the longest hole is sixty-five yards.

Another statewide guide is *Florida Golf Guide* ($14.95) by Jimmy Shacky, well organized with all the basics. *Golfweek,* "America's Golf Newspaper," puts out an excellent annual statewide course list. Free to subscribers, it's $7.50 to the general public (407/345-5500). The Florida Sports Foundation publishes *Fairways in the Sunshine, the Official Florida Golf Guide.* It's free with a phone call to 904/488-8347.

*Ready Golf* has Central Florida news you can use. The masthead announces, IT'S WHAT THE LOCALS READ. No wonder. The tabloid is comprehensive and well written (407/351-4897). In Orlando, on WGTO, Talkradio AM 540, Rick Karlson and Ed Schmidt, Jr., host "GolfTalk," Fridays at 4 P.M.

Snead's Tavern in Orlando is lively, though mobbed on weekends. Supposedly the numerous PGA stars who make their homes here pop in whenever they're in town. The decor is early, modern, and postmodern Snead memorabilia (407/295-9999).

*Florida's Golf Newspaper* covers an area roughly from Orlando to Lake Placid, Kissimmee to Tampa. The monthly freebie has a course guide, golf on TV schedule, a few small features, and coupons (813/858-8190).

*FGN* publisher Bill Carter told me, "Central Florida is just bursting wide open" with new courses. A handful of development-affiliated courses have opened to the public, or at least will be open until the real estate moves. Of these, Bill suggests Ridgewood Lakes (off Highway 27 about halfway to Orlando from Lakeland), with lots of water, great scenery, and greens, and Sandpiper (about 6,000 yards, but with some real challenging holes). He also likes Huntington Hills, an "up-and-coming course in the Lakeland area" that's hosted minitours and has a nice restaurant, good range, and a huge practice putting green.

Golfer's Guide Inc. publishes bimonthly guides under different names for Tampa Bay, Orlando, Jacksonville, Naples, and Palm Beach. They're like little *TV Guides*, crammed with maps, features, coupons, range listings, and more. Free or $3 by mail—$9.95 for all (800/864-6101).

*The Miami Herald* publishes *South Florida Golf.* It includes scorecards with chiseled blurbs on every public course in Dade and Broward counties. There's even some reporting. Excellent maps, readability, and gloss make this more than your average puff piece. Call 305/376-GOLF for a free issue.

Florida's First Coast of Golf is trying to do for North Florida what Myrtle Beach Golf Holiday has done for the South Carolina coast. Its promotional brochure, Golf's Best Kept Secret, although geared to the package traveler, is still a handy course guide (800/877-PUTT).

The tabloid *North Florida Golf News* is down-home enough to even make snowbirds feel welcome. In-depth scuttlebutt. Best tip: Courses will be less crowded on Sundays during football season, at least until the novelty of the NFL Jags wears off. Favorite feature: "Grazing on the Greens" by "Golf Chef" Betty Smith. "TPC week can be very iffy weather-wise," she observes before introducing Liz Taylor's Favorite Chili recipe. From editor Fred Sealy: "Our office will be glad to advise [presumably on area course recommendations or recipes!], if anyone wants to call us. Jacksonville really overbuilt back when S&L money was flowing, so we have many courses and excellent prices." Give Fred a call at 904/739-3251.

The *St. Petersburg Times* runs an annual list of Pinellas County courses each March. It's available from circulation for $1 (800/333-7505).

*Golf Guide* is a glossy advertorial quarterly devoted to Sarasota, Manatee, and Charlotte counties (Florida's west coast). It includes detailed course listings (everything but prices) with a foldout four-color map to courses, ranges, golf shops, even the Center for Chinese Medicine and Wings 'N Weenies (813/792-2737). *U.S. GolfNews* also covers the west coast. It's a free but fancier tabloid with lots of insider PGA and Senior Tour news and equipment updates (813/398-5111).

Fore Better Golf offers golf maps for Miami/Fort Lauderdale, Boca Raton/Palm Beach, Orlando and Central Florida, Tampa/St. Petersburg, Naples, and Fort Myers. They're $3.95 at most pro shops or by mail (708/893-8672).

Among the state's oldest courses are a dozen or so attributed to Donald Ross and any number of public courses you can file under affordable, walkable, scenic, enjoyable; simple as that. The tee might be a little too close to the preceding hole's green, fairways may intersect, but the courses convey a comforting sense of permanence. Development isn't quite so evident, the homes are farther back from the course, and the trees are grand. On a good day with the breeze swaying the Spanish moss through the live oaks, without much imagination one sees what folks here think of as real Florida.

A Time Line of Florida Golf

1908 Tarpon Springs, Tarpon Springs
1912 Winter Park, Winter Park
1915 Bartow, Bartow
1920 Ocala, Ocala
1920 Clearwater, Clearwater
1921 Cleveland Heights, Lakeland
1921 Daytona Beach, Daytona Beach (Donald Ross)
1924 Lake Worth, Lake Worth
1924 Dubsdread, Orlando
1924 Hollywood, Hollywood
1925 Granada, Coral Gables
1925 Biltmore, Coral Gables (Donald Ross)
1925 Hyde Park, Jacksonville (Donald Ross)
1925 Palatka, Palatka (Donald Ross)
1926 Osceola, Pensacola
1926 Pinecrest, Avon Park (Donald Ross)
1926 Bobby Jones, Sarasota (Donald Ross)
1927 Punta Gorda, Punta Gorda (Donald Ross)
1928 Fort Myers, Fort Myers (Donald Ross)

Two other munys designed by Donald Ross are Delray Beach and New Smyrna Beach.

The University of South Florida course, a trek from downtown but still in Tampa, is another typical upper-level course: good enough to frustrate better players (6,900+ from the tips), cheap enough for students. Jeez, even its yardage book comes with coupons. I loved it: well tended, interesting holes, pretty scenery. Beware the "claw" on the nasty fourteenth. With specials from sunup to sundown, no wonder it's been voted "Best of the Bay" in the category "Best Golf Course or Best Place to Act Like Landed Gentry" by the readers of *Creative Loafing,* the local arts rag.

Another Ross design, the University of Florida's course in Gainesville, is ostensibly open only to those affiliated with UF. A couple of years back, however, an official told *The Tampa Tribune:* "You can also play if you are a guest of a Gator, which includes just about everyone." If the man still has a job, it's worth a shot. You could fill a Ryder Cup team with former Gators. Jacksonville University also has a nine-holer.

In the panhandle, The Moors (Milton) hosts the Nike Pensacola Open. The road hole at St. Andrews and number eight at Royal Troon are mimicked.

Off the beaten track, there's the Florida State Hospital's Seminole Valley Golf Course in Chattahoochee. You'll find it just past the horticultural therapy buildings and around the bend from the guard towers and razor-wire fences of the River Junction Correctional Facility. Why the state hospital maintains a golf course is a question the state of Florida is apparently now asking. The nine-hole course is nifty, winding through some lovely forest and terrain. Finally, Rolling Hills in Fort Lauderdale (the official hotel and resort of the Miami Dolphins) is where *Caddyshack* was shot. It's on the $30 bubble, but I thought you'd like to know anyway. Be the ball.


## More Local Knowledge

*Tee Times USA* offers a free golf information and reservation service in Tampa, St. Pete, Sarasota, and Orlando/Kissimmee. It will book tee times in advance, is privy to some discounts, and says it's got ins at several private clubs. It makes its money from the courses. Club rentals, directions, even transportation (800/374-8633).

*Tee Times*'s Roseanne Stocker says she often gets calls from folks looking to play near the ocean. This is a pricey proposition on the west coast, but she said courses on the east side, especially in and around Daytona and a little north, offer some great values. Ocean Palm in Flagler Beach is right across the street from the ocean, "a little on the short side." It also offers clubs you can borrow for free.

Limited but free golf info is available from *Official Florida Golf Guide* (904/487-1462), Tampa (800/44-TAMPA), Central Florida (800/828-7655), Lee Island Coast (800/733-7935), Fort Lauderdale (800/22-SUNNY), Panama City (800/PC-BEACH), and Palm Beach (800/242-1774).

## Discount Cards

American Cancer Society Big Book of Golf Discounts. "Hundreds and hundreds of discounted rounds on more than 325 courses." May 1–October 31. 800/ACS-2345. $25.

American Lung Association Golf Privilege Card. Free or reduced fees at over four hundred courses throughout Florida. 800/940-2933 or 904/743-2933 or 813/962-4448. $25.

Arthritis Foundation Golf Card. Free or discounted green fees at over three hundred courses, May–October. 305/563-0027 or 800/850-9455. $15.

Big Summer Golf Card. Up to 55 percent off carts and fees at 25 top courses in Manatee and Sarasota counties, May–October. 813/923-2232. $35.

Flag Winter Golf Membership. "Up to 50 percent off Green Fees at over 40 championship courses in South Florida," November 1–April 30. 305/389-2105. $65.

North & South Florida PGA Section Passport. "The Card for the Avid Discriminating Golfer" is only available to Florida residents. Shame on you. 250+ courses. 407/894-4653 or 800/833-7421. $52.95.

## Shopping

The Lord & Taylor Clearance Center in Plantation has golf shirts, boxers, robes, a mixed bag of golf-related apparel, all routinely 50 percent off. Listed as one of the two hundred best buys by *South Florida* magazine. 7067 W. Broward Blvd. (305/581-8205).

Sawgrass Mills bills itself as the world's largest outlet mall. It's in Sunrise, fifteen minutes from Fort Lauderdale Executive Airport (305/846-2350).

## FINDING THE GREEN IN FLORIDA

Bartow Golf Course ($13.50/$14.50) 6,024 yds. (68.9/113)
150 Idlewood Ave.
Bartow 813/533-9183

Bella Vista Golf & Yacht Club ($21.50/$23*) 6,072 yds. (67.1/116)
Hwy. 48
Howey-in-the Hills 904/324-3233

Biltmore Golf Course ($20/$20*) 6,259 yds. (70.1/123)
1210 Anastasia Ave.
Coral Gables 305/460-5366

Bobby Jones ($18/$18) 36 holes
British Course: 6,265 yds. (69.2/110)
American Course: 5,502 yds. (68.4/117)
1000 Azinger Way
Sarasota 813/955-8097

Citrus Springs Country Club ($22/$22) 6,242 yds. (70.1/125)
8690 N. Golfview Dr.
Citrus Springs 904/489-5045

Clearwater Country Club ($22/$25.75*) 6,000 yds. (68.0/120)
525 N. Betty Ln.
Clearwater 813/443-5078

Cleveland Heights Country Club ($8/$13) 27 holes
Course A/B: 6,004 yds. (68.6/115)
Course A/C: 6,125 yds. (69.4/116)
Course B/C: 6,063 yds. (68.8/116)
2900 Buckingham Ave.
Lakeland 813/682-3277

Coral Oaks Golf Course ($8.95/$8.95) 6,078 yds. (69.2/118)
1800 N.W. 28th Ave.
Cape Coral 813/283-4100

Daytona Beach Golf & Country Club ($12/$12)
North Course: 6,059 yds. (69.0/111)

*Off season or twilight

South Course: 5,950 yds. (68.6/106)
600 Wilder Blvd.
Daytona Beach 904/258-3119

Delray Beach Municipal ($9.75/$9.75*) 6,201 yds. (69.2/114)
2200 Highland Ave.
Delray Beach 407/243-7380

Dubsdread Golf Course ($20.50/$20.50) 5,865 yds. (68.0/113)
549 W. Par Ave.
Orlando 407/246-2551

Fort Myers Country Club ($27/$27) 6,006 yds. (68.7/115)
3591 McGregor Blvd.
Fort Myers 813/936-2457

Foxfire Golf Club ($29/$29) 27 holes
Palm/Oak Course: 5,903 yds. (68.3/119)
Pine/Palm Course: 5,835 yds. (67.9/114)
Pine/Oak Course: 5,670 yds. (67.7/121)
7200 Proctor Rd.
Sarasota 813/921-7757

Golf Club of Jacksonville ($13.50/$28*) 6,181 yds. (68.9/115)
10440 Tournament Ln.
Jacksonville 904/779-0800

Granada Golf Club ($14/$14) 3,081 yds. (na/109)
2001 Granada Blvd.
Coral Gables 305/460-5367

Hollywood Golf & Country Club ($25/$25) 6,345 yds. (69.0/na)
1650 Johnson St.
Hollywood 305/927-1751

Huntington Hills ($18/$20*) 6,226 yds. (70.9/119)
2626 Duff Rd.
Lakeland 813/859-3689

Hyde Park Golf & Country Club ($15/$29) 6,153 yds. (68.8/117)
6439 Hyde Grove Ave.
Jacksonville 904/786-5410

*Off season or twilight

Jacksonville University Golf Course ($6/$7) 1,700 yds. (na/na)
2800 University Blvd. North
Jacksonville 904/745-7560

King's Point Par 3 ($7/$7) 2,723 yds.
7000 Atlantic Ave.
Delray Beach 407/499-0140

Lake City Country Club ($16/$18*) 6,364 yds. (70.2/118)
Hwy. 90
Lake City 904/752-2266

Lake Worth Municipal ($25/$25) 5,744 yds. (67.1/112)
7th Ave. North and Lakeside
Lake Worth 407/582-9713

Marion Oaks Country Club ($21/$21) 6,469 yds. (70.6/122)
430 Marion Oaks Golfway
Ocala 904/347-1271

Million Dollar Mulligan Pitch'n'Putt ($10.50/$10.50)
2850 Florida Plaza Blvd.
Kissimmee 407/396-8180

The Moors Country Club ($20.50/$20.50) 6,100 yds. (69.5/118)
3220 Avalon Blvd.
Milton 904/995-4653

Myakka Pines Golf Club ($11/$11*) 27 holes
Red/White Course: 6,094 yds. (68.6/122)
Red/Blue Course: 6,136 yds. (69.4/123)
White/Blue Course: 6,110 yds. (69.1/120)
2550 S. River Rd.
Englewood 813/474-3296

New Smyrna Beach Municipal ($18.50/$18.50) 6,008 yds. (68.2/110)
1000 Wayne Ave.
New Smyrna Beach 904/424-2192

Ocala Municipal ($15/$15) 5,966 yds. (69.5/125)
3130 E. Silver Springs Blvd.
Ocala 904/622-8681

*Off season or twilight

Ocean Palm Golf Course ($12/$12*) 2,660 yds. (62.2/103)
3600 Central Ave. South
Flagler Beach 904/439-2477

Osceola Municipal ($14/$14) 6,284 yds. (68.6/111)
300 Tonawanda Dr.
Pensacola 904/456-2761

Palatka Municipal ($16/$16) 6,551 yds. (70.3/119)
1715 Moseley Ave.
Palatka 904/329-0141

Pinecrest Golf Club ($20/$20*) 6,247 yds. (69.4/117)
2250 S. Little Lake Bonnet Rd.
Avon Park 813/453-7555

Punta Gorda Country Club ($25/$25*) 6,085 yds. (68.8/114)
6100 Duncan Rd.
Punta Gorda 813/639-1494

The Ridge at Ridgewood Lakes ($20/$25*) 6,031 yds. (68.6/116)
Hwy. 27
Davenport 813/424-8688

Sandpiper Golf & Country Club ($20/$20*) 6,017 yds. (68.5/118)
6001 Sandpiper Dr.
Lakeland 813/859-5461

Seminole Valley Golf Course ($8/$11) 9 holes/6,238 yds. (69.7/119)
Florida State Hospital
Main St.
Chattahoochee 904/663-8700

Seville Golf & Country Club ($15/$15*) 6,185 yds. (70.5/131)
18200 Seville Clubhouse Dr.
Brooksville 904/596-7888

Tarpon Springs Golf Course ($18/$18) 5,819 yds. (71.5/110)
1310 S. Pinellas Ave.
Tarpon Springs 813/937-6906

*Off season or twilight

*Better make a safe approach to Seminole Valley Golf Course.*

Twisted Oaks Golf Club ($20/$20) 6,410 yds. (69.7/118)
4801 Forest Ridge Blvd.
Beverly Hills 904/746-6257

University of Florida ($15/$15) 5,823 yds. (67.3/115)
2800 SW 2nd Ave.
Gainesville 904/375-4866

University of South Florida ($18/$20) 6,243 yds. (69.8/125)
13120 N. 46th St.
Tampa 813/974-2071

Winter Park Municipal ($12.50/$12.50) 9 holes/5,302 yds.
(64.5/100)
761 Old England Ave.
Winter Park 407/623-3339

# GEORGIA

*Local Knowledge*

Browns Mill in Atlanta, says Tom McCollister at the *Journal and Constitution,* is "probably the best of the four city courses." Rather flat, it's "always in great shape." The course, particularly the short and memorable par fours, "test your whole game. There's bunkers, water, doglegs." It always hosts sectional USGA publinks qualifying as does North Fulton. Slow play is not unknown on the difficult track. Tom puts it this way: "There are a lot of people out there who shouldn't be."

Mystery Valley, run by De Kalb County, was another of his recommendations. "The better player you are, the better you'd like it." It does get a lot of senior play, to the point that some regulars have near standing tee times. Bobby Jones Golf Course, he says, "just gets so much play, it stays beaten up all the time."

Around the state, Nob North near Dalton is, in Tom's opinion, "probably one of the best public courses in the state. It's awfully good." He also suggests the courses at Stone Mountain. Carts are mandatory so you'll only get nine holes for under $30. Tom's guidebook, *Golf in Georgia* ($7.95), reviews every public and private course in the state. At golf shops, it's also available from Longstreet Press in Marietta (404/980-1488). A new edition is planned.

*Georgia Golf News* is a free tabloid. Courses, Atlanta sports bars, and visitor centers stock it. A free copy is available by mail; the annual "Best of" rankings appears in the July issue. For a good time, call 404/442-9630. (The staff is glad to help with questions, tips, you name it.) Favorite column: "Bogey Man's Bargain Golf" lists all the twilight rates and other specials on courses throughout Georgia, a great idea.

Several of *GGN*'s Top 10 public courses for under $30: The Landings (Warner Robins), University of Georgia (Athens), Bull Creek (Columbus), and Barrington (Macon).

Macon has become something of a hotbed of strong amateur play, Ed Grisamore at *The Macon Telegraph* told me. Snowbirds on their way to Florida will enjoy Bowden, the city's muny, which Ed says "suits the public golfer very well." It's very wide open, which is not entirely surprising as it was an airport before the WPA built the course in 1942. Not in the best of neighborhoods anymore, the course does have an advantage. Ed says it drains exceptionally well.

"Even when there's a real gully washer and they have to suspend play, as soon as it quits, they can get right back on." At other courses, with the clay soil typical of Georgia, when it rains, "That's it, you just can't play." A new irrigation system has helped put the Bowden course in "as good shape as it's ever been." Bowden has been a past host to the Georgia State Golf Association's Public Links Championship.

Ed also recommends Barrington Hall and Houston Lake in Perry ("both great courses, sort of upscale daily fees") and Golf Club of Macon.

In Savannah, Tim Guidera at the *Evening Press* told me that sixteen of the original holes Donald Ross designed at Bacon Park in the late 1920s are still there, interspersed among the twenty-seven hole complex now managed by American Golf.

Willowpeg in Rincon (about twenty minutes from Savannah), "if it's in shape," is, in Tim's opinion, "the best layout in town." Willowpeg hosted the TC Jordan minitour three years running. It can be a tough walk, as some greens are five hundred to six hundred yards from the next tee. Tim did say the club runs good specials, including cart.

Southbridge, in Savannah, is a Rees Jones design with heavy bunkering around often enormous and undulating greens. There has been talk that the club, which now permits public play, may go private. It's been a *Georgia Golf News* Top 10 and is worth looking into.

Georgia also has excellent state park golf. Both Ed and Tom say Hard Labor Creek in Rutledge, Georgia Veterans Memorial in Cordele, and Wallace Adams at Little Ocmulgee State Park are all very good. *Georgia Golf News* has rated Georgia Veterans among the top five public courses in the state. A brochure on the five Georgia State Park golf courses (with slope, yardage, directions, etc.) is available from 404/656-2770; general tourism info is yours with a call to 800/VISIT-GA.

Frustrated Augusta visitors will find the town's muny is "nothing great," according to Ward Clayton at *The Augusta Chronicle*. Jones Creek, however, is "your upper type, higher green fee place." You can walk during the week for under $30. It's been named *Georgia Golf News*'s best public course in the state. For public Augusta golf info, call 800/726-0243.

A Donald Ross course, Forest Hills, run by Augusta College, held the Southeastern Open, the last tournament Bobby Jones won before the Grand Slam. Ward recommends it but warns, "They probably get more play than anywhere else."

Finally, Jekyll Island has three courses and a nine-holer, Oceanside, an honest and sterling test of true links golf (800/841-6586).

### Discount Card

See "Stalking the Elusive Deep Discount" in Finding the Green introduction.

### Shopping

The Augusta GreenJackets, a single-A team of the Pittsburgh Pirates, wear their trademark hunter green cap with deep purple bill for home games. You can too. The team has a great selection of official merchandise: embroidered golf shirts ($30/$27), T-shirts ($20—they're purple and two-sided), wool fitted caps ($20), pennants ($3), even seat cushions ($5). Plastic accepted (800/689-7889).

Peach Festival Outlet Center in Byron (near Macon), off I-75, has Van Heusen, Bass, The Dress Barn, and Reebok. The Tanger outlet in Commerce (near Athens) has Reebok, Bass, Liz Claiborne, and more.

## FINDING THE GREEN IN GEORGIA

**Bacon Park Golf Course ($11.75/$13.75) 27 holes**
Cypress/Magnolia Course: 5,916 yds. (67.9/114)
Magnolia/Live Oak Course: 6,175 yds. (68.9/116)
Cypress/Live Oak Course: 6,333 yds. (68.3/115)
Shorry Cooper Rd.
Savannah 912/354-2625

**Barrington Hall Golf Club ($19/$29) 6,196 yds. (69.9/129)**
7100 Zebulon Rd.
Macon 912/757-8358

Bobby Jones Golf Course ($19/$22) 5,700 yds. (67.3/116)
384 Woodward Way
Atlanta 404/355-1009

Bowden Golf Course ($9/$10) 6,620 yds. (68.8/117)
3111 Millerfield Rd.
Macon 912/742-1610

Brazell's Creek Golf Course ($13/$13) 9 holes/6,068 yds. (69.0/127)
Gordonia-Alatamaha State Park
Reidsville 912/557-6445

Browns Mill Golf Course ($19/$22) 6,260 yds. (69.6/120)
480 Cleveland Ave.
Atlanta 404/366-3573

Bull Creek Golf Course ($14/$16) 36 holes
East Course: 6,420 yds. (69.4/120)
West Course: 6,480 yds. (70.8/126)
7333 Lynch Rd.
Columbus 706/561-1614

Forest Hills Golf Club ($15/$22) 6,450 yds. (68.8/120)
1500 Comfort Rd.
Augusta 706/733-0001

Georgia Veterans Memorial State Park ($15/$20) 6,623 yds.
(71.8/126)
2315 US Hwy. 280 West
Cordele 912/276-2371

Golf Club of Macon ($12/$15) 5,847 yds. (66.7/118)
Thomaston Rd.
Macon 912/474-8080

Hard Labor Creek State Park ($17/$17) 6,269 yds. (68.7/119)
Knox Chapel Rd.
Rutledge 706/557-3006

Houston Lake Country Club ($29/$27*) 5,819 yds. (68.5/121)
2323 Hwy. 127
Perry 912/987-3243

*Twilight

Jones Creek Golf Club ($21/$30) 6,126 yds. (70.0/124)
4101 Hammonds Ferry
Evans 706/860-4228

The Landings Golf Course ($26.25/—) 27 holes
Trestle/Bluff Course: 6,297 yds. (70.3/129)
Trestle/Creek Course: 6,238 yds. (69.9/124)
Bluff/Creek Course: 6,061 yds. (69.4/123)
309 Statham's Way
Warner Robins 912/923-5222

Mystery Valley Golf Course ($17/$20) 6,329 yds. (69.0/118)
6094 Shadowrock Dr.
Lithonia 404/469-6913

Nob North Golf Course ($17/$17) 6,100 yds. (69.5/123)
298 Nob North Drive
Cohutta 706/694-8505

North Fulton Golf Course ($20.50/$23.50) 6,301 yds. (70.4/121)
216 West Wieuca Rd.
Atlanta 404/255-0723

Oceanside Golf Course ($15.75/$15.75) 3,023 yds. (69.6/123)
Beachview Drive
Jekyll Island 912/635-2170

Southbridge Golf Club ($16.50/$23) 6,002 yds. (69.4/128)
415 Southbridge Blvd.
Savannah 912/651-5455

Stone Mountain Golf Course ($19/$19) 36 holes
Stonemont Course: 6,094 yds. (71.2/128)
Lakemont Course: 6,093 yds. (69.0/119)
Stone Mountain Park
Stone Mountain 404/498-5715

University of Georgia Golf Course ($18/$20) 6,083 yds. (69.7/126)
Riverbend Rd.
Athens 706/369-5739

Victoria Bryant State Park ($13/$13) 2,967 yds. (68.7/122)
Hwy. 327
Royston 706/245-6770

Wallace Adams Golf Course ($15/$15) 6,312 yds. (69.0/na)
Little Ocmulgee State Park
Hwy. 441
McRae 912/868-6651

Willowpeg Golf Club ($17/$29) 6,185 yds. (68.7/116)
1 Clubhouse Dr.
Rincon 912/826-2092

# HAWAII

### Local Knowledge

Consumer costs 30 percent higher than on the mainland might deflate all but the most ardent aloha spirit. Never fear. *Golf on $30 a Day (or Less)* can't get you on at *kamaaina* (local) rates, but how's $5 all day for a beautiful nine-holer with ocean views?

Affordable golf in Hawaii is not as well known as it might be. One theory holds that, in deference to the resorts, munys don't advertise. Jim Kozy, publisher of *Hawaii Golf,* assures me the bargains are out there. "You just have to know about them." Well, yeah.

Okay, first the publinks qualifying sites for the recent past. Courses used, "year in and year out," according to Harold Okita, president of the Hawaii State Golf Association, are Hilo Municipal on The Big Island, Waiehu on Maui, and Wailua on Kauai. On Oahu, Ala Wai, Ted Makalena, and West Loch have been used. Women's qualifying has been held at Pali and West Loch. (NOTE: At the time of publication, several of these courses are right on the $30 bubble.)

### Hawaii

Hilo, Jim writes, "is a lush 18-hole course with great views, popular among the locals."

Hamakua Country Club in Honokaa is a nine-holer where you can play all day for $10. Jim calls it "an old-fashioned course in a friendly Hawaiian atmosphere." It was built in the mid-1920s. It's not a big course—there are no par fives—but the views are said to be spectacular.

### Oahu

Ala Wai averages more rounds per day than many courses will over a holiday weekend. The oldest municipal course in Hawaii, it recently got a new clubhouse and a lighted range. Kahuku, on the north shore, is, according to Jim, "an unassuming nine-hole seaside course that is inexpensive, [with] great views, and fun. There are no carts to ride or other amenities, but there is community golf, Hawaii style."

Ted Makalena is near Pearl Harbor. Pali is nestled in next to the mountain across the Pali Highway. "Plenty of play and rain—so plan accordingly," Jim advises. West Loch is the newest muny, "one of the better layouts, with numerous water hazards."

### Maui

Waiehu is Maui's only muny. It's near Kahului on the windsurfing coast. The front side follows the water; the wind adds challenge on the upper nine.

### Kauai

Above the little sugar town of Kalaheo in Kukuiolono Park is a gem acknowledged as "one of Hawaii's best-kept secrets." It's Kukuiolono Golf Course, and it's $5 all day, "a beautiful ocean layout." Dave Mills, who pens the superlative *Golfer's Guide to Southern California,* loves Kukuiolono. Its views, he writes, are "nothing short of sensational." He also loves taking lessons from Toyo Shirai, an island legend and member of the Hawaii Golf Hall of Fame. (The lessons with Toyo are $12 for a half hour and come highly recommended.) Dave has turned his attention to Kauai and has plans to return. Subscribers to his guide can also take advantage of several resort specials (310/841-4866).

*Hawaii Golf* mixes national features and exquisite graphics with local maps, a course directory, and a local perspective. Subscriptions are $9.95 for four issues, $14.95 for eight issues. The cover price is $2.95 (800/942-4871). Two guidebooks to look for: George Fuller's *Hawaii Golf: The Complete Guide* ($12.95, Foghorn Press, 800/842-7477) and Steve Harper's (see also Arizona) *Hawaii Golf Guide* ($12.95, 602/919-2980).

## FINDING THE GREEN IN HAWAII

Ala Wai Golf Course ($30/$30) 5,806 yds. (66.8/115)
404 Kapahulu Ave.
Island of Oahu
Honolulu 808/734-3656

Hamakua Country Club ($10/$10) 2,460 yds. (63.8/101)
Island of Hawaii
Honokaa 808/775-7244

Hilo Municipal Golf Course ($6/$8) 6,006 yds. (68.8/118)
340 Haihai St.
Island of Hawaii
Hilo 808/959-7711

Kahuku Golf Course ($30/$30) 9 holes/5,398 yds. (65.2/na)
Island of Oahu
Kahuku 808/293-5842

Kukuiolono Golf Course ($5/$5) 2,981 yds. (70.0/na)
Papalina Rd.
Island of Kauai
Kalaheo 808/335-9940

Pali Golf Course ($30/$30) 6,524 yds. (70.4/126)
40-050 Kamehameha Hwy.
Island of Oahu
Kaneohe 808/296-7254

Ted Makalena Golf Course ($30/$30) 5,946 yds. (67.9/110)
93-059 Waipio Pt. Access Rd.
Island of Oahu
Waipahu 808/296-7888

Waiehu Municipal Golf Course ($25/$30) 6,330 yds. (69.8/111)
Island of Maui
Wailuku 808/244-5934

Wailua Golf Course ($18/$20) 6,585 yds. (71.9/134)
3-5351 Kuhio Hwy.
Island of Kauai
Lihue 808/241-6666

West Loch Golf Course ($30/$30) 5,849 yds. (67.8/119)
91-1126 Okupe St.
Island of Oahu
Ewa Beach 808/296-5624

# IDAHO

*Local Knowledge*

Dan MacMillan's *Golfing in Idaho* ($7.95) substantiates its subtitle, *The* Complete *Guide to Idaho's Golf Facilities* with a section for senior golfers, a bushel of suggested weekend getaway ideas (with *après* golf tips), the skinny on golf shops and club-repair centers, even driving-range info (with directions!). That's the potatoes. The meat is capsule reviews on nearly ninety courses. It's available from Mac Productions (206/333-4641).

Some of Dan's favorites, and these from a man who loves his work, are, in northern Idaho: Avondale in Hayden Lake ("Fairways are impeccably groomed") and Hidden Lakes in Sandpoint, which, he says, "Plays much tougher than yardage indicates [and is] worth a special trip anytime."

The Highlands in Post Falls offers beautiful views with "demanding tee shots on nearly every hole." He also recommends McCall, in McCall: "You cannot beat this championship caliber course at this price." Other recommendations: Purple Sage in Caldwell ("One of the best courses in the state . . . 5-time host to Idaho State Open and host to 1994 publinks qualifying") and Soldier Mountain in Fairfield ("Great getaway spot for the whole family. A best kept secret").

Jeff Shelley, author of *Golf Courses of the Pacific Northwest* ($19.95), told me that "there are only three courses that I'd eliminate because of their higher fees." Zowie. He went on to suggest that two of the three probably have off-season rates under $30. Prices are certain to change, and they can only go in one direction, but Shelley's statement gives you some idea of how far a dollar can stretch in this beautiful corner of the woods.

*Golf Courses of the Pacific Northwest* reviews twenty-eight courses in Idaho. It's available from Fairgreens Media and is reviewed in greater detail in other state sections (206/525-1294).

Leo Chandler, a golf shop designer and correspondent for *Back Nine* magazine, recommends Twin Lakes Village ("short but fun") in Rathdrum and Stoneridge in the Mount Spokane foothills at Blanchard.

The University of Idaho's course in Moscow gets a thumbs-up from the experts. Shelley notes "magnificent views" and describes it as a "mountain goat–type course." MacMillan warns that "tough windy conditions and hilly terrain put a premium on shot making." Among *Golf Digest*'s Top 5: Coeur d'Alene and Quail Hollow (Boise). A brochure on courses in southwest Idaho is available from the Boise Convention & Visitors Bureau (208/344-7777).

### Discount Card

See "Stalking the Elusive Deep Discount" in Finding the Green introduction.

### Shopping

Boise Factory Outlets—I-84 at Gowan Rd.—has Bass, Cape Isle, Levi's, SunLet SunGlasses, and more (208/331-5000).

## FINDING THE GREEN IN IDAHO

**Avondale Golf Club ($20/$20) 6,319 yds. (70.4/118)**
10745 Avondale Loop Rd.
Hayden Lake 208/772-5963

**Coeur d'Alene Golf Club ($18/$18) 6,040 yds. (68.6/113)**
2201 Fairway Dr.
Coeur d'Alene 208/765-0218

**Hidden Lakes Golf Course ($20/$20) 6,109 yds. (69.5/123)**
8838 Lower Pack River Rd.
Sandpoint 208/263-1642

The Highlands Golf & Country Club ($21/$23) 6,041 yds. (68.9/122)
N. 701 Inverness Dr.
Post Falls 208/773-3673

McCall Golf Course ($19/$22) 5,861 yds. (67.3/119)
Reedy Lane
McCall 208/634-7200

Purple Sage Golf Course ($12/$14) 6,337 yds. (68.6/113)
15192 Purple Sage Rd.
Caldwell 208/459-2223

Quail Hollow Golf Club ($16/$19) 5,953 yds. (68.1/120)
4520 N. 36th
Boise 208/344-7807

Soldier Mountain Ranch and Resort ($15/$15) 3,105 yds. (70.5/124)
Fairfield 208/764-2506

Stoneridge Golf Course ($20/$20) 6,141 yds. (69.4/123)
277 Blanchard Rd.
Blanchard 208/437-4682

Twin Lakes Village Golf Course ($20/$20) 5,836 yds. (67.5/116)
2600 East Village Blvd.
Rathdrum 208/687-1311

University of Idaho Golf Course ($13/$15) 6,154 yds. (69.8/123)
1215 Nez Perce Dr.
Moscow 208/885-6171

# ILLINOIS

## *Local Knowledge*

Tim Tully's revised edition of *Chicago Area Golf Course Guide* ($9.95) reprints scorecards for 150 courses with concise descriptions and general directions. Not unexpectedly, he warns of five-hour weekend rounds and advises playing during the week, the earlier the better. Some of his recommendations: Balmoral Woods in Crete ("A real nice course in excellent shape"), Bon Vivant in Bourbonnais ("One of the longest courses in the area"), Bonnie Brook in Waukegan ("Scottish-style, a former private club, heavily wooded"), George Dunne in Oak Forest ("Beautifully laid out, well worth it"), Midlane Country Club in Wadsworth ("Country club–type treatment"), Minnie Monesse in Grant Park ("Easy to get to, real short, real challenging"), Naperbrook Golf Course in Naperville ("relatively flat and wide open with 45 sand traps"), Poplar Creek Country Club in Hoffman Estates ("Water in play on 14 holes . . . OB on 15 holes"), and Springbrook Golf Course in Naperville ("Well-kept secret . . . in excellent condition").

The preeminent public golf empire of the Jemsek family is driven by an intense distaste for litter and a firm belief that "golfers today are customers tomorrow." Cog Hill's Dubsdread, host to the PGA Tour's Western Open, costs a packet (no doubt well worth it), but courses number one and number three are still reasonably priced.

The *Chicago Tribune* does an annual special section. The snappily titled *Public Golf Course Guide* usually appears in the first two weeks of April. Back issues, available for ninety days, are a hefty $10 (312/222-3232).

The excellent free tabloid *Chicagoland Golf* runs a readers' poll of Top 40 public courses with its first issue of the year (concurrent with the February Chicago Golf Show). Copies are free at 350 local northwest Chicagoland courses. The tabloid is published twice a month from the end of March through Labor Day. Back issues are $3 (708/485-GOLF). Publisher/editor Phil Kosin hosts a weekly golf radio show on WMVP. It airs Saturday mornings from six to eight.

Illinois's Top 125 Public Golf Courses as selected by *Chicago Metro Golfer* Magazine are noted in a list available from the Central Illinois Tourism Council (800/262-2482 or 217/525-7980). This is an inordinately high number of entrees for your typical course pageant list (ten I can see, or forty or seventy-five, okay, but 125?). That said, unfortunately, they are presented in alphabetical rather than meritorious order, a dubious method. Surely, someone will concede, as nice as these courses may be, there is a difference between course number 1 and course number 125.

The Chicago Convention and Tourism Bureau's *Chicago Southland Visitor's Guide* provides information, including a map to thirty-two courses. A response card to receive specific materials directly from the courses themselves, if you're so inclined, is also available (800/873-9111). General tourist information with phone numbers for thirty-five tourism boards statewide is yours by calling 312/814-4732. And if you're wondering how it plays in Peoria, Newman Golf Course hosted '94 publinks sectional qualifying, so did White Pines in Bensenville (which has a dome for winter practice).

Now that he's hit the big time, business at Tom Wargo's course in Centralia, Greenview Golf Club, is picking up. It has the reputation of being the best public course in the area. In an incredible story, PGA Seniors champion Wargo took up the game at twenty-five.

Several courses in southern Illinois noted in the *St. Louis Post-Dispatch* annual readers' poll of Top 10 courses include Belk Park, The Legacy, The Orchards, and Fox Creek.

Two Illinois state parks have golf courses. Eagle Creek, however, does not allow walking and has already eclipsed $30. In sight of the Arch in East St. Louis, Frank Holten State Park has eighteen holes, Grand Marais, and two lakes.

University courses open to all comers in the land of Lincoln are the University of Illinois in Savoy, Illinois State University in Normal, and Western Illinois University in Macomb.

If you have some time to kill in Palatine, or if you're just passing through, ahem, Ahlgrim & Sons Funeral Home has a course that's . . . been in the ground for thirty years. What kind of funeral home has a golf course and is booked solid almost every day and most evenings with fortieth-birthday parties, Indian Guides, Cub Scouts, Girl Scouts, and family gatherings? Why, one offering free miniature golf (and bumper pool, hockey, shuffleboard, Ping-Pong, and some old video games). You heard right, it's free, though reservations are required to avoid mixing family business with pleasure.

Roger Ahlgrim sent along descriptions of several holes: "Hole #1 has a metal skull with blinking red eyes in a sand trap [Roger, that's a bunker] which the player must shoot the ball over. Hole #2 is an old shipping box (which we used to use for shipping casketed remains on trains to out-of-town cities but since we fly everything now, we don't need shipping boxes) [Question: Will they work for shipping clubs?] Hole #3 is a guillotine." Ahlgrim is family-owned and -operated since 1892 (708/358-7411).

Fore Better Golf has a golf map covering greater Chicago. It's $3.95 in pro shops or by mail (708/893-8672).

### Discount Card

American Lung Association Golf Privilege Card. 145 courses, April–November. 800/788-LUNG or 217/528-3441. $30.

### Shopping

Gurnee Mills Outlet Mall (I-94 and Rte. 132) should satisfy any cravings with over two hundred stores (800/YES-SHOP). Irv's Men's Clothing (2841 N. Laramie Ave., Chicago) has men's sportswear 30 to 40 percent below retail. There's also more in Kenosha (see "Finding the Green in Wisconsin"). The book *Never Pay Retail: CHICAGOLAND* is your personal passport to area bargains. At bookstores or from 815/226-8355.

## FINDING THE GREEN IN ILLINOIS

Balmoral Woods Country Club ($26/$30) 6,477 yds. (71.2/128)
2500 Balmoral Woods Dr.
Crete 708/672-7448

Belk Park Golf Course ($19/$21) 6,415 yds. (71.0/118)
Belk Park Rd.
Wood River 618/251-3115

Bon Vivant Golf Club ($14/$20) 7,014 yds. (73.8/122)
Career Center Rd.
Bourbonnais 815/935-0403

Bonnie Brook Golf Course ($22/$27) 6,341 yds. (70.8/122)
2800 North Lewis Ave.
Waukegan 708/336-5538

Cog Hill Golf & Country Club ($26/$30)
Course One: 6,224 yds. (68.3/114)
Course Three: 6,193 yds. (69.1/114)
119th St. and Archer Ave.
Lemont 708/257-5872 or 312/242-1717

Fox Creek Golf Club ($20/$25*) 6,045 yds. (71.2/132)
Rte. 159
Edwardsville 618/692-9400 (Mo.: 800/692-9401)

George Dunne National Golf Course ($15/$20*) 6,175 yds.
(70.2/121)
16310 S. Central Ave.
Oak Forest 708/429-6886

Grand Marais ($12/$14) 6,224 yds. (na/na)
Frank Holten State Park
4500 Pocket Rd.
East St. Louis 618/398-9999

Greenview Golf Club ($17/$17) 6,400 yds. (69.2/114)
2801 Putter Lane
Centralia 618/532-7395

Illinois State University Golf Course ($11/$11) 6,081 yds. (68.7/116)
Gregory St.
Normal 309/438-8065

The Legacy Golf Course ($17/$20) 6,021 yds. (na/110)
3500 Cargill Rd.
Granite City 618/931-4653

Midlane Country Club ($17/$20*) 6,427 yds. (71.2/125)
14565 Yorkhouse Rd.
Wadsworth 708/244-1990

Minnie Monesse ($17/$23) 6,120 yds. (68.1/115)
Hwy. 17
Grant Park 815/465-6653

Naperbrook Golf Course ($21/$29) 6,089 yds. (68.2/115)
111th St. and Plainfield Rd.
Naperville 708/378-4215

*Twilight

Newman Golf Course ($12.25/$13.25) 6,475 yds. (69.9/114)
2021 W. Nebraska Ave.
Peoria 309/674-1663

The Orchards ($19/$28) 5,800 yds. (66.6/116)
Greenmount Rd.
Belleville 618/233-8921

Poplar Creek Country Club ($23/$26) 5,773 yds. (67.9/119)
1400 Poplar Creek Dr.
Hoffman Estates 708/884-0219

Springbrook Golf Course ($21/$29) 6,459 yds. (70.9/120)
2240 83rd St.
Naperville 708/420-4215

Western Illinois University Golf Course ($8.25/$9.50) 3,005 yds.
(68.0/111)
1215 Tower Rd.
Macomb 309/837-3675

White Pines Golf Course ($26/$27) 36 holes
East Course: 6,100 yds. (69.5/121)
West Course: 6,400 yds. (70.7/117)
500 W. Jefferson St.
Bensenville 708/766-0304

University of Illinois Golf Course 36 holes
Orange Course: ($14.50/$14.50) 6,596 yds. (71.1/118)
Blue Course: ($12.50/$12.50) 6,423 yds. (70.4/114)
800 Hartwell
Savoy 217/359-5613

# INDIANA

*Local Knowledge*

In Indianapolis, Sarah Shank, Royal Hylands, and Deer Creek have all hosted recent state publinx championships. Royal Hylands has been described as "a stern test for even the best area golfers," with owners pledging country club–like service "never seen at a public course before." The course begins with the number one handicap hole, a par five, and there are three par threes on the front side.

Deer Creek is out in the country (about twenty to thirty minutes from Indianapolis), more scenic than the courses in town. I was warned that because of a propensity for wayward shots, some golfers tend to think of it as "Duck Creek."

The women have used Martinsville Country Club for sectional qualifying for their national publinks. Otter Creek hosted the whole shebang for the men, in 1991. It's over $40 a round, but Eagle Creek, where the '82 national publinks championship was played, and Coffin (host in 1935, 1955, and 1972 and perhaps the toughest local area course) are still affordable. Coffin will reopen in July of '95 after a complete renovation, new greens, tees, irrigation system—the works. "A whole new layout," I was told. "You won't even recognize it." Fees should be comparable to Eagle Creek. Coffin was tragically the scene of a murder several years ago (the killer got two hundred years). Wisely, the new design is being given a chance to grow in before reopening. Pleasant Run and South Grove have held recent sectional publinx qualifying for the men.

Pleasant Run is very short, wide open on the front and narrow on the back, with small greens. A friend who's played it for thirty years says it's in good shape in the spring, hard as a rock all summer, and okay in the fall. It's in the nice historic neighborhood of Irvington in Indianapolis. South Grove, only a few minutes from downtown, might be a little tougher, and a little more fun, with comparable conditions.

He's since moved on—and no one would mistake his early work for Crooked Stick—but there are several early Pete Dye courses open to the public for under $30: Eagle Creek (1974) and William Sahm in Castleton (1963).

North of Indianapolis, Rick Teverbaugh, sports editor at the

*Herald Bulletin* in Anderson, likes Yule in Alexandria. The front's on the flat side but the back nine offers something of the feel of a Scottish linksland course. There's a good mix of holes, with one par four, number 13, that Rick says is as "long and as difficult as any par four in the county." He describes it as the best of the inexpensive. Find college courses at Indiana University (about a half mile past the football stadium), Indiana State, Purdue, Notre Dame, and Tri-State University in Angola (home of the Thunder). Play It Again Sports stores carry *The Indiana Golfer's Guide* ($9.99). It provides details on 400 courses across the state (317/299-8015).

Finally, it's officially $4 for nine holes at White Lick Golf Course, off radar somewhere north of Brownsburg ($2.50 for a second nine), but a friend once played as many holes as he could swing for the princely sum of a quarter a hole. What a deal.

## Discount Cards

American Lung Association Golf Privilege Card. Free green fees for over 140 weekday rounds, January 1–December 31. 800/LUNG-USA. $35.

Indiana Golf Association, PGA Section Gold Card. Complimentary or reduced green fees at over fifty courses, fifteen months, 317/738-9696. $45.

## Shopping

Michigan City Factory Outlet, about an hour and a half from Chicago and two hours from Indianapolis, has Brooks Brothers, Eddie Bauer, Polo/Ralph Lauren, J Crew, and more.

## FINDING THE GREEN IN INDIANA

Coffin Golf Course ($17/$20) 6,300 yds. (na/na)
2209 W. 30th
Indianapolis 317/327-7266

Deer Creek Golf Course ($17/$22) 6,225 yds. (69.6/126)
7143 South S.R. 39
Clayton 317/539-2013

Eagle Creek Golf Club ($16/$16) 6,600 yds. (71.3/123)
8802 W. 56th St.
Indianapolis 317/297-3366

Indiana State University Golf Course ($5/$6) 2,163 yds. (na/na)
3300 Wabash
Terre Haute 812/237-3633

Indiana University Golf Course ($16/$17) 6,538 yds. (72.0/126)
S.R. 46 Bypass East
Bloomington 812/855-7543

Martinsville Country Club ($16/$19) 6,244 yds. (69.3/112)
1510 State 37 North
Martinsville 317/342-4336

Pleasant Run Golf Course ($11/$11) 5,501 yds. (66.6/109)
601 N. Arlington Ave.
Indianapolis 317/357-0829

Purdue University Golf Course 36 holes
North Course: ($8/$10) 6,682 yds. (72.4/116)
South Course: ($10/$13) 5,903 yds. (70.5/122)
1201 Cherry Lane
West Lafayette 317/494-3139

Royal Hylands Golf Club ($15/$20) 5,948 yds. (68.0/125)
7629 South Greensboro Pike
Knightstown 317/345-2123

Sarah Shank Golf Course ($11/$11) 6,200 yds. (68.9/106)
2901 S. Keystone Ave.
Indianapolis 317/784-0631

South Grove Golf Course ($11/$11) 6,100 yds. (69.3/108)
1800 W. 18th St.
Indianapolis 317/327-7350

University of Notre Dame Golf Course ($14/$17) 6,129 yds.
(68.4/113)
Notre Dame 219/631-6425

White Lick Golf Course ($6.50/$6.50) 2,622 yds. (na/na)
White Lick Lane/S.R. 267
Fayette 317/852-2931

William Sahm Golf Course ($12/$12) 6,060 yds. (67.3/102)
6800 E. 91st St.
Indianapolis 317/849-0036

Yule Golf Club ($12/$14) 6,353 yds. (69.3/113)
1800 S. Harrison
Alexandria 317/724-3229

Zollner Golf Course ($15/$18) 6,320 yds. (69.7/121)
Tri-State University
300 West Park St.
Angola 219/665-4269

# IOWA

## Local Knowledge

*Golf Courses of Iowa* ($15.50) surveys 365 courses across the state.
Author Roger Aegerter considers playability, aesthetics, and several
other benchmarks. Disappointments are not sugar coated. A poor
course is clinically defined as one "Not up to expectations, lacking in
resource development, unsatisfactory, a detraction to the course."
Ouch.

The oversized paperback reprints scorecards and hole layouts.
Roger also asks the timeless question: Was a course worth the trip?

In Des Moines, Waveland garners four stars and excellent ratings
across the board. Bunker Hill in Dubuque is just a step behind.
Roger calls it "probably one of the best municipal courses in the
state." Ellis Municipal in Cedar Rapids also gets four stars and similar
high marks.

Several others Roger feels are definitely worth the trip: Beaver Run
in Grimes ("Evergreens dominate the course . . . bent grass fairways
. . . four ponds . . . good mix of holes . . . very scenic"), Pine Lake
Country Club near Eldora ("Surrounded by Pine Lake State Park.
Built in 1927 . . . . . . cut out of thick woods . . . by a variety of polls
as one of the most beautiful in Iowa"), Primghar Golf and Country

Club in Primghar ("In immaculate shape, definitely one of THE best in western Iowa . . . one of the best facilities in the entire state . . . really a thing of beauty"), Three Lake Municipal in Lenox ("One of the five remaining sand green courses . . . short and open to any kind of swing . . . 1925"), and Timberline in Peosta ("Carved right out of the woods").

Wapsipinicon State Park in Anamosa has nine holes. Roger thought the course, built in 1923, with its log-cabin clubhouse and beautiful surroundings, worth the trip.

The *Iowa Visitors Guide* includes a partial list of course names and addresses, broken down by region (800/345-IOWA). *Golf Courses of Iowa* is available from: Roger Aegerter, P.O. Box 88, Jefferson, IA 50129.

### Discount Card

See "Stalking the Elusive Deep Discount" in Finding the Green introduction.

### Shopping

Tanger Factory Outlet Center in Williamsburg has Brooks Brothers, Bass, Reebok and Polo/Ralph Lauren. On I-80, between Des Moines and Iowa City.

## FINDING THE GREEN IN IOWA

**Beaver Run Golf Course ($15.50/$17.50) 6,041 yds. (64.8/113)**
**11200 Northwest Towner Dr.**
**Grimes 515/986-3221**

**Bunker Hill Golf Course ($9.50/$10.50) 4,964 yds. (63.9/109)**
**Bunker Hill Rd.**
**Dubuque 319/589-4261**

**Ellis Municipal Golf Course ($9.25/$10.50) 6,410 yds. (70.8/120)**
**1401 Zika Ave. NW.**
**Cedar Rapids 319/398-5180**

Pine Lake Country Club ($12/$12) 2,696 yds. (na/na)
County Rd. S56
Pine Lake 515/858-3031

Primghar Golf & Country Club ($12/$14) 3,040 yds. (69.7/110)
Second St. NE.
Primghar 712/757-6781

Three Lake Municipal Golf Club ($3/$3) 2,121 yds. (na/na)
Lenox 515/333-2990

Timberline Golf Club ($10/$13) 6,142 yds. (70.9/118)
19804 E. Pleasant Grove Rd.
Peosta 319/876-3422

Wapsipinicon Country Club ($8/$12) 2,362 yds. (na/na)
Wapsipinicon State Park
Anamosa 319/462-3930

Waveland Golf Course ($14/$16) 6,171 yds. (71.2/121)
4908 University
Des Moines 515/242-2902

# KANSAS

*Local Knowledge*

Alvamar in Lawrence continues to uphold its reputation as one of the
Midwest's, and the nation's, nicest public courses. Publinks qualifying, Big 8 tournaments, and the Kansas Open are all held here. The
quality and the challenge, not surprisingly, attract a lot of business.

Green fees at Alvamar, according to Jim Misunas of *The
Hutchinson News,* are about as high as you'll find them for public
golf in the state, which is another way of saying you can do very well
here for under $20, even under $15. Sunflower Hills in Bonner
Springs hosted recent sectional qualifying for the women's publinks.

Wichita used to claim more public holes per capita than any other
city in the nation. Jim recommends McDonald Park, (the old Wichita
Country Club), Turkey Creek in McPherson, and Pawnee Prairie,

right by the airport—in that order. He also likes Buffalo Dunes in Garden City and Rolling Meadows in Junction City. Buffalo Dunes has hosted Kansas Golf Association Championships in the recent past. Publinks qualifying has also been held at Quail Ridge in Winfield. Wichita State's course was the former Crestview Country Club.

Another private club that's opened its doors is Victory Hills in Kansas City. After extensive improvements, it went public in 1993, pledging "country club services at a public course price."

Kansas City also has Dub's Dread, designed and built by Byron Nelson's "Gold Dust" twin, Harold McSpaden. "Jug" turned up at the Legends of Golf one year; he was in his mid-eighties and easily bested his age. The course originally topped out at over eight thousand yards with a course rating of 78.8, something of a sensation when it opened, but it's since been shortened.

Bob Hentzen at *The Topeka Capital-Journal* also talks up the affordability of Kansas golf. "Kansas is just a good place to play golf," he says. Bob recommends Lake Shawnee ("very scenic and playable for the average person"). Colly Creek is harder, fairly new, and still "a little rough around the edges," but a "severe test"—so much so that it offers attractive used-ball specials at the door. You might also want a cart. Topeka Public is "not a bad course at all." Western Hills is a former country club, Forbes Public an old military base course (nine holes).

There's talk the Kansas Golf Association will revise its *Kansas Golf Course Directory*. In the meantime, while supplies last, the association will send out free copies of the early nineties edition (913/842-4833).

### Discount Card

American Lung Association Golf Privilege Card. Fifty-eight courses, some range discounts, March 1–October 31. 800/432-3957 or 913/272-9290. $35.

### Shopping

Riverfront Plaza in the north end of downtown Lawrence has fifty outlet stores (800/913-4567). There's also a Tanger Factory Outlet Center in East Lawrence (913/842-6290). Off I-70 at Exit 53, Colby has a White's Factory Outlet Center offering a "Shopping Oasis on the Plains" (913/462-7387).

## FINDING THE GREEN IN KANSAS

Alvamar Golf Club ($20/$30) 6,474 yds. (70.6/130)
1800 Crossgate
Lawrence 913/492-GOLF

Buffalo Dunes Golf Course ($10/$12) 6,443 yds. (70.9/122)
South Hwy. 83
Garden City 316/276-1210

Colly Creek Golf Club ($11/$14) 5,832 yds. (69.6/125)
3720 SW. 45th St.
Topeka 913/267-7888

Dub's Dread Golf Club ($19/$26.25) 6,385 yds. (71.4/128)
12601 Hollingsworth Rd.
Kansas City 913/721-1333

Forbes Public Golf Course ($7/$8) 9 holes/6,476 yds. (70.2/128)
700 Capehart Rd.
Topeka 913/862-0114

Lake Shawnee Golf Course ($8.25/$9.75) 6,013 yds. (68.9/107)
4141 SE. East Edge Rd.
Topeka 913/267-2295

McDonald Park Golf Course ($12/$12) 6,347 yds. (67.4/115)
840 N. Yale Ave.
Wichita 316/688-9391

Pawnee Prairie Men's Club ($12/$12) 6,863 yds. (71.0/117)
1931 S. Tyler
Wichita 316/721-7474

Quail Ridge Golf Course ($11/$13) 6,600 yds. (71.1/125)
3805 Quail Ridge Dr.
Winfield 316/221-5645

Rolling Meadows Golf Club ($8.50/$10.50) 6,370 yds. (71.5/128)
Old Milford Rd.
Junction City 913/238-4303

Sunflower Hills Golf Course ($14/$15) 5,800 yds. (72.6/124)
122nd and Riverview
Bonner Springs 913/721-2727

Topeka Public Golf Course ($10.45/$10.45) 6,124 yds. (69.0/112)
2533 Urish SW.
Topeka 913/272-0511

Turkey Creek Golf Course ($8/$10) 5,750 yds. (68.9/120)
1000 Fox Run
McPherson 316/241-8530

Victory Hills Golf Course ($8/$8) 5,685 yds. (67.0/112)
7101 Parallel Pkwy.
Kansas City 913/334-1111

Western Hills Golf Course ($10.50/$13) 5,540 yds. (68.0/na)
8533 SW. 21st St.
Topeka 913/478-4000

Wichita State University Golf Course ($13/$13) 5,800 yds.
(69.7/122)
4201 E. 21st
Wichita 316/685-6601

# KENTUCKY

*Local Knowledge*

*Kentucky Golf: The Complete Guide to Golfing in the Bluegrass* ($9.95) describes over two hundred courses. It's at most book and golf stores and also available from Stoneham Communications, Inc., P.O. Box 6603, Louisville, KY 40207.

Some of editor Lane Stoneham's favorites in Lexington: Players Club, Kearney Hill, and Campbell House Country Club. Kearney Hill, designed by Pete and P. B. Dye, hosts the Senior Tour. No surprise, it's very tough, with everything narrowing to the greens (definitely spring for the yardage book). Quality, service—it's all first-rate, from the condition of the course to the large soda cups on the coolers. It's closed from around the end of August through most of September to prepare for the Bank One. Set amongst the horse farms, Kearney will host the national publinks championship in 1997. This course pushes all the right buttons. It's certainly one of the best affordable public golf values anywhere, assuming your game is up to snuff.

The Lexington City Championship is on a rota with Tates Creek and Lakeside. You can certainly spray the ball at Lakeside without facing the adversity you have at Kearney Hill. A par five of 634 yards (that's from the whites!) is an experience. The finishing hole requires a slight downhill carry over water to a peninsula green. Power lines mar a couple of holes, but this is a strong municipal course. The only blemish: $1 for a rather small soda. Tuesday morning tee times are blocked out for women from eight to ten.

Gibson Bay in Richmond is an outstanding public facility, indicative of the positive direction public golf is headed. You can easily pay twice as much, and probably have, for considerably less. This is just another public course masquerading as a resort. It's a hike to walk, rated 74.1 from the back. There are four tees. The only question is what optimist decided a yardage marker was needed 346 yards away on a hole? Gibson Bay is right around the corner from Eastern Kentucky University. The café serves a decent sandwich.

In and around Louisville, Lane suggests Nevel Meade and Seneca (the site of Gary Player's first PGA Tour win in 1957), next to Bowman Field. Shawnee in Louisville hosted the publinks back in 1932. Lane notes that the course has undergone a $5 million renovation.

Quail Chase, perennially lauded by *Louisville Magazine,* is, in Lane's opinion, "A public course with country club standards." About each of the previous suggestions, he says: "They're all really good." Charlie Vettiner in Louisville is a sectional publinks qualifying site.

Kentucky State Park courses came as something of a revelation. Beautiful scenery, friendly folks, and the golf is cheap and unhurried. At Lincoln Homestead, the opportunity presents itself to flub one into the reproduction blacksmith shop where Abraham Lincoln's father, Thomas, learned his trade. Of the five state parks I played in Kentucky, only Jenny Wiley, a nine-holer in eastern Kentucky, disappointed. Barren River offers panoramic views of the lake from several holes. Sixty-four hundred yards from the blues, the lamb of the older front side turns into a longer lion on the back. The club also

*Looking down off the third tee at Lincoln Homestead.*

has an active demo program. Almost all of the parks with golf courses have lodges and cottages and offer discount travel packages.

The Kentucky Department of Parks has a pile of useful golf information related to the state parks (800/255-PARK). *The Kentucky Travel Guide* is only mildly helpful. *The Lexington Visitors Guide* won't help you any more than the phone book, in fact less.

*Divots, Tri-State Area Golf Course News* covers eastern Kentucky, parts of West Virginia, and Ohio. It's free, if you can find it, from April through October at courses, chambers of commerce, even YMCAs (614/867-6376).

## Discount Cards

American Cancer Society Golf Pass. Free green fees on eighty-nine courses, some in Indiana and Tennessee. 800/ACS-2345. $35.
American Lung Association Golf Tour Card. Free green fees at over 100 Kentucky courses. 502/363-2652 or 800/366-LUNG. $35.

## Shopping

On I-75 between Cincinnati and Lexington, the Dry Ridge Outlet Center has Bass, Nike, Van Heusen, and North Face.

## FINDING THE GREEN IN KENTUCKY

Barren River State Resort Park ($15/$15) 5,942 yds. (68.4/122)
1149 State Park Rd.
Lucas 502/646-4653

Ben Hawes State Park ($15/$15) 6,372 yds. (71.0/116)
400 Booth-Field Rd.
Owensboro 502/684-9808

Campbell House Country Club ($27/—) 5,804 yds. (68.1/119)
427 Parkway Dr.
Lexington 606/254-3631

Carter Caves State Resort Park ($10/$10) 2,756 yds. (66.7/na)
State Rd. 182
Olive Hill 606/286-4411

Charlie Vettiner Golf Course ($7/$8) 6,000 yds. (68.5/115)
10207 Mary Dell
Jeffersontown 502/267-9958

General Burnside State Park ($13/$13) 5,905 yds. (67.5/108)
U.S. 27
Burnside 606/561-4104

General Butler State Resort Park ($10/$10) 2,745 yds. (na/na)
Hwy. 227
Carrollton 502/732-4384

Gibson Bay Golf Course ($10/$14) 6,508 yds. (71.3/122)
2000 Gibson Bay Dr.
Richmond 606/623-0225

Jenny Wiley State Resort Park ($10/$10) 2,347 yds. (60.9/92)
Kentucky Hwy. 3
Prestonburg 606/886-2711

John James Audubon State Park ($10/$10) 3,120 yds. (68.7/111)
US Hwy. 41 North
Henderson 502/826-5546

Kearney Hill Golf Links ($20/$20) 6,501 yds. (70.5/122)
3403 Kearney Rd.
Lexington 606/253-1981

Kenlake State Resort Park ($10/$10) 1,909 yds. (na/na)
Hwy. 94
Hardin 502/474-2211

Kentucky Dam Village State Park ($15/$15) 6,307 yds. (71.0/131)
Hwy. 641
Gilbertsville 502/362-4271

Lake Barkley State Resort Park ($15/$15) 6,448 yds. (70.1/120)
Blue Springs Rd.
Cadiz 502/924-9076

Lakeside Golf Club ($10/$10) 6,521 yds. (70.9/120)
3725 Richmond Rd.
Lexington 606/263-5315

Lincoln Homestead State Park ($15/$15) 6,350 yds. (69.8/118)
5079 Lincoln Rd.
Springfield 606/336-7461

My Old Kentucky Home Country Club ($15/$15) 5,836 yds.
(68.3/117)
My Old Kentucky Home State Park
Hwy. 49
Bardstown 502/349-6542

Nevel Meade Golf Club ($15/$21) 6,516 yds. (69.4/114)
10509 Hwy. 329
Prospect 502/228-9522

Pennyrile Forest State Resort Park ($10/$10) 3,270 yds. (70.2/113)
Kentucky 109
Dawson Springs 502/797-3421

Pine Mountain State Resort Park ($10/$10) 2,150 yds. (62.0/na)
203 Kentucky Ave.
Pineville 606/337-6195

Players Club of Lexington ($20/$30) 6,385 yds. (73.2/116)
4850 Leestown
Lexington 606/255-1011

Quail Chase Golf Club ($14/$17) 27 holes
Course One: 6,440 yds. (70.4/121)
Course Two: 6,421 yds. (70.3/122)
Course Three: 6,371 yds. (69.6/115)
7000 Cooper Chapel Rd.
Louisville 502/239-2110

Seneca Golf Course ($7/$8) 6,621 yds. (70.8/113)
2300 Pee Wee Reese Rd.
Louisville 502/458-9298

Shawnee Golf Course ($7/$8) 6,072 yds. (66.7/100)
460 Northwestern Parkway
Louisville 502/776-9389

Tates Creek Golf Course ($10/$10) 5,870 yds. (67.9/117)
1400 Gainesway Dr.
Lexington 606/272-3428

# LOUISIANA

*Local Knowledge*

Bayou Oaks, old City Park, goes back a long way; the original nine holes date to 1902. It's not the same course that held the New Orleans Open for many years, a course Byron Nelson recalled fondly in his autobiography as "a fine municipal facility that I always liked. I always played well there, and especially liked the long par threes, since I was a good long-iron player." He won it twice; in 1946, first place was good for all of $1,500.

The old number one course has been broken up, fragmented into the West and East courses, but, according to Dave Lagarde, who covers the game for *The Times-Picayune*, there are still some "lovely older holes on the East Course." To give an indication of how busy the four Bayou Oaks courses are, Dave recalled a recent spring weekend. Walking up around four-thirty he was told the courses together had sold some 1,700 tickets *that day,* which breaks down to something like 425 rounds on each course! Not to despair, though; he assures me that getting on is really not that hard. By no means expensive, Bayou Oaks gets cheaper after 3 P.M. The West Course is the championship course, longer, with more water. The East has got more trees, narrower fairways, and smaller greens. It's also a little cheaper. The South Course is executive length. The North, Dave says, has a lot of sameness, which allows the ball to be struck "pretty much anywhere you want."

Dave's column runs in Sunday's paper. He suggests two other courses: Oak Harbor in Slidell ("A nice little track . . . when the wind blows it's as tough as any around") and Bayou Barriere ("pretty decent . . . fairly demanding"), not as tough as the West Course but a step up in difficulty from the East at Bayou Oaks. During the week the club runs attractive specials.

The Gulf States PGA section will fax anyone interested a list of member courses in the New Orleans area with approximate travel time from downtown (504/245-7333). The golf and tennis brochure from the New Orleans Tourist Convention Commission includes a map and prices (504/566-5011).

Baton Rouge may very well have the most affordable city golf in the country. Would you believe $5 for eighteen holes (that's all day) at three of the city's six munys? The fairways are not irrigated at Howell, City Park, or Webb (which once was the Baton Rouge Country Club and then LSU's course), but the layouts are sufficient that the city amateur tournament can be shared amongst them all. The tees and greens, I'm told, are fine. A very civilized ten-minute interval is used for tee times at the city courses.

Almost a decade ago, a private club designed by Trent Jones went under. The course never opened, and the city wisely bought it at auction. Santa Maria is more expensive, though still under $30, and offers an obvious upper-niche experience. For a Baton Rouge golf brochure, call 800/LA-ROUGE.

LSU's course is open to the public. Louisiana Tech in Grambling also has nine holes.

### Discount Card

Gulf States Section PGA Golf Pass. Discounts to about 50 courses in Louisiana and Mississippi, twelve months. 800/844-0844 or 504/245-7333. $49.

### Shopping

Tanger Factory Outlet Center in Gonzales has Liz Claiborne; VF in Iowa has Van Heusen; in Arcadia, there's also Cape Isle. Slidell Factory Outlets has Arrow, Bugle Boy, Cape Isle, Van Heusen, Levi's, and several shoe stores that carry discounted golf shoes.

### FINDING THE GREEN IN LOUISIANA

**Baton Rouge City Park ($3.50/$3.50) 9 holes/5,716 yds. (na/na)**
1442 City Park Ave.
Baton Rouge 504/387-9523

**Bayou Oaks 72 holes**
West Course: ($12/$15) 7,160 yds. (71.5/116)
East Course: ($9/$12) 6,968 yds. (70.5/111)
North Course: ($9/$12) 6,054 yds. (68.5/110)
South Course: ($7/$10) 4,921 yds. (66.5/106)
1040 Fillmore Ave.
New Orleans South Course 504/483-9390; all others 504/483-9396

Bayou Barriere Golf Club ($10/$16) 27 holes
Holes 1–18: 6,143 yds. (69.2/124)
Holes 10–27: 6,037 yds. (na/na)
Holes 1–9, 19–27: 5,862 (na/na)
7427 Hwy. 23
Bellchase 504/394-0662

Howell Park Golf Course ($5/$5) 5,779 yds. (na/na)
5511 Winbourne Ave.
Baton Rouge 504/357-9292

LSU Golf Course ($8/$8) 5,995 yds. (69.4/na)
Louisiana State University
Baton Rouge 504/388-3394

Louisiana Tech Golf Course ($10/$10) 2,700 yds. (na/na)
Hwy. 150
Grambling 318/247-8331

Oak Harbor Golf Club ($20/$20*) 5,305 yds. (69.6/118)
201 Oak Harbor Blvd.
Slidell 504/646-0110

Santa Maria Golf Club ($16/$20) 5,758 yds. (74.0/127)
19301 Old Perkins Rd.
Baton Rouge 504/752-9667

Webb Park Golf Course ($5/$5) 6,400 yds. (na/na)
1351 Country Club Dr.
Baton Rouge 504/383-4919

*Twilight

# MAINE

### Local Knowledge

*The Maine Golf Guide* ($15) is the latest and best of the New England trilogy of guides by Bob Labbance and David Cornwell. The course descriptions and historical background make pleasant and informative reading. Where the black flies are particularly vexing, Labbance and Cornwell will tell you. Available from New England Golf Specialists (802/234-9220). The annual *New England Golf Guide* ($14.95), compiled by Michael Sugarman and Jack Albin, is less descriptive but chock-full of information including prices, coupons, and directions (800/833-6387).

In season, look for *Fairway Focus,* Maine's golf newspaper. It's got a statewide course list and a separate directory. Call and ask if the MGM Card has been reprised. It was a good deal for $15, half off once a season at twenty-five courses statewide. (207/989-1722).

The Maine Publicity Bureau has a handy golf brochure with rates and amenities. It's reprinted in the official state tourism magazine, 207/989-6555.

Maine has a handful of public Donald Ross courses. Lake Kezar in Lovell has hosted the state amateur. Labbance and Cornwell note that except for the relocation of one green, the layout is unchanged and well maintained. Biddeford-Saco got nine holes in 1921 and the second nine, using Ross's original plans, in 1987.

Cape Neddick in Ogunquit and Poland Spring are a couple of other venerable courses that trace their lineage to the turn of the century. Cape Neddick will let you in if you're staying at a local hotel. Northeast Harbor is Labbance's unabashed favorite.

Springbrook, in Leeds, hosts the Women's Maine State Golf Association Championship, a "frequent venue for the Maine Open and other top tournaments," according to Labbance and Cornwell.

The Greater Bangor Open, which offers the largest purse in the state, is held at Kebo Valley. Sectional publinks qualifying has also been held there. President William Howard Taft, who once refused a diplomatic appointment with the rejoinder "I'll be damned if I will give up my game of golf to see this fellow," is reputed to have taken a twenty-two on the seventeenth hole at Kebo.

Bangor's heralded muny has hosted the National Amateur Public Links Championship.

Sable Oaks in South Portland, ranked number two in the state by *Golf Digest,* has entertained the Oldsmobile Scramble and is home of the Maine Golf Hall of Fame. Fred Martin, publisher of *Fairway Focus,* told me that not only is it a great course but "You can always get on." A couple of other Portland-area recommendations: Dutch Elm and Willowdale. Pressed for out-of-the-way gems, under duress, Fred let slip the name of the nine-hole Country View in Brooks. "The scenery," he says, "is absolutely gorgeous."

### Discount Card

American Lung Association Golf Privilege Card. Free rounds at over fifty courses, including Sugarloaf and Samoset (add $10), *Golf Digest's* Top 2 best in state, although Samoset is available only after October 1. 800/499-5864 or 207/622-6394. $70.

### Shopping

*Vogue* once suggested a name for the inevitable burnout that overcomes even the most ardent outlet shopper. "Chronic Outlet Fatigue Syndrome (COFS)" is a real concern in Freeport. To help pick your shots, get the map from the visitors' bureau. The real question is what will give out first: your feet, your wallet, or your will to resist a bargain.

Benetton, Patagonia, L.L. Bean, Gant/Izod/Evan-Picone, Fila, Reebok, Nike, Brooks Brothers, they're all here. Titleist apparel is 35 to 55 percent off at Corbin, 15 Main St., at Shopper's Landing, across the street from the Freeport Police Station. Golf Day's in the Freeport Crossing Outlet Center. Kittery has Polo/Ralph Lauren, J Crew, and Brooks Brothers.

## FINDING THE GREEN IN MAINE

**Bangor Municipal Golf Course ($16/$17) 6,500 yds. (69.2/115)**
**278 Webster Ave.**
**Bangor 207/941-0232**

Biddeford-Saco Country Club ($25/$25) 6,192 yds. (68.2/119)
101 Old Orchard Rd.
Saco 207/282-5883

Cape Neddick Country Club ($30/$30) 9 holes/5,485 yds. (65.8/108)
Shore Rd.
Ogunquit 207/361-2011

Country View Golf Club ($15/$15) 9 holes/5,770 yds. (66.4/115)
Rte. 7
Brooks 207/722-3161

Dutch Elm Golf Course ($20/$25) 5,942 yds. (69.0/119)
RR. 4, Brimstone Rd.
Arundel 207/282-9850

Kebo Valley Golf Club ($30/$30) 6,100 yds. (69.0/129)
Eagle Lake Rd., Rte. 233
Bar Harbor 207/288-3000

Lake Kezar Country Club ($18/$20) 5,850 yds. (67.1/116)
Rte. 5
Lovell 207/925-2462

Northeast Harbor Golf Club ($30/$30) 5,360 yds. (68.0/na)
Sargeant Dr. NE.
Northeast Harbor 207/276-5335

Poland Spring Country Club ($16/$16) 6,196 yds. (67.2/117)
Rte. 26
Poland Spring 207/998-6002

Sable Oaks Golf Club ($22/$28) 6,056 yds. (70.2/129)
505 Country Club Dr.
South Portland 207/775-6257

Springbrook Golf Club ($16/$16) 6,163 yds. (71.2/120)
Rte. 202
Leeds 207/946-5900

Willowdale Golf Club ($20/$20) 5,980 yds. (67.9/110)
Willowdale Rd.
Scarborough 207/883-9351

# MARYLAND

### Local Knowledge

Queenstown Harbor Golf Links racks up the accolades. A *Metro Golf* magazine Readers' Choice winner for Best Public or Daily-fee Course, "it's probably the best public course in Maryland," says editor John Holmes. Right on the Potomac, the scenic and challenging course is also a Top 10 *Tee Time* magazine Best Course in the Mid-Atlantic. Eagle's Landing, just outside of Ocean City, was second runner-up in the *Metro Golf* poll. It also cracked *Tee Time*'s Top 10. One of the anonymous panelists for *Golf Digest*'s rankings called it "the best public course on the eastern shore."

Other *Tee Time* winners: Mount Pleasant in Baltimore (where Arnold Palmer won the 1956 Eastern Open and which was highly regarded over fifty years ago when it hosted the National Publinx in 1939), Pine Ridge in Lutherville (once home of the Eastern Open and the LPGA Lady Carling Open), and Hog Neck in Easton (a Top 10 best in the Mid-Atlantic).

On the basis of slope and course rating alone, *Metro Golf* determined Enterprise in Mitchellville, Redgate in Rockville, and Hog Neck to be near the top of any list of the region's hardest courses. Holmes says that some liken Enterprise to a poor man's Augusta. Redgate has hosted sectional publinks qualifying. Oakland Golf Club in Oakland hosted the Western Maryland Men's Amateur Golf Championship in 1993. Upper-level courses can be found at the University of Maryland in College Park and in Westminster at Western Maryland College.

For metro areas suffering from a dearth of public golf, the Mid-Atlantic is very well served by *Metro Golf* and *Tee Time*. Both are a cut above. *Tee Time* includes a regional sixteen-page course directory with the first issue of the year. It's also for sale for $3.50. Back issues are $4.50 (301/913-0081). *Metro Golf* profiles its Readers' Choice winners in the January/February issue. The magazine is free at courses (202/663-9015). Back issues are $3. Both offer subscriptions. T-Time Maps has a Maryland and Delaware edition, which is basically a state golf encyclopedia that fits inside a #10 envelope. The fine print includes course ratings, par, amenities, driving ranges, etc. ($3.95, 410/667-6738).

The Maryland Office of Tourism Development's *Destination Maryland* contains some golf info, though not enough. *The Travel and Outdoor Guide* is better (800/543-1036). Better still is the *Maryland Golf Guide*. Worcester County produces the brochure A Guide to Golfing (800/852-0335).

Ocean City is taking a page from Myrtle Beach. Umpteen packages, one-stop reservations, and tee times are available from 800/4-OC-GOLF.

### Discount Cards

Chesapeake Golf Association. Discounted regional green fees, travel packages, other goodies, including bag tag and membership card. 410/392-0552. $45.

Mid-Atlantic Golf & Travel Association. Discounts at courses in seven states, equipment, car rentals, travel, free year's subscription to *Tee Time*. 301/884-4475. $35.

### Shopping

A few miles east of the Chesapeake Bay Bridge, Kent Narrows Factory Stores has Izod/Gant, Bass, and Van Heusen (410/643-5231). There's also an "upscale designer outlet center" in Perryville (410/378-9399). Chesapeake Village in Queenstown has Brooks Brothers, J Crew, and Nike.

## FINDING THE GREEN IN MARYLAND

Eagle's Landing Golf Course ($22/$22) 6,306 yds. (70.8/121)
12367 Eagle's Nest Rd.
Berlin 410/213-7277

Enterprise Golf Course ($17/$22) 6,500 yds. (70.1/124)
2802 Enterprise Rd.
Mitchellville 301/249-2040

Hog Neck Golf Course ($28/$28) 6,000 yds. (68.7/115)
10142 Old Cordova Rd.
Easton 410/822-6079

Mount Pleasant Golf Club ($10.50/$11.50) 6,395 yds. (70.3/117)
6001 Hillen Rd.
Baltimore 410/254-5100

Oakland Golf Club ($22/$27.50) 6,356 yds. (69.9/115)
Sang Run Rd.
Oakland 301/334-3883

Pine Ridge Golf Course ($10.50/$11.50) 6,390 yds. (70.0/117)
2101 Dulaney Valley Rd.
Lutherville 410/252-1408

Queenstown Harbor Golf Links ($25/$30*) 36 holes
River Course: 6,599 yds. (71.8/132)
Lakes Course: 6,001 yds. (68.4/118)
Rte. 301
Queenstown 410/827-6611 or 800/827-5257

Redgate Municipal Golf Course ($17.50/$20) 6,100 yds. (70.2/128)
14500 Avery Rd.
Rockville 301/309-3055

University of Maryland Golf Course ($13/$13*) 6,271 yds. (69.5/116)
University Blvd.
College Park 301/403-4299

Western Maryland College Golf Course ($10/$15) 9 holes/5,324 yds.
(64.0/100)
Pennsylvania Ave. and Sullivan Rd.
Westminster 410/848-7667

*Twilight

# MASSACHUSETTS

### Local Knowledge

For the cost of a phone call, the Massachusetts State Golf Association will post you a copy of *Mass Golfer,* its official publication, which does a great job of focusing in on an area, say the Cape, and providing course reviews and well-written features. The association also makes its member course list available (617/891-4300).

George Wright Golf Course, perennial host to sectional publinks qualifying and designed by Donald Ross, entertains fifty thousand-plus rounds a year. When asked about the course's condition, Jack O'Leary, who covers the game for the *Boston Herald,* said: "For a public course that gets that amount of play, it's in great shape." Ross spoke to reporters when Hyde Park, as it was then known, opened in the thirties. "I am positive that a city cannot expend its money for a better, more worthy cause than a municipal course such as this," he said.

Lord knows what he would say if he could see what's become of another of his area public works, Ponkapoag in Canton. Celebrated in *Sports Illustrated*'s classic tale "Golf's Missing Links" by Rick Reilly (included in the 1989 edition of *Best Sports Stories*), edited by Tom Barnidge, it's inspiring muny bedside reading; if you haven't read it, do so, you'll love it.

Apparently, Ponkapoag is showing signs of improvement. It is "getting better," Jack says. "They're actually doing something condition-wise." Rest assured, such are the time-honored traditions of Metro District politics, Ponky is and will always be Ponky.

Larry Gannon, north of Boston, fits Jack's definition of a "good public course," plain and simple. So does Beverly Golf & Tennis Club, where a young amateur named Julius Boros once played for the United Shoe industry team. Built by the WPA on a former family estate, the terms are such that the city can use the land only as long as a public golf course rests upon it. The day that ends is the day the property reverts to private ownership.

Stow Acres Country Club, about thirty miles from Boston, will host the National Amateur Public Links Championship in 1996. There are thirty-six holes, and each course is distinct. Franklin Park in

Dorchester went in the ground in 1896, the second oldest public course in the country. In an 1899 article, George Sargeant noted that "here he [the beginner] may cut divots to his heart's content, and freely does he avail himself of the privilege." Fifty miles southwest of Boston, Nichols College in Dudley (home of the Bison) admits the public unless there are leagues or tournaments. The *Herald* runs its annual golf special section each April.

From W. Pete Jones's *Directory of Golf Courses Designed by Donald J. Ross* come the following courses reputed to bear the stamp of the famed architect:

Ellinwood, Athol
Greenock, Lee
Newton Commonwealth, Newton
Sandy Burr, Wayland
Tekoa, Westfield
Wachusett, West Boylston
Wyckoff Park, Holyoke

Cape Cod now has a promotional association modeled on Myrtle Beach's successful Golf Holiday (800/TEE-BALL). Almost to Provincetown, until erosion claims the historic lighthouse and the course, Highland Golf Links in North Truro is worth the trip. Geoff Converse, who covers golf for the *Cape Cod Times* in Hyannis, mentions that the course is so far out that not a lot of visitors know about it. "It's a beautiful course," he says. "They just can't irrigate." The authentic nine-hole links course dates to 1892.

Geoff's "Golf Notes" column appears every Saturday. A special section, "The Cape Cod Golf Guide," runs each May. Other suggestions: Falmouth Country Club and Bass River in South Yarmouth, an upper-crust muny that holds the distinction of being "the busiest course in the Commonwealth." There are forty-nine courses on Cape Cod, accounting for 2 million rounds of golf. You might try two nationally recognized executive courses: Kings Way at Yarmouthport and Tara Hyannis. To really enjoy the Cape, Geoff says—no surprise here—come in September and October, "the best time of year." For more strategy, check *The Complete Guide to Golf on Cape Cod, Nantucket and Martha's Vineyard* ($9.95) by Paul Harber (Peninsula Press).

Glen Waggoner, author of the seminal *Divots, Shanks, Gimmes,*

*Mulligans, and Chili Dips,* once effectively derailed U.S. foreign policy by engaging then secretary of state George Shultz in a discussion of the Worthington Golf Course. Mr. Shultz belongs to Cypress Point, Augusta National, and Pine Valley. Worthington, though less exclusive, nevertheless ranks high on his list. And on Glen's too. Worthington is in the Berkshires, about thirty miles from Northampton.

Among a slew of affordable recommendations, in and around western Mass, Jim Regan, longtime sportswriter for the Springfield *Daily News,* recommends Oak Ridge near Agawam, host of the Miller Eastern Amateur, a top amateur event; Westover, built by the air force and now owned by the town of Ludlow; Waubeeka in Williamstown; and Franconia in Springfield, one of the oldest public courses in New England. It's also used for publinks qualifying, as is Veterans, also in Springfield.

The current edition of *Powers Northeast Golf Guide* ($14.95) includes sixty-eight course listings in Massachusetts with a handful of coupons, 800/446-8884. *New England GolfGuide* ($14.95) surveys the region, providing reprinted scorecards, readers' choice winners, coupons, directions, and other good stuff (800/833-6387).

The Mass Office of Travel and Tourism puts out a juicy statewide directory covering details for public and semiprivate courses (617/727-3201). Range, credit card info, prices, and amenities are covered. The *Getaway Guide* lists regional tourism councils for obtaining more specifics. The Greater Boston Convention and Visitors Bureau, for instance, has a list of courses in and around the hub it will be happy to mail you (800/888-5515).

### Discount Card:

American Lung Association Golf Privilege Card. Free green fees at eighty courses across the state. 508/947-7204. $39.95.

### Shopping

There are flea markets, and then there are flea markets. Brimfield (near Sturbridge) is a monster, good enough to attract dealers from all along the East Coast. They do *their* buying here. Second Tuesday through the following Monday of May, July, and September (800/628-8379).

There are outlets in Fall River and New Bedford; Reebok/ Rockport's in Avon and Marlborough; Lenox has Bass and Izod Lacoste; Lawrence has Polo/Ralph Lauren.

## FINDING THE GREEN IN MASSACHUSETTS

Bass River Golf Course ($28/$28) 5,702 yds. (68.4/124)
Highbank Rd.
South Yarmouth 508/398-9079

Beverly Golf and Tennis Club ($24/$30) 5,965 yds. (70.1/123)
134 McKay St.
Beverly 508/922-9072

Ellinwood Country Club ($18/$23) 5,737 yds. (69.0/110)
1928 Pleasant St.
Athol 508/249-7460

Falmouth Country Club ($20/$30) 6,227 yds. (68.8/114)
630 Carriage Shop Rd.
East Falmouth 508/548-3211

Franconia Golf Course ($11.50/$13.50) 5,825 yds. (67.1/113)
619 Dwight Rd.
Springfield 413/734-9334

Franklin Park Golf Course ($19/$22) 6,095 yds. (68.6/113)
One Circuit Dr.
Dorchester 617/265-4084

George Wright Golf Course ($21/$24) 6,166 yds. (68.6/123)
420 West St.
Hyde Park 617/361-8313

Greenock Country Club ($18/$30) 9 holes/6,027 yds. (67.4/123)
W. Park St.
Lee 413/243-3323

Highland Golf Links ($25/$25) 9 holes/5,114 yds. (63.5/97)
Highland Rd.
North Truro 508/487-9201

Kings Way Golf Club ($20.50/$20.50\*) 4,100 yds. (58.9/93)
Kings Circuit
Yarmouthport 508/362-8870

Larry Gannon Municipal Golf Course ($21/$24) 6,036 yds.
(67.9/113)
42 Great Woods Rd.
Lynn 617/592-8238

New England Country Club ($25/—) 5,665 yds. (67.2/125)
180 Paine St.
Bellingham 508/883-2300

Newton Commonwealth Golf Course ($18/$25) 5,590 yds.
(67.0/121)
212 Kenrick St.
Newton 617/630-1971

Nichols College Golf Course ($16/$22) 9 holes/6,482 yds. (70.6/115)
46 Dudley Hill Rd.
Dudley 508/943-9837

Oak Ridge Golf Club ($20/$25) 6,390 yds. (70.0/120)
850 S. Westfield St.
Feeding Hills 413/786-9693

Ponkapoag Golf Course ($13/$15) 36 holes
Course One: 6,726 yds. (71.9/123)
Course Two: 6,332 yds. (69.9/121)
2167 Washington St.
Canton 617/828-5828

Sandy Burr Country Club ($27/$29) 6,730 yds. (69.9/117)
103 Cochituate Rd./Rte. 27
Wayland 508/358-7211

Stow Acres Country Club ($15/$18\*) 36 holes
South Course: 6,520 yds. (70.5/120)
North Course: 6,907 yds. (72.4/124)
58 Randall Rd.
Stow 508/568-8690

\*Twilight

Tara Hyannis Golf Course ($20/$20) 18 holes/2,621 yds. (na/na)
West End Cir.
Hyannis 508/775-7775

Tekoa Country Club ($17/$20) 6,081 yds. (69.3/114)
459 Russell Rd.
Westfield 413/568-1064

Veterans Golf Course ($11.50/$13.50) 6,115 yds. (69.9/116)
1059 South Branch Pkwy.
Springfield 413/783-9611

Wachusett Country Club ($25/$28) 6,608 yds. (71.2/117)
187 Prospect St.
West Boylston 508/835-4484

Waubeeka Golf Links ($17/$22) 6,024 yds. (69.5/124)
137 New Ashford Rd.
Williamstown 413/458-8355

Westover Golf Club ($13/$15) 6,610 yds. (71.7/123)
South Street
Ludlow 413/583-8456

Worthington Golf Club ($18/$22) 9 holes/5,629 yds. (66.8/115)
Ridge Rd.
Worthington 413/238-4464

Wyckoff Park Golf Course ($30/—) 5,360 yds. (67.4/113)
233 E. Hampton Rd.
Holyoke 413/536-3602

# MICHIGAN

*Local Knowledge*

A color magazine guide, *Tee Up Michigan* divvies up the state's seven hundred-plus courses into three regional issues. Each has feature articles, detailed maps, and color photos along with the meat and potatoes. The annuals are sold at the usual outlets for $6.95 each. Save four bucks by ordering all three, and if you order one copy, *Tee Up* will send another copy free to a friend. You pay only the postage (810/792-6359).

The annual *Michigan Golfers Map and Guide* ($17.95) follows the standard coupon book format. It promises five hundred free rounds (mostly two-for-ones during the calendar year on the cover) (800/223-5877 or 313/416-5300).

A useful insider's guide, though there are no plans to update it, is retired *Detroit News* golf writer Jack Berry's *1993 Guide to Michigan Golf*. Jack doesn't waste or mince words. Thirty years of experience comes cheap at $9.95. Perhaps it will be reprised.

*Michigan Golfer Magazine* is "Michigan's Only Statewide Golf Magazine." It comes out six times a year. A copy is $2 at newsstands, a year's subscription is $10 (810/227-4200). Single issues or back copies are available. The first two issues usually highlight new openings. Its 1994 annual muny Top 10 ranking included Binder Park (Battle Creek), Cascades (Jackson), Groesbeck (Lansing), Kensington (Milford), L. E. Kaufman (Wyoming), Leslie Park (Ann Arbor), Milham Park (Kalamazoo), Rackham (outside Detroit), Warren Valley (Dearborn Heights), and White Lake Oaks (Pontiac).

Rackham and Warren Valley were designed by Donald Ross, as were other Detroit munys Rogell and Rouge Park. In his guide, Jack Berry applauds American Golf Corporation's efforts at restoring Rackham. (The corporation manages all the munys except Rogell.) Warren Valley's courses, he writes, "still show some Ross touches." Elk Rapids, upstate, is also a Ross course.

The Hill Brothers are known for more than coffee in Michigan. Mike Hill won three times in thirteen years on the PGA Tour, but he went crazy on the mulligan circuit, raking in more than a million as the Senior Tour's leading money winner in 1991. With his winnings, he bought a nine-holer in Brooklyn, then added another nine and an automatic sprinkler system. He told *Golf Digest* one hundred trees a year are being planted. Hill's Heart of the Lakes was described as being in "immaculate condition."

Deer Run in Lowell hosts the Michigan Public Links Championship. Other courses used in the recent past for sectional USGA publinks qualifying include Tyrone Hills in Fenton, The Pines in Weidman, the aforementioned Cascades in Jackson, and Michigan State's Forest Akers course. Other upper-level courses that allow public play are Eastern Michigan University's Huron Golf Club in Ypsilanti, Grand Valley State's The Meadows in Allendale, Katke at Ferris State in Big Rapids, and Portage Lake at Michigan Tech in Houghton.

Both *The Detroit News* and the *Detroit Free Press* produce annual golf specials in early April. They're available for $1.25 from Back Issues (313/222-6876). For info on the West Michigan Golf Show (usually in late February in Grand Rapids), call 616/247-1931; for info on the Southeast Michigan Golf Show (mid-March), call 810/348-5600.

Along with movie listings, Math Quest, and Gardening Tips, *Detroit News* readers can check out golf writer Vartan Kupelian's insights on the News Now free touchtone service. Contact numbers are different throughout the area. From Detroit, it's 252-2200, ext. 0937.

Two other freebie golf tabloids, available at courses, ranges, etc., are *Great Lakes Golf* (810/253-3219) and *Michigan Golf News,* published nine times a year (810/792-9800).

Free golf travel information is available from Michigan's Sunrise Side (800/424-3022), Northwest Michigan Golf Council (800/937-7272), and Gaylord Golf Mecca (800/345-8621). The emphasis is on packages, but there is also some useful daily-fee info. Michigan's general tourism magazine is one of the best (not an ad to be seen, just honest-to-goodness information), but golf's upper crust is emphasized (800/5432-YES).

Fore Better Golf covers Detroit, Ann Arbor, and Flint in its Southeast Michigan golf map, $3.95 at pro shops, $4 by mail (minimum purchase two) (708/893-8672).

Finally, if you happen to be in Southfield, Walter Hagen is in the mausoleum at Holy Sepulchre. Visiting hours are 9 A.M. to 4 P.M. daily, (810/350-1900).

## Discount Cards

American Lung Association Golf Privilege Card. Free green fees for over one hundred fifty-five rounds, May–October. 800/678-LUNG or 810/559-5100. $35.

Gaylord Golf Passport. Two-for-ones, including cart at seventeen resort courses. Gaylord Area Convention & Tourism Bureau. 800/345-8621. $99.

## Shopping

A laundry list of top outlet locations for, among others, Eddie Bauer, Bass, and Reebok, includes Birch Run, Holland, Monroe, Port Huron, Traverse City, and West Branch.

## FINDING THE GREEN IN MICHIGAN

Binder Park Municipal ($12/$13) 6,098 yds. (69.8/112)
6723 B Drive S.
Battle Creek 616/966-3459

Cascades Golf Course ($13/$16) 6,385 yds. (70.8/120)
1992 Warren Ave.
Jackson 517/788-4323

Deer Run Golf Club ($16/$18) 6,626 yds. (71.9/123)
13955 Cascade
Lowell 616/897-8481

Elk Rapids Golf Course ($10/$10) 3,000 yds. (67.8/111)
7204 Ames
Elk Rapids 616/264-8891

Forest Akers Golf Course 36 holes
Michigan State University
East Course: ($18/$20) 6,132 yds. (69.0/112)
West Course: ($30/—) 6,413 yds. (71.0/130)
Harrison Rd. at Mount Hope
East Lansing 517/355-1635

Groesbeck Golf Course ($15/$15) 6,082 yds. (69.4/118)
1600 Ormond Rd.
Lansing 517/483-4333

Hill's Heart of the Lakes Golf Course ($11/$14) 5,635 yds. (na/na)
500 Case Rd.
Brooklyn 517/592-2110

Huron Golf Club ($25/—) 6,150 yds. (70.7/131)
1275 Huron St.
Ypsilanti 313/487-2441

Katke Golf Course ($18/$20) 6,108 yds. (69.6/118)
Ferris State University
Big Rapids 616/592-3765

Kensington Metropark Golf Course ($16/$18) 6,378 yds. (70.8/115)
I-96, Kensington Rd.
Milford 810/685-9332

L. E. Kaufman Golf Course ($16/$16) 6,338 yds. (70.3/121)
4829 Clyde Park SW.
Wyoming 616/538-5050

Leslie Park Golf Course ($14/$17) 6,435 yds. (70.9/122)
2120 Traver Rd.
Ann Arbor 313/994-1163

The Meadows ($18/$28) 6,000 yds. (68.3/120)
Grand Valley State University
One Campus Dr.
Allendale 616/895-1000

Milham Park Golf Course ($14/$14) 6,304 yds. (70.2/118)
4200 Lovers Lane
Kalamazoo 616/344-7639

The Pines at Lake Isabella ($16/$20) 6,279 yds. (70.3/120)
7231 Clubhouse Dr.
Weidman 517/644-2300

Portage Lake Golf Course ($18/$18) 6,063 yds. (68.3/115)
Michigan Tech University
1400 Townsend
Houghton 906/487-2641

Rackham Golf Course ($16/$23) 6,253 yds. (69.8/115)
10100 Ten Mile Rd.
Huntington Woods 810/543-4040

Rogell Golf Course ($15/$18) 5,828 yds. (69.2/125)
18601 Berg Rd.
Detroit 313/935-5331

Rouge Park Golf Course ($15/$19) 6,100 yds. (69.4/118)
11701 Burt Rd.
Detroit 313/837-5900

Tyrone Hills Golf Course ($14/$20) 6,048 yds. (68.8/121)
8449 US 23 at Center Rd.
Fenton 810/629-5011

Warren Valley Golf Course ($16/$19) 36 holes
East Course: 5,880 yds. (67.7/110)
West Course: 5,827 yds. (67.6/113)
26116 W. Warren Ave.
Dearborn Heights 313/561-1040

White Lake Oaks Golf Course ($20/$24) 5,572 yds. (67.0/106)
991 S. Williams Lake Rd.
White Lake 810/698-2700

# MINNESOTA

*Local Knowledge*

*Minnesota Golfer,* the official publication of the Minnesota Golf
Association (and a good read it is), puts out a comprehensive annual
course directory with yardage and slope from every tee. It's free from
the Minnesota Office of Tourism (800/657-3700).

Broomball may have a longer season, but, befitting its ranking as
a top state in golfer participation, Minnesota has a bumper crop of
very good, affordable courses. Edinburgh USA in Brooklyn Park
plays to 6,141 yards when the LPGA Tour comes through in August.
*Golfweek* rated the Robert Trent Jones, Jr., course among the Top 10

in the state, heady company alongside Olympian layouts like Interlachen and Hazeltine. The Senior Tour now storms Bunker Hills in Coon Rapids; Chi Chi Rodriguez won the inaugural Burnet Senior Classic there in 1993 with a 201 (fifteen under par). Both courses have been honored in the recent past by the National Golf Foundation with the Public Golf Achievement Award. Other Minnesota winners: Rich Acres in Richfield and Brookview in Golden Valley.

A passel of courses have shared sectional qualifying for the USGA Amateur Public Links Championships, won incidentally in its fifth year, 1926, by Golden Gopher golfing legend Lester Bolstad. (The University of Minnesota's course bears his name.) They are:

Anoka Greenhaven, Anoka
Braemar, Edina
Bunker Hills, Coon Rapids
Elk River, Elk River
Francis A. Gross, Minneapolis
Hiawatha, Minneapolis
Highland Park, St. Paul
Keller, St. Paul
Majestic Oaks, Ham Lake
River Oaks, Cottage Grove

Minnesota courses have participated in national publinks competition almost from the beginning. Keller Golf Course, which also had the 1954 PGA Championship, hosted the 1931 national publinks, Meadowbrook the 1947, Francis A. Gross the 1964, and Bunker Hills the 1976.

Qualifying for the USGA Women's Amateur Publinx has been held at many of the above-named sites. Braemar hosted the championship in 1979. Others are Hollydale in Plymouth, Phalen Park in St. Paul, and The Links at Northfork in Ramsey.

State publinx championships have been held at Baker National in Medina, Ortonville Golf Course in Ortonville, Francis A. Gross in Minneapolis, Pokegama in Grand Rapids, Northern Hills in Rochester, and Meadowbrook in Hopkins.

Winter may slow Minnesota golfers down but only just. The Twin Cities are dotted with indoor domes. No matter the chill factor, the opportunity exists to hit a shot from under a hundred yards and to use your imagination. Indoor golf centers are in Edina, Spring Lake

Park, Cottage Grove, and Lakeville (see course listings). Rates are typically computed on the clock. A half hour to forty-five minutes goes for about $10. Club selection varies, and the centers often run hourly all-you-can-hit specials and even free clinics.

*Minnesota Greens—Places to Play* ($15.95) is a homegrown guide that stretches north to the Iron Range and east into western Wisconsin. Along with the nuts and bolts, there's also a word on which skill level the course best suits. It's available at the usual outlets, also Scheel's Sporting Goods in Mankato and St. Cloud and from Minnesota Greens, 1220 Conway, St. Paul, MN 55106.

*Minnesota Golf Magazine* is published six times during the season from April to September. Publisher/editor Tom O'Callaghan recommends Willinger in Northfield, Dwan in Bloomington, and Mille Lacs in Garrison. *MGM* is free at courses, a subscription is $5 (612/890-7037).

There's a state park course at Fort Ridgely State Park in Fairfax, the first course in Minnesota with something called ModSod artificial grass greens.

### Discount Card

See "Stalking the Elusive Deep Discount" in Finding the Green introduction.

### Shopping

Medford Outlet Center, about sixty miles south of Minneapolis off I-35, has Bass, Geoffrey Beene, Nike, North Face, and Van Heusen.

## FINDING THE GREEN IN MINNESOTA

**Airena Golf Center ($6 per half hour)**
7833 NE. Hwy. 65
Spring Lake Park 612/780-3663

**All Seasons Golf Center ($7.50 per half hour)**
(Four miles south of 494 on Hwy. 61)
Cottage Grove 612/459-2135

Anoka Greenhaven ($18/$20) 6,120 yds. (68.7/122)
2800 Greenhaven Rd.
Anoka 612/427-3180

Baker National Golf Course ($20/$20)
Lake/Lea Course: 6,271 yds. (71.5/128)
2935 Parkview Dr.
Medina 612/473-0800

Braemar Golf Club ($18/$18) 6,360 yds. (70.6/121)
6364 Dewey Hill Rd.
Edina 612/941-2072

Braemar Golf Dome ($7.75 per half hour)
7420 Braemar Blvd.
Edina 612/944-9490

Brookview Golf Course ($18/$18) 6,109 yds. (69.0/120)
200 Brookview Pkwy.
Golden Valley 612/544-8446

Bunker Hills Golf Course ($22/$24) 27 holes
North/East Course: 6,428 yds. (71.0/126)
East/West Course: 6,574 yds. (71.7/129)
North/West Course: 6,534 yds. (71.5/131)
Hwy. 242 and Foley Blvd.
Coon Rapids 612/755-4141

Dwan Golf Club ($15/$15) 5,275 yds. (64.5/107)
3361 W. 110th St.
Bloomington 612/948-8702

Edinburgh USA Golf Course ($29/$29) 6,335 yds. (68.7/122)
8700 Edinbrook Crossing
Brooklyn Park 612/424-7060

Elk River Country Club ($19/$22) 6,150 yds. (69.6/118)
20015 Elk Lake Rd.
Elk River 612/441-4111

Fort Ridgely Golf Course ($7/$9) 2,772 yds. (na/na)
Hwy. 4
Fairfax 507/426-7840

Francis A. Gross Golf Course ($16.50/$16.50) 6,237 yds. (70.8/120)
2201 St. Anthony Blvd.
Minneapolis 612/789-2542

Hiawatha Golf Club ($16.50/$16.50) 6,630 yds. (71.0/115)
4553 Longfellow Ave. South
Minneapolis 612/724-7715

Highland Park Golf Course ($17/$17) 6,113 yds. (69.3/118)
1403 Montreal Ave.
St. Paul 612/699-3650

Hollydale Golf Club ($16/$18) 5,922 yds. (67.9/107)
4710 Holly Lane
Plymouth 612/559-9847

Keller Golf Course ($18/$18) 6,075 yds. (69.6/123)
2166 Maplewood Dr.
St. Paul 612/484-3011

The Links at Northfork ($25/$28) 6,344 yds. (70.2/114)
9400 153rd Ave. NW.
Ramsey 612/241-0506

Majestic Oaks Golf Course 36 holes
Platinum Course: ($18/$22) 6,548 yds. (71.8/125)
Gold Course: ($16/$19) 5,879 yds. (68.6/117)
701 Bunker Lake Blvd.
Ham Lake 612/755-2140

Meadowbrook Golf Club ($16.50/$16.50) 6,315 yds. (68.7/111)
201 Meadowbrook Rd.
Hopkins 612/929-2077

Mille Lacs Golf Course ($16/$16) 6,355 yds. (68.2/115)
Hwy. 169 South
Garrison 612/692-4325

Northern Hills Golf Club ($16/$16) 5,971 yds. (68.8/120)
4800 41st Ave. NW.
Rochester 507/281-6170

Ortonville Golf Course ($13/$15) 6,014 yds. (68.1/111)
Golf Club Rd.
Ortonville 612/839-3606

Phalen Park Golf Course ($17/$17) 5,872 yds. (67.7/119)
1615 Phalen Dr.
St. Paul 612/778-0424

Pokegama Golf Course ($18/$18) 6,526 yds. (71.7/126)
3910 Golf Course Rd.
Grand Rapids 218/326-3444

Rich Acres Golf Course ($15.75/$16.75) 6,336 yds. (69.9/114)
2201 E. 66th St.
Richfield 612/861-9341

River Oaks Municipal ($15/$18) 6,018 yds. (68.3/117)
11099 West Point Douglas
Cottage Grove 612/438-2121

Second Season Indoor Golf ($8.25 per half hour)
(South of the Burnsville Center off 35W, exit Hwy. 50)
Lakeville 612/892-1661

University of Minnesota Course ($17/$20) 6,123 yds. (69.3/117)
2273 W. Larpenteur Ave.
St. Paul 612/627-4000

Willinger Golf Course ($21/$27) 5,859 yds. (69.4/132)
6900 Canby Trail
Northfield 612/652-2500

# MISSISSIPPI

*Local Knowledge*

The informative and well-organized *Mississippi Travel Planner* is available from the state office in Jackson and from visitor centers. Listings for over 120 courses are broken down by region with the laudable inclusion of the nearest larger city to each course. So, for instance, if you're trying to find the Copiah-Lincoln Community College Golf Course, which, as far as the post office is concerned, is in Wesson, you'll know Brookhaven is the nearest city (800/927-6378).

Pine Island Golf Club in Ocean Springs is a Pete Dye design (walking's allowed after 11 A.M.). Both Ole Miss and Mississippi State's courses have gotten recent face-lifts. MSU's was described to me as "absolutely immaculate." Other college courses are in Cleveland (Delta State), and Hattiesburg (University of South Mississippi).

The *Mississippi Golf Association Membership Directory* is available for $6 (601/649-0570). Although there's no statewide publinks championship, sectional qualifying is held annually at Clear Creek Golf Club in Vicksburg. The muny in Greenville is right at the airport, the only eighteen-hole course between Memphis and Jackson. The Mississippi Beach Convention and Visitors Bureau sends a package of golf information for the thirty to forty south Mississippi coast courses (800/237-9493).

### Discount Card

See "Stalking the Elusive Deep Discount" in Finding the Green introduction.

## FINDING THE GREEN IN MISSISSIPPI

Clear Creek Golf Club ($12/$12) 6,287 yds. (69.3/114)
1566 Tiffentown Rd.
Vicksburg 601/638-9395

Copiah-Lincoln Community College Golf Course ($6/$9)
9 holes/6,249 yds. (na/na)
Hwy. 51
Wesson 601/643-8379

Delta State University Course ($7/$10) 9 holes/6,094 yds. (69.4/119)
Sunflower Rd.
Cleveland 601/846-4585

Greenville Municipal Golf Course ($8/$10) 6,085 yds. (70.0/na)
Airbase Rd.
Greenville 601/332-4079

Pine Island Golf Club ($13/$13) 5,863 yds. (67.6/116)
Gulf Park Estates
Ocean Springs 601/875-1674

Mississippi State University Course ($13/$15) 6,400 yds. (71.0/121)
Old Highway 82
Starkville 601/325-3028

University of Mississippi Golf Course ($10/$14) 6,396 yds.
(71.3/127)
College Hill Rd.
Oxford 601/234-4816

Van Hook Golf Course ($10/$12.50) 5,680 yds. (na/na)
University of South Mississippi
One Golf Course Rd.
Hattiesburg 601/264-1872

# MISSOURI

*Local Knowledge*

*The Midwest Golfer's Guide* evinces solid spadework. Regular course features mix with typical instruction tips and coupons. It's free, and courses and golf shops stock it; so do St. Louis–area Schnuck, National, Dierberg supermarkets, and visitor centers.

The magazine's publisher, Krista Berry, passed along several recommendations: Victory Hills, a former private club turned public (see Kansas), Royal Meadows in Kansas City, Country Creek in Pleasant Hill, and Paradise Pointe in Smithville.

In Kansas City, traditionalists will enjoy Swope Park, a Tillinghast course revitalized and restored, after a prolonged period of neglect, using the original plans. Its pot, cross and deep greenside bunkers demand a steely sand game. Longview Lake is newer, well designed, with gorgeous fairways. Tom Kuhl, the editor of the *Golf Collectors Society Bulletin,* recommends it as a hilly course with lots of character.

Annual outbreaks of ballot stuffing notwithstanding, (high jinks ferreted out and reported), the *St. Louis Post-Dispatch* runs an annual readers' poll of Top 10 courses. The list appears in a comprehensive special section each April (available for $2.25 from circulation: 314/340-8812).

Several perennial favorites: Crystal Highland, Forest Park, Innsbrook Estates, and Quail Creek. Normandie Park and St. Andrews also made the list, if you include the ballot stuffers (see also Illinois). Crystal Highlands was the sectional publinks qualifying course in 1994.

Several top nine-holers are Ballwin, Ruth Park, and Creve Coeur. Needless to say, conditions will depend on the docility of the Meramec, not to mention the Missouri and the Mississippi rivers.

*Golf Scene Magazine* ($3.95 at newsstands) covers the St. Louis area. The quarterly also produces a directory of three hundred courses within a two-hundred-mile radius of St. Louis ($5.95). Back issues, including the year-end "Best of" rankings, are $3.95 (314/621-0170).

*Golf: The Missouri Challenge* ($7.95) bills itself as "The Real Golfers Guide" to Kansas City and Lake of the Ozarks. Written by average golfers (and not a quiche eater in the bunch from the looks of them), the book's in area stores or available from Ah! Plause! Productions (800/934-9205).

Several upper-level courses open to all are the University of Missouri's A. L. Gustin, Jr., Golf Course in Columbia and Central Missouri State University (Keth Memorial) in Warrensburg, which also has eighteen holes. Hannibal-LaGrange College in Hannibal has a free course with sand greens and has added a driving range. The University of Missouri at Rolla also has nine holes.

The Grandview muny in Springfield has been renamed to honor Payne Stewart and his father, Bill. Payne played the course in high school. He told me he was delighted with the honor. When I asked about the course, he was judicious; if he was tuning up for the British Open, he said, he'd practice there rather than at the country club. Take from that what you will.

The state travel guide breaks down course listings regionally (so much better than by county): 800/877-1234. And if you fly into Lambert International in St. Louis, you might wonder whether any other airport is named after a golfer.

Albert B. Lambert, from whom the airport takes its name, was an aviator and an investor in Lindbergh's flight across the Atlantic. He was also an avid amateur golfer, the only man to compete in both Olympics when golf was contested. He won the men's handicap tournament at the 1900 games in Paris and naturally defended in 1904 when the games were held in his hometown of St. Louis.

Despite 295 "playable golf days a year" in St. Louis, as calculated by the Palmer Management Company ("playable" is defined as 50° with less than an inch of rain; heat and humidity, however, are not indexed), if the weather isn't cooperating, you can always go down to the National Video Game & Coin-Op Museum. It's got ninety games from 1947 to the present, pinball and lots of early video, Nintendo golf for the deprived. It's at 801 North Second at Laclède's Landing (314/621-2900).

## Discount Cards

American Heart Association/Hale Irwin's Golf Passport. Three hundred rounds of discounted golf in Missouri and Illinois. 4643 Lindell Blvd., St. Louis, MO 63108. (800/775-GOLF). $69.

American Lung Association of Western Missouri Golf Privilege Card. Seventy-five courses, eight ranges, evenly divided between KC, Springfield, Central/Lake, and Northwest. Calendar year. 800/638-8670 or 816/842-5242. $40.

American Lung Association of Eastern Missouri Golf Privilege Card. Complimentary green fees at fifty-one courses. 800/467-LUNG or 314/645-5505. $50.

Missouri Fairways Club. Discounts at forty courses statewide, twelve months. 167 Lamp & Lantern, Ste. 200, Chesterfield, MO 63017. $32.50.

## Shopping

Anheuser-Busch has all kinds of stuff: golf towels, head covers, gloves, you name it. A beer can containing two logoed balls (though no beer) is $3.95, a Michelob-emblazoned tour bag is $269.95. The catalog of official A-B merchandise is available from 800/742-5283.

The outlet in Sikeston, two hours south of St. Louis off I-55, has Levi's, Van Heusen, Duck Head, Cape Isle, and Farah (800/908-7467). Reebok is at Factory Merchants Malls in Osage Beach (314/348-4600). Warrenton on I-70, east of St. Louis, has Bass, Nike, and Champion.

## FINDING THE GREEN IN MISSOURI

A. L. Gustin, Jr. Golf Course ($11/$13.50) 6,400 yds. (na/123)
University of Missouri
Stadium Blvd.
Columbia 314/882-6016

Ballwin Golf Course ($18/$22) 3,155 yds. (69.1/122)
333 Holloway Rd.
Ballwin 314/227-1750

Country Creek Golf Club ($11/$13) 6,251 yds. (69.8/116)
P Hwy.
Pleasant Hill 816/540-5225

Creve Coeur Golf Course ($13.50/$15.00) 3,000 yds. (68.0/106)
11400 Olde Cabin Rd.
Creve Coeur 314/432-1806

Crystal Highland Golf Course ($20/$27) 6,158 yds. (69.1/130)
US 61 and Weaver Rd.
Crystal City 314/931-3880

Forest Park Golf Course ($16/$19) 5,840 yds. (67.8/113)
5591 Grand Dr.
St. Louis 314/367-1337

Hannibal-LaGrange College Golf Course (free) 9 holes
2800 Palmyra Rd.
Hannibal 314/221-3675

Innsbrook Estates Country Club ($20/$20*) 5,697 yds. (68.8/127)
One Innsbrook Estates Dr.
Wright City 314/928-3366

Keth Memorial Golf Course ($11/$12) 5,792 yds. (68.7/113)
Central Missouri State University
Warrensburg 816/543-4182

Longview Lake Golf Course ($14/$16) 6,200 yds. (68.5/113)
1100 View High Dr.
Kansas City 816/761-9445

*Twilight

Normandie Park Golf Course ($24/$30) 6,534 yds. (71.1/120)
7605 St. Charles Rock Rd.
St. Louis 314/862-4884

Paradise Pointe Golf Course 36 holes
Posse Course: ($14.50/$16) 6,375 yds. (71.1/121)
Outlaw Course: ($17/$19) 6,798 yds. (72.3/129)
18212 Golf Course Rd.
Smithville 816/532-4100

Quail Creek Golf Course ($25/$30) 6,460 yds. (71.3/138)
6022 Wells Rd.
St. Louis 314/487-1988

Royal Meadows American Golf Club ($13/$15) 4,200 yds. (68.8/113)
10501 E. 47th St.
Kansas City 816/353-1323

Ruth Park Golf Club ($17/$20) 2,808 yds. (65.7/109)
8211 Broby Rd.
St. Louis 314/727-4800

St. Andrews Golf Course ($19/$26) 5,442 yds. (65.3/100)
2121 St. Andrews Ln.
St. Charles 314/946-7777

Stewart Golf Course ($10/$11) 6,043 yds. (68.3/113)
1825 E. Norton
Springfield 417/833-9962

Swope Memorial Golf Course ($11/$13) 5,780 yds. (70.9/128)
6900 Swope Memorial Dr.
Kansas City 816/523-9081

University of Missouri-Rolla Golf Course ($10/$10) 9 holes/6,048
yds. (68.6/111)
10th St.
Rolla 314/341-4217

# MONTANA

## *Local Knowledge*

Eagle Bend has held several recent national amateur championships, including the publinx in 1994. It's over $30, but Fraser McDonald, executive director of the Montana State Golf Association, says two of the "best public courses we have" are in the neighborhood: Buffalo Hill in Kalispell and Whitefish. Both, he says, are "outstanding," well run and well maintained, though Buffalo Hill is "probably the busiest course in Montana."

Jeff Shelley, who reviews and chronicles the development of twenty-two northwest Montana courses in *Golf Courses of the Pacific Northwest* ($19.95), agrees. He calls Buffalo Hill one of the region's "most challenging golf courses." Whitefish, he writes, "is a wonderful spot for a relaxed round." Both have been in *Golf Digest*'s Top 5 Best in State. Jeff's book, a masterful reference, is available from Fairgreens Media in Seattle: 206/385-0752.

He also has glowing comments for Hamilton Golf Club in Hamilton ("wonderful alpine views . . . very well-tended") and Larchmont in Missoula, annual host to the Montana Open. Fraser also mentions RO Speck in Great Falls and Mission Mountain in Ronan, a sectional publinks qualifying site. "It's gonna be a real good golf course," Fraser says. (It opened in 1988; a second nine opened in 1992.) "It is now."

The University of Montana in Missoula has nine holes open to the public.

The *Montana Travel Planner* lists course names and phone numbers by region (800/541-1447).

State parks are within range of Whitefish (Whitefish State Recreation Area) and Buffalo Hill (Wayfarers State Park). A number of country clubs do allow public play for those living outside the area.

## *Discount Card*

See "Stalking the Elusive Deep Discount" in Finding the Green introduction.

*Shopping*

In Dillon, an hour south of Butte on I-15, Patagonia has an outlet store. You can't miss it.

## FINDING THE GREEN IN MONTANA

Buffalo Hill Golf Course ($25/$25) 6,247 yds. (70.2/128)
North Main St.
Kalispell 406/756-4547

Hamilton Golf Club ($15/$17) 6,545 yds. (69.6/115)
Golf Course Rd.
Hamilton 406/363-4251

Larchmont Golf Course ($16/$18) 6,696 yds. (69.8/113)
3200 Old Fort Rd.
Missoula 406/721-4416

Mission Mountain Country Club ($20/$20) 6,251 yds. (68.7/112)
640 Stagecoach Tr.
Ronan 406/676-4653

RO Speck Municipal Golf Course ($16/$16) 6,586 yds. (69.6/111)
29th and River Drive North
Great Falls 406/761-1078

University of Montana Golf Course ($15/$17) 9 holes/6,450 yds.
(68.6/110)
515 S. Avenue East
Missoula 406/728-8629

Whitefish Lake Golf Club ($28/$28) 36 holes
North Course: 6,297 yds. (68.7/116)
South Course: 6,144 yds. (69.0/120)
Hwy. 93 North
Whitefish 406/862-4000

# NEBRASKA

*Local Knowledge*

A *Golf Digest* survey once pegged Nebraska as the cheapest state in the union in which to play golf. Now it can be told. "Public golf here is a tremendous value," says Mike Osborne, author of *Walt's Guide to Nebraska Public Golf* ($8.95). "Ten to twelve dollars is average in Lincoln. The courses always get compliments from out of staters . . . really incredible value."

Mike's book is updated annually, and directions are often noted from Lincoln and Omaha. It's available from courses and golf stores, also Four Star Drug, Lawlor's, Wal-Mart, and Shopko. You can order direct from P.O. Box 5273, Lincoln, NE 68505. (800/230-3831).

Besides giving you the basics, Walt can sometimes get playful. At College Heights in Crete, for instance, one learns: "You can eat your way around the course at different times of the year between the apple, cherry, plum and mulberry trees."

The Nebraska State Travel and Tourism Division sends out the previous year's *Walt's* for free to those requesting golf info (800/228-4307). That's the good news. At worst, it will send you a June 1988 list of public and private courses with phone numbers and, inexplicably, their acreage.

Walt loves Woodland Hills in Eagle, twenty miles east of Lincoln. Surrounded by an award-winning tree nursery, Walt waxes poetic about the rolling, tree-lined fairways, gaping bunkers, and scenic vistas. It's hosted sectional publinks qualifying and has been a *Golf Digest* Best in State. HiMark in Lincoln has also hosted. Quail Run in Columbus is, according to Walt, "The finest municipal course I have encountered anywhere." It has four tee boxes and measures over seven thousand yards from the tips. Quail Run and Woodland Hills also rates a thumbs-up from Randy Jensen, a man who can hit a drive 285 yards with hickories (see Shopping).

Other recommendations: Deer Park Country Club, up near the Sandhills, abuts a wildlife refuge and is crisscrossed by the crystal-clear waters of Minnechaduza Creek. (Walt's tip: Putts break toward the creek.) Also Applewood, Heritage Hills in McCook (a Best 75 Public Course, *Golf Digest,* 1984), Benson Park, Miracle Hill, Shoreline, Tiburon.

In Lincoln, Walt suggests Holmes Lake, Mahoney, and Pioneers (past host to the Nebraska Open). As far as state parks go, Mahoney, opened in 1991, also has a range. Kids will love the Jim Ager Junior Golf Club in Lincoln. The nine-hole par three course sports a model junior golf program, dedicated to letting kids pick up the game in a comfortable setting.

## Discount Card

American Lung Association Golf Privilege Card. Free rounds or substantial discounts at courses in Nebraska, South Dakota, and North Dakota, including lessons and miniature golf. 402/572-3030. $30.

## Shopping

Randy Jensen runs Classic Golf on Dodge Street, near downtown Omaha, and features an exceptional selection of new, classic, and antique clubs (402/554-0202). Factory-outlet stores in Gretna, outside of Omaha on I-80, include Izod and Champion/Hanes. Ashworth Warehouse is also in Gretna (402/332-5577).

## FINDING THE GREEN IN NEBRASKA

The Jim Ager Junior Golf Club ($2 kids/$6 adults/$4.75 seniors)
1,181 yds. (na/na)
3761 Normal Blvd.
Lincoln 402/441-8963

Applewood Golf Course ($12/$13) 6,510 yds. (70.4/113)
6111 S. 99th St.
Omaha 402/444-4656

Benson Park Golf Course ($12/$13) 6,371 yds. (70.1/116)
5333 N. 72nd St.
Omaha 402/444-4626

College Heights Country Club ($13/$16) 5,564 yds. (66.2/114)
1225 E. 4th St.
Crete 402/826-4653

Deer Park Country Club ($18/$20) 9 holes/6,022 yds. (68.7/115)
Hwy. 12
Valentine 402/376-1271

Heritage Hills Golf Course ($20/$20) 6,095 yds. (68.7/125)
6000 Clubhouse Rd.
McCook 308/345-5032

HiMark Golf Course ($9.50/$16) 6,591 yds. (71.1/120)
9001 Pioneers
Lincoln 402/488-8486

Holmes Lake Golf Course ($10.75/$12) 6,438 yds. (69.1/112)
3701 S. 70th St.
Lincoln 402/441-8960

Mahoney Golf Course ($10.75/$12) 6,020 yds. (68.5/115)
7900 Adams St.
Lincoln 402/441-8969

Miracle Hill Golf Course ($15.25/$20.25) 5,736 yds. (67.4/118)
1401 N. 120th St.
Omaha 402/498-0220

Pioneers Golf Course ($10.75/$12) 6,176 yds. (68.3/110)
3403 W. Van Dorn
Lincoln 402/441-8966

Quail Run Golf Course ($12/$15) 6,057 yds. (70.7/131)
327 South 5th St.
Columbus 402/564-1313

Shoreline Golf Course ($13/$14) 6,049 yds. (69.0/113)
210 E. Locust St.
Carter Lake, IA 712/347-5173

Tiburon Golf Club ($15/$21) 6,530 yds. (72.1/133)
10302 S. 168th St.
Omaha 402/895-2688

Woodland Hills Golf Club ($12/$20) 6,245 yds. (69.7/121)
6000 Woodland Hills Dr./Hwy. 43
Eagle 402/475-GOLF

# NEVADA

### Local Knowledge

Most state visitor guides include something about golf. Nevada's is no different; in fact, it's one of the better guides. It is to my recollection also the only state guide that offers marriage information on the inside back cover (800/NEVADA-8).

In Las Vegas, Angel Park's courses are approaching $100 green fees, which is certainly taking municipal golf to new heights. "Their twilight rate's probably $50," a local scribe told me. Another sectional publinks qualifying site, Incline Village in Reno, is $85 a round. Yikes. The putting course at Angel Park is thankfully still under $30; it's under $10, actually, and really fun. It's eighteen natural holes with bunkers, water, and rough. The longest hole is about 180 feet.

The par three course, Cloud Nine, mimics famous holes from St. Andrews, Royal Troon, Sawgrass, Pebble Beach, and others. At night (the last tee time is at eight), the course is shortened somewhat, but you'll still have some shots of up to 170 yards. Green fees for nine holes won't break the bank. Good grief, you can even rent a cart.

Mark Edwards, who writes for *Las Vegas Golf* magazine (available at courses, visitor centers, and the convention bureau), told me that Craig Ranch, "if you look at it from a value standpoint is tremendous." Several contacts told me essentially the same story about "muny," the Las Vegas Golf Club, where a sprout named Robert Gamez could once be seen whacking balls at age seven. The general (although unenthusiastic) consensus was that for the dollar, it's a good golf course.

Los Prados is in a private community; tell the guard you're playing golf and you may pass. "It's not really a tough course," Mark says, "but it's in great shape"—a good course for pumping up the ole self-esteem. There's also North Las Vegas Golf Course, a par three nine-holer. Take the subject up with Mark Tuesday nights from ten to midnight on "Beyond the Neon" on KDWN, AM-720.

Eagle Valley in Carson City has hosted the Nevada State Women's Amateur and USGA Junior Amateur qualifying. The West Course requires a cart; after four, it's $15. You can walk the East anytime.

Francis Haase has been involved with publinks golf in northern

Nevada for over twenty years, as a past president of the Nevada State Golf Association and a sports reporter of twenty-three years' standing before retiring in 1982. Around Reno, Washoe County, a WPA course, is "pretty good for ordinary play," he says, and is routinely used for publinks qualifying. Same with Sierra Sage, closed down as a military base in 1965. Francis also recommends Rosewood Lakes ("a good test of golf"). There's also Glenbrook, built in the 1920s.

Burning Sands, in the mining town of Downtown Empire, is free; so is Sandy Bottom Golf Course in Gabbs. If there's any truth in advertising, better check your antifreeze before starting out to play these courses. Toana Vista in Wendover is often used for Utah Golf Association events.

## Discount Card

American Lung Association Golf Privilege Card. Three Las Vegas courses. 702/454-2500. $25.

## Shopping

Sierra Trading Post, noted in "Saving the Green," has an outlet store in the Reno/Sparks area. It's right off I-80 at Exit 20 (Sparks Blvd.).

## FINDING THE GREEN IN NEVADA

**Burning Sands Golf Course** (free) 2,007 yds. (na/na)
Downtown Empire 702/557-2341

**Cloud Nine at Angel Park** ($20/$20) 1,465 yds. (na/na)
100 S. Rampart
Las Vegas 702/254-4653

**Craig Ranch Golf Course** ($13/$13) 6,000 yds. (66.8/105)
628 W. Craig Rd.
N. Las Vegas 702/642-9700

**Eagle Valley Golf Course** 36 holes
East Course: ($18/$18) 6,314 yds. (67.3/114)

West Course: ($25/$25*) 5,819 yds. (69.0/123)
3999 Centennial Park Dr.
Carson City 702/887-2380

Glenbrook Golf Course ($20/$20*) 9 holes/5,700 yds. (66.3/121)
Pray Meadow Rd.
Glenbrook 702/749-5201

Las Vegas Golf Club ($20.50/$20.50) 6,337 yds. (70.3/114)
4300 W. Washington
Las Vegas 702/646-3003

Los Prados Country Club ($20/$20*) 4,900 yds. (62.2/101)
5150 Los Prados Cir.
Las Vegas 702/645-5696

North Las Vegas Golf Course ($10/$12) 1,128 yds. (na/na)
324 E. Brooks Ave.
N. Las Vegas 702/649-7171

Rosewood Lakes Golf Course ($24/$24) 5,481 yds. (65.8/119)
6800 Pembroke Dr.
Reno 702/857-2892

Sandy Bottom Golf Course (free) 3,010 yds. (na/na)
(just west of town)
Gabbs (no phone)

Sierra Sage Golf Course ($21/$24) 6,207 yds. (67.9/118)
6355 Silver Lake Blvd.
Reno 702/972-1564

Toana Vista Golf Course ($25/$29) 6,048 yds. (67.3/107)
2319 Pueblo Blvd.
Wendover 800/852-4330

Washoe County Golf Course ($20/$23) 6,450 yds. (68.9/116)
2601 S. Arlington
Reno 702/828-6640

*Twilight

# NEW HAMPSHIRE

### Local Knowledge

The New Hampshire Golf Association prints out an alphabetical list of seventy-eight NHGA member clubs to anyone requesting state information. It simply lists course name, phone number, and number of holes (603/623-0396). The state guidebook provides course names and phone numbers (800/639-2731).

*The Golf Courses of New Hampshire* ($15) puts golf in historical context. Features on famous architects, courses that no longer exist, and assorted facts and figures fill out the second in their series on New England golf by Bob Labbance and David Cornwell. The meat and potatoes, however, is playing the courses, a task undertaken with a welcome sense of golfing pathos and humor (802/234-9220).

*New England Golf Guide* ($14.95) is the region's better-than-average coupon book (800/833-6387).

Every Monday in *The Portsmouth Herald,* Mike Hassel Shearer, an avid historian and collector, pens "Niblicks from the Rough." He recommends Beaver Meadow in Concord, the oldest course in the state. Tall, thin pines line the fairways. The original holes were laid out in 1897. William Robinson and Geoffrey Cornish lengthened several holes and added the back nine in the late 1960s.

The magisterial Mount Washington Hotel offers eighteen holes of circa 1915 Donald Ross with inspirational views of the Presidentials. In the summer, a swim in the Kangamangus can be similarly uplifting. Other courses where Ross is credited with some facet of design and construction and that are open to all comers are Kingswood in Wolfeboro, Maplewood in Bethlehem, and Tory Pines in Francestown. Bretwood won a Top 5 Best in State from *Golf Digest.* A handful of courses that Labbance and Cornwell date before 1900: Waumbek (1895), Wentworth Resort (1898), Waterville Valley (1898), Exeter (1895), and Monadnock (1899).

The *Boston Herald's* Jack O'Leary is effusive about Overlook Country Club in Hollis. "A wonderful golf course, reasonably priced. It's got everything, just a fun place to play golf," he says. Jack also likes Souhegan Woods in Amherst and the thirty-six holes at Green Meadow, both owned by the Friel family.

Finally, for the skinny on the sport truly taken seriously in New

England, your toll-free foliage hot line, during peak season, is
800/258-3608. "A Leaf Peeper's Guide to the White Mountains," no
less, is available by calling 800/346-3687.

### Discount Card

American Lung Association Golf Privilege Card. Free rounds at thirty-
seven courses. 800/835-8647. $60.

### Shopping

Within reach of Laconia, visit the Allen-Rogers Factory Store. Tees
are two cents apiece (1-7/8″ or 2-1/8″), or a bag of 150 to 170 (you
bag 'em yourself) is $2. You won't find them any cheaper. Quantities
are limited, however. Vice president Dave McKay told me the store
price is the real deal: "Even some of our bulk rates are higher."
Hours are 10 A.M. to 3 P.M., Monday through Friday, 9 A.M. to noon
on Saturday.

> Directions: In NH, Exit 20 East off I-93, 7 1/2 miles to Laconia. Take
> the downtown loop, Beacon Street, head west on Beacon Street.
> Look for the outlet sign at the large brick factory building (603/524-
> 2060).

Dexter Shoe has over a dozen factory stores in New Hampshire.
Here's a few locations: Amherst (Route 101A), Hampton Falls (Route
1, Lafayette Rd.), Keene (Route 12), Littleton (Route 302), Nashua
(195 D.W. Highway). Outlet centers are in Laconia, North Conway,
and North Hampton, (L.L. Bean, Patagonia, Benetton, Banana
Republic, etc.).

## FINDING THE GREEN IN NEW HAMPSHIRE

**Beaver Meadow Golf Club ($23/$25) 6,034 yds. (68.5/118)**
**One Beaver Meadow Dr.**
**Concord 603/228-8954**

**Bretwood Golf Course ($22/$24) 5,822 yds. (68.4/120)**
**E. Surry Rd.**
**Keene 603/352-7626**

Exeter Country Club ($17/$19) 9 holes/5,428 yds. (66.9/110)
Jady Hill Ave.
Exeter 603/772-4752

Green Meadow Golf Club ($20/$26) 36 holes
North Course: 6,088 yds. (67.6/109)
South Course: 6,182 yds. (69.3/113)
59 Steele Rd.
Hudson 603/889-1555

Kingswood Country Club ($25/$25) 5,800 yds. (67.5/116)
Rte. 28/S. Main
Wolfeboro 603/569-3569

Maplewood Golf Club ($18/$20) 6,001 yds. (67.4/109)
Rte. 302
Bethlehem 603/869-3335

Monadnock Country Club ($12/$15) 3,152 yds. (54.0/76)
49 High St.
Peterborough 603/924-7769

Mount Washington Hotel Golf Course ($20/$24) 6,156 yds.
(70.1/118)
Rte. 302
Bretton Woods 603/278-1000

Overlook Country Club ($17/$20*) 6,051 yds. (69.0/128)
5 Overlook Dr.
Hollis 603/465-2909

Souhegan Woods Golf Club ($22/$28) 6,100 yds. (68.7/117)65
Thornton Ferry Rd.
Amherst 603/673-0200

Tory Pines Golf Resort ($22/$29) 5,296 yds. (66.1/116)
Rte. 47
Francestown 603/588-2923

Waterville Valley Golf Club ($20/$20) 9 holes/4,700 yds. (na/na)
Rte. 49
Waterville Valley 603/236-4805

*Twilight

Waumbek Country Club ($15/$15) 5,874 yds. (66.0/107)
Rte. 2
Jefferson 603/586-7777

Wentworth Resort Golf Course ($24/$30) 5,360 yds. (64.6/108)
Rte. 16
Jackson 603/383-9641

# NEW JERSEY

*Local Knowledge*

Those who've never gotten off the Jersey Turnpike or strayed from
the casinos, never eaten sweet corn picked fresh that morning, or
admired the small towns along the upper stretches of the Delaware
River have no idea how pleasant a place the Garden State can be.
Baltusrol and Pine Valley, after all, aren't exactly chopped liver.

The *Jersey Golfer* magazine comes out three times a year and
includes a statewide course directory in the back of each issue. It's
free at courses, ranges, and bookstores. Publisher Lowell Schmidt
uses words like "decent," "good public layout," and "really nice public course" to describe the following:

Buena Vista, Buena
Cedar Creek, Bayville
Jumping Brook, Neptune
Old Orchard, Eatontown
Quail Brook, Somerset
Spring Meadow, Farmingdale
Warrenbrook, Warren
Willowbrook, Moorestown

Down the shore, Spring Meadow is a well-tended older-style
course. It's a "muny in the boonies" with some memorable short par
fours. The National Golf Foundation gave it a Public Golf
Achievement Award in 1990.

Rancocas was the old Willingboro Country Club, a Robert Trent
Jones, Sr., course somewhat down on its luck, bought by American

Golf Corporation. Trees were apparently causing the greens some problems and a bunch have been taken out, which is a shame, but a cash infusion and attention can only help matters in the long run. This course is definitely a cut above. Perhaps its new owners will even install some water fountains. Another Jones course, in Jacobstown, not far from Great Adventure, is the Hanover Country Club. Rutgers University has an old course typically described as a good course for beginners and seniors (whatever that means—I suppose that it's easier to walk and, perhaps, shorter).

The bimonthly tabloid *19th Hole!* is chock-full of coupons. It's free at courses, ranges, and golf shops throughout south Jersey. The first issue every year includes a regional course directory. A listing of over two hundred public and private courses (name, address, phone number, organized by county) is available for the asking from the New Jersey State Golf Association (201/338-8334). It also includes driving ranges.

*Golf Greens* ($9.95) features listings on over four hundred courses in the Delaware Valley. One dollar from each sale benefits the Leukemia Society of America (800/394-GOLF or 609/547-4747). *Powers Northeast Region Golf Guide* ($14.95) ups the ante with 275 free (two-for-one) green fees. Course information from eastern Pennsylvania to southern Massachusetts is included, one hundred seventeen listed for New Jersey. (800/446-8884). Both books get bigger and better with each edition.

The state travel guide lists courses by city and town and includes a highway map, pages of travel, and coupons not related to golf (800/JERSEY7). Fore Better Golf has a golf map for northern New Jersey (708/893-8672).

The USGA is headquartered in a beautiful, if remote, corner of the state, Far Hills. (It's a good two hours from Philadelphia, the same from Manhattan.) The mechanical marvel Iron Byron performs his repeatable perfect swing daily at the research and test center, behind the museum and library. The library is often bypassed. With permission, one can amble through turn-of-the-century publications and much, much more. It's uncanny how unchanged the ads are over the years (908/234-2300).

*Shopping*

There are outlet centers in Flemington (908/782-8550), Secaucus, Manasquan (908/223-0340), and Wall Township (908/223-2300).

## FINDING THE GREEN IN NEW JERSEY

Buena Vista Country Club ($12/$15*) 6,422 yds. (71.5/127)
Country Club Lane/Rte. 40
Buena 609/697-3733

Cedar Creek Golf Course ($20/$22) 6,003 yds. (69.6/112)
Tilton Blvd.
Bayville 908/269-4460

Hanover Country Club ($14/$16*) 6,392 yds. (70.0/120)
133 Larrison Rd.
Jacobstown 609/758-0300

Jumping Brook Country Club ($22/$29) 6,250 yds. (69.6/118)
210 Jumping Brook Rd.
Neptune 908/922-6140

Old Orchard Country Club ($22/$27) 6,183 yds. (68.6/112)
Rte. 71 and Monmouth Rd.
Eatontown 908/542-7666

Quail Brook Country Club ($30/$—) 5,835 yds. (67.9/113)
New Brunswick Rd.
Somerset 908/560-9528

Rancocas Golf Course ($18/$26*) 5,979 yds. (68.9/122)
Clubhouse Dr.
Willingboro 609/877-5344

Rutgers University Golf Course ($16/$23) 5,800 yds. (68.3/112)
777 Hoes Lane
Piscataway 908/932-2631

Spring Meadow Golf Course ($13/$16) 5,953 yds. (68.1/113)
4181 Atlantic Ave.
Farmingdale 908/449-0806

*Twilight

Warrenbrook Golf Course ($20/$24) 6,300 yds. (69.6/124)
500 Warrenville Rd.
Warren Township 908/754-8402

Willowbrook Country Club ($18.50/$28) 6,204 yds. (71.2/118)
Bridgeboro Rd.
Moorestown 609/461-0131

# NEW MEXICO

*Local Knowledge*

Even if the grading were on a curve, the Championship Course at the University of New Mexico in Albuquerque would still top an impressive list of college courses open to the public. Rated in the state's Top 5 by *Golf Digest,* it's hosted the NCAA Championships, several major state tournaments, and PGA and LPGA qualifying. The views of downtown are said to be as impressive as the course itself. There's also a three-hole beginner's course and an elaborate practice facility. Another nine holes are open to the public on UNM's North Campus. New Mexico Highlands in Las Vegas has nine holes. New Mexico State has an eighteen-hole course in Las Cruces, and, in Roswell, the New Mexico Military Institute, for crying out loud, does too, both reportedly with bent-grass greens.

For $5, the Sun Country Amateur Golf Association in Albuquerque mails out *New Mexico Golf, A Course Guide for the Land of Enchantment* (1993) plus photocopies of course listings from *The National Golf Course Directory* (505/897-0864). In it you'll learn the Nike Tour stops at Valle Grande, north of Albuquerque, and get some fairly valuable, if exuberant, insight to the state, broken down by region. Cochiti Lake, designed by Robert Trent Jones, offers spectacular views. It's described as "not long but it eats golf balls." After a $2 million renovation, Paradise Hills boasts a country club atmosphere at public golf prices.

Sectional public links qualifying in northern New Mexico has also been held at Valle Grande in Bernalillo and Arroyo del Oso in Albuquerque.

The annual state vacation guide provides addresses and phone numbers for a handful of private and public courses (800/545-2040).

*Shopping*

Sante Fe Factory Shops on I-25 has Brooks Brothers, Jones New York, and Gant.

## FINDING THE GREEN IN NEW MEXICO

Arroyo del Oso Golf Course ($13/$13) 6,545 yds. (70.4/121)
7001 Osuna Rd. NE.
Albuquerque 505/884-7505

Cochiti Lake Golf Course ($18/$20) 5,996 yds. (68.3/115)
5200 Cochiti Hwy.
Cochiti Lake 505/465-2239

New Mexico Highlands University Course ($9.45/$9.45)
9 holes/6,109 yds. (67.3/107)
Mills Avenue
Las Vegas 505/425-7711

New Mexico Military Institute Course ($12/$12) 6,374 yds.
(69.3/115)
201 W. 19th St.
Roswell 505/622-6033

New Mexico State University Course ($16/$18) 6,659 yds.
(72.1/129)
University and I-25
Las Cruces 505/646-4131

Paradise Hills Golf Course ($18/$26) 6,629 yds. (70.8/116)
10035 Country Club Dr.
Albuquerque 505/898-7001

University of New Mexico at Albuquerque
Championship Course: ($18/$21) 6,480 yds. (70.3/121)
3601 University Blvd. SE.
Albuquerque 505/277-4546

University of New Mexico at Albuquerque
North Course: ($13/$13) 3,333 yds. (69.2/114)
2201 Tucker Ave. NE.
Albuquerque 505/277-4146

Valle Grande Golf Course ($16/$21) 27 holes
Tamaya/Rio Grande Course: 5,870 yds. (66.7/108)
Rio Grande/Coronado Course: 5,894 yds. (66.4/106)
Tamaya/Coronado Course: 5,922 yds. (66.8/108)
288 Prairie Star Rd.
Bernalillo 505/867-9464

# NEW YORK

*Local Knowledge*

New York City can be disheartening for a golfer. Nevertheless, even
at its foulest, when the slush rises to the top of the curb and winter
winds trumpet up the avenues, Manhattan still offers several quiet
preserves to savor the game.

Dick Metz's Golf, down a few doors and across the street from
*Newsweek* on Madison Avenue, has a number of netted hitting stations. You can escape the crowds and hack away with a variety of
demo clubs to your heart's content. Eight bucks per half hour, on
your honor; it's best to call ahead as no reservations are taken.

The Museum of Television & Radio, also in midtown, has some
entertaining golf footage. For five bucks, you get your own Trinitron
and a comfortable lounger. Kick back, slip on the headphones, and
marvel at the 1958 Masters or two hours of "Bing Crosby & His
Friends" (his 1958 clambake at Pebble Beach). The broadcast opens
with your host crooning "Straight Down the Middle" ("It headed for
two but bounded off nine"). Wind reverberates in the headsets, conveying an enviable sense of realism from today's broadcasts. The ads
are hilarious; you'll know all about the Easy Laundry Combomatic
Washer/Dryer before long.

Jim McKay and John Derr have the call at the twenty-second

Masters. Snead, Palmer, defending champion Doug Ford, and Fred Hawkins battle for the green "coat," as Claude Harmon calls it. Amateur champ Palmer, he notes, is a "very strong boy," as indeed he was. Claude also does double duty with Jimmy Demaret with a word on behalf of American Express (Peter Thomson prefers the $20 denominations).

Other telecasts include the 1960, 1963, and 1980 Masters. There's also lots of other sports footage and all the Ernie Kovacs and *Honeymooners* you can stand. Like all New York City museums, it does a lot of business. Closed Mondays, the Museum of Radio & Television is at 25 West Fifty-second Street (212/621-6800). Get there early.

Van Cortlandt Park, managed by American Golf, is bereft of car parts and muggers, but two of the pins were AWOL the day I played it and a gaggle of geese definitely copped a New York attitude. Obviously, there is still much work to be done, but the setting is surprisingly pleasant, especially in autumn.

Aggrievance is something of a public golf tradition in New York. James Skardon wrote in *The Saturday Evening Post* nearly thirty years ago: "Golfers come, sign up and then go home while their numbers are slowly working up to the top of the list. They may get in some more sleep, take their families for rides, attend church or go shopping. A man once drove almost seventy miles, to Bridgeport, Connecticut, played eighteen holes there and returned to Brooklyn before the foursome he had originally signed up with had gone more than a few holes."

Dozens of courses were plowed under for housing on Long Island during post–WWII prosperity. *Long Island Golfer* publisher John Glozek, Jr., chuckled when I asked for any diamonds in the rough.

"We're an island," he reminded me. "The wait's anywhere from three to six hours on the weekend." One glimmer of hope: avoid prime time and "you can play anywhere you want, anytime."

Should you luck out, the highlights would surely include Tillinghast's legacy at Bethpage State Park, renowned for the long par fours and enormous bunkers on the famed Black Course. For the money, John says, "You can't get any better." The other four courses are not treated any differently, he adds, and they are just as mobbed. Mightn't Montauk Downs, all the way at the tip of the island, remodeled by Trent Jones, be any less crowded? "No," he said. "We've got

150 courses on Long Island, about half of that is country clubs, and they're all full."

While you wait, pick up a copy of *Long Island Golfer* ($2), which follows the continuing exploits of local-boys-made-good Jim Albus and Larry Laoretti. There's also product news, book reviews, instruction, etc. It also has a fax newsletter: 516/249-2445. Brainstorming aloud, John also mentioned Spring Lake in Middle Island.

Both Bethpage and Montauk Downs are part of an extensive network of premier state park courses. Call Albany for *The Guide to New York State Operated Parks, Historic Sites and Their Programs* (518/474-0456). The state travel package includes a tourism map, which, if you can unfold it without tearing it to pieces, notes golf courses. The *I Love NY Travel Guide* orients courses to the map (a great idea, 800/CALL-NYS).

Not so much a guidebook, although it is a marvelous resource and a fun read, *Adirondack Golf Courses . . . Past and Present* by J. Peter Martin, weaves entertaining tales from a century of upstate golfing history.

Early photos, maps, and scorecards transport the reader back in time to the region's glory days as a summer resort. The area remains a blissful retreat. Peter recommends as an interesting and affordable place to play Loon Lake, "off the beaten path" and one of the first courses built in the Adirondacks, in 1895. Four presidents escaped the heat in Washington there; the course is all that remains of a resort that dates back to the 1870s. "*Golf Digest* used to mention it years ago as a place to play," Peter says.

Westport Golf Course, in the small town of Westport, overlooking Lake Champlain, is another of Peter's favorites: "in good shape and challenging." The first six holes were laid out in the 1890s. A demanding back nine was added in the 1920s. Peter also mentions Adirondack Golf & Country Club, a Cornish design, built in 1987, in Peru (it's included on the Vermont Golf Links Card).

In the Lake Placid area, he likes Craig Wood, Lake Placid Club, and Whiteface Inn. Although it's not in the Adirondacks, Peter writes glowingly of Bluff Point Golf and Country Club in Plattsburgh, a fun ferry ride across Lake Champlain from Burlington, Vermont. It claims to be the third oldest course in the U.S. (1890). Four Ross courses open to the public are Thendara, Rip Van Winkle (Palenville), Chautauqua, and Mark Twain (Elmira).

Peter's book is available in area bookstores or from the author for $14.95: Box 492, Lake Placid, NY 12946. *Powers Northeast Region Golf Guide* ($14.95) lists 150 courses, many offering coupons of one sort or another (800/446-8884).

Insider tips on Syracuse and golf in the Finger Lakes appear every third Friday in season in the *Herald American* and the *Herald-Journal.* Chuck Harty pens "Hidden Treasures" from May to September. Hard by the Budweiser plant, Radisson Greens, designed by R. T. Jones, Sr., hosts the New York State Open. Fox Fire got an infusion of cash from a local supermarket mogul. While it gets a little "bedraggled" in August (who doesn't?), Chuck says it's an exceptional golf course. The eighteen holes at Green Lakes State Park, one of Trent Jones's first courses, was built by the Works Projects Administration in the early thirties. The view from the clubhouse, north and west over the six-hundred-foot-deep lake, is "one of the most beautiful views in New York State," enthuses Chuck.

En-Joie in Endicott hosts the PGA Tour's B.C. Open. Cartoonist Johnny Hart, an area native, still lives in Ninevah. In Rochester, look for Rochester *Golf Week,* the official publication of the Rochester District Golf Association (716/427-2468). It has a good mix of news and features. A year's subscription, fifty-two issues, is $25.

In Buffalo and southern Ontario, Rick Zurak spreads the message through several mediums. His *Niagara Golfer* magazine is available in golf shops from St. Catherine to the Pennsylvania border and east to Batavia. His radio show, "Let's Talk Golf," airs on WHTT Friday afternoons from five to five-thirty P.M., and his cable show, "Niagara Golf Report," is carried throughout the region on Adelphia and TCI Cable.

Whirlpool, run by the provincial government in Niagara Falls, Ontario, took top honors when Rick was compiling a "Best of" list for the local ABC affiliate. He calls it "probably the best public course in the entire area." Number two was a toss-up between Glen Oak, a Robert Trent Jones, Jr., course in East Amherst, and River Oaks, on Grand Island, between Niagara Falls and Buffalo. Across the border, he also likes Willo-Dell ("excellently manicured, not overly long but in terrific condition"), the International Country Club of Niagara in Stevensville, Ontario, and Sawmill Golf Course in Fenwick, Ontario.

There are university courses all over the state. Vassar has nine holes, SUNY at Delhi and Wells College in Aurora do, too.

## *Shopping*

Tender Buttons (see Through the Green) is on the Upper East Side, not far from Bloomingdale's. Downtown, there's a remarkable store for men's hats. Whether your tastes run from Snead to Hogan to Norman, Young's Stetsons, at the corner of Nassau and Beekman streets, offers exceptional selection and value. Within walking distance is another New York shopping landmark, Century 21, near Wall Street, one of those places that gets the name labels. They just charge a lot less. Century 21 is at 22 Cortland Street (212/227-9092) and in Brooklyn (718/748-3266).

Competitive Edge Golf, the catalog, has a store at 526 West Twenty-sixth St., between Tenth and Eleventh, on the tenth floor.

## FINDING THE GREEN IN NEW YORK

**Adirondack Golf & Country Club** ($24/$28) 6,359 yds. (69.0/117)
Rock Rd.
Peru 518/643-8403

**Battle Island State Park Golf Course** ($12/$14) 5,998 yds. (67.1/107)
Rte. 48
Fulton 315/593-3408

**Beaver Island State Park Golf Course** ($12/$14) 6,595 yds. (69.8/108)
Grand Island 716/773-4668

**Bethpage State Park 90 holes**
Red Course: ($14/$16) 6,537 yds. (72.0/125)
Blue Course: ($14/$16) 6,513 yds. (71.4/124)
Green Course: ($14/$16) 6,267 yds. (69.8/121)
Yellow Course: ($14/$16) 6,171 yds. (69.5/120)
Black Course: ($16/$18) 6,556 yds. (73.1/140)
Quaker Meetinghouse Rd.
Farmingdale 516/249-0700

**Bluff Point Golf and Country Club** ($24/$29) 6,309 yds. (70.6/122)
Rte. 9
Plattsburgh 518/563-3420

Bonavista State Park Golf Course ($12/$14) 3,208 yds. (na/112)
Hwy. 964
Willard 607/869-5482

Chautauqua Golf Course ($20/$25) 36 holes
Lake Course: 6,148 yds. (69.6/113)
Hill Course: 6,034 yds. (70.6/115)
Rte. 394
Chautauqua 716/357-6211

Chenango Valley State Park Golf Course ($12/$14) 5,878 yds.
(68.9/na)
State Park Grounds
Rte. 369
Chenango Forks 607/648-9988

Craig Wood Golf Course ($17/$17) 6,554 yds. (70.9/114)
Rte. 73
Lake Placid 518/523-9811

En-Joie Golf Course ($18/$20) 6,088 yds. (69.1/120)
722 W. Main St.
Endicott 607/785-1661

Foxfire Golf & Tennis Club ($18/$20) 6,440 yds. (70.4/123)
1 Village Blvd.
Baldwinsville 315/638-2930

Glen Oak Country Club ($30/$30*) 6,232 yds. (70.8/122)
711 Smith Rd.
East Amherst 716/688-5454

Green Lakes State Park Golf Course ($12/$14) 5,920 yds. (67.0/110)
7000 Green Lakes Rd.
Fayetteville 315/637-0258

James Baird State Park Golf Course ($12/$14) 6,201 yds. (71.3/124)
Taconic Pkwy.
Pleasant Valley 914/473-1052

*Twilight

Jones Beach State Park Golf Course ($3/$3) 1,010 yds. (na/na)
Ocean Drive
Wantagh 516/785-1600

Lake Placid Club ($20/$20) 36 holes
Upper 18 Course: 5,900 yds. (69.0/115)
Lower 18 Course: 6,200 yds. (70.2/115)
Lake Placid 518/523-4460

Loon Lake Golf Course ($15/$15) 5,200 yds. (na/na)
Rte. 99
Loon Lake 518/891-3249

Mark Twain Golf Course ($12/$14) 6,300 yds. (70.1/117)
Rte. 14
Elmira 607/737-5770

Montauk Downs State Park Course ($16/$18) 6,289 yds. (70.5/128)
S. Fairview Ave.
Montauk 516/668-5000

Pinnacle State Park Course ($12/$14) 3,234 yds. (71.2/na)
Ackerson Rd.
Addison 607/359-2767

Radisson Greens Golf Course ($22/$22) 6,360 yds. (71.9/128)
8055 Potter Rd.
Baldwinsville 315/638-0092

Richard Metz's Golf
425 Madison Ave. (at 49th St.)
New York 212/759-6940

Rip Van Winkle Golf Club ($13/$16) 3,120 yds. (68.5/na)
Rte. 23A
Palenville 518/678-9779

River Oaks Golf Club ($15/$20) 6,588 yds. (71.0/122)
201 Whitehaven Rd.
Grand Island 716/773-3336

Robert Moses State Park Golf Course ($3/$3) 18 holes/1,435 yds.
(na/na)
Fire Island 516/669-0449

Rockland Lake State Park Golf Course ($16/$18) 6,347 yds.
(70.2/121)
Rte. 9W
Congress 914/268-7275

St. Lawrence State Park Golf Course ($12/$14) 9 holes/5,386 yds.
(na/na)
Riverside Dr.
Ogdensburg 315/393-9850

Saratoga Spa State Park Golf Course ($12/$14) 6,344 yds. (70.6/125)
Rte. 9
Saratoga 518/584-2006

Soaring Eagles Golf Course ($12/$14) 6,327 yds. (70.2/115)
Mark Twain State Park
Rte. 14
Horse Heads 607/739-0551

Spring Lake Golf Course ($23/$25)
Thunderbird Course: 6,455 yds. (70.5/123)
950 Bartlett Rd./Rte. 25
Middle Island 516/924-5115

Sunken Meadows State Park Golf Course ($16/$18) 27 holes
Red/Green Course: 6,165 yds. (na/116)
Green/Blue Course: 6,185 yds. (na/129)
Red/Blue Course: 6,100 yds. (na/128)
Sunken Meadow Pkwy.
Kings Park 516/269-4333

SUNY at Delhi Golf Course ($13/$16) 3,085 yds. (69.2/122)
Scotch Mountain Rd.
Delhi 607/746-4281

Thendara Golf Club ($20/$20) 6,213 yds. (69.1/121)
Fifth Ave.
Thendara 315/369-3136

Van Cortlandt Park Golf Course ($19/$21) 5,913 yds. (67.7/110)
Van Cortlandt Park
Bronx 718/543-4595

Vassar College Golf Course ($12/$14) 2,790 yds. (na/na)
Raymond Ave.
Poughkeepsie 914/473-1550

Wellesley Island State Park ($12/$14) 2,730 yds. (na/na)
Wellesley Island 315/482-9622

Wells College Golf Course ($10.80/$12.80) 2,650 yds. (69.5/na)
Rte. 90
Aurora 315/364-8024

Westport Country Club ($25/$30) 6,203 yds. (70.0/118)
Liberty St.
Westport 518/962-4470

Whiteface Inn Resort Golf Course ($24/$26) 6,293 yds. (70.6/123)
Whiteface Inn Rd.
Lake Placid 518/523-2551


## AND ACROSS THE BORDER

International Country Club of Niagara ($Can 18/$Can 22) 27 holes
Red/White Course: 6,579 yds. (70.9/121)
Red/Blue Course: 6,650 yds. (71.3/122)
White/Blue Course: 6,529 yds. (71.4/123)
College Rd.
Stevensville, Ontario 905/382-2000

Sawmill Golf Course ($Can 21/$Can 25) 5,569 yds. (69.2/122)
Sawmill Rd.
Fenwick, Ontario 905/562-4041

Whirlpool Golf Course ($Can 20/$Can 20) 6,500 yds. (71.3/122)
Niagara Falls Pkwy.
Niagara Falls, Ontario 905/356-4717

Willo-Dell Golf Course ($US 12/$US 15) 6,181 yds. (69.3/121)
Willo-Dell Rd.
Niagara Falls 905/295-8181

# NORTH CAROLINA

*Local Knowledge*

Two Donald Ross courses on opposite ends of the state, in Asheville and Wilmington, remain vivid to a memory addled from months on the road. The nines at Buncombe in Asheville are completely different, the front side flat and inviting, the back side hilly and deceiving.

The eleventh, 357 yards up an intermediate ski slope, took a well-struck three wood to reach the green's summit from 150 yards. Long ago there was a tuberculosis hospital along the side of "hemorrhage hill." Patients who could negotiate the climb were released. I'd rather not think about the fate of those who couldn't.

The elevated sixteenth tee is set behind Edgewood Road. Tee shots may require a pause to let a car play through. On the steep downhill finishing hole, a 219-yard par three, a bunker to the left of the green is—somehow—invisible from the tee, a wonderful sleight of hand.

Cart paths now crisscross Wilmington Municipal, but the course is lovely, especially in the spring around Azalea Festival time. Every hole is different. Every hole is interesting. The greens are tiny and well framed. Trouble lurks in the piney, sandy soil off the narrow fairways, but it doesn't come after you. Seniors mob it during the week. It must've been my lucky day because I walked right on Sunday morning. Both of these courses called for every club in the bag; both conveyed the uplifting feeling that comes from realizing one has landed on a course that conveys the game's essence. Other North Carolina courses with the Ross imprimatur for under $30 are Monroe Golf Club (Monroe), Richmond Pines (Rockingham), and Waynesville Country Club (Waynesville).

There were problems with drainage in the past, but Duke's course is an excellent layout. Rees Jones, who designed it, has been back, moving a couple of greens and making some other improvements. There's also a course at UNC, Finley, in Chapel Hill.

Paschal Golf Club in Wake Forest, just at the bottom of the hill below the old campus, was where Arnold Palmer and Buddy Worsham palled around. Nine holes are still there. As students the two actually replaced the sand greens and installed Bermuda.

Nearby, the semiprivate Wake Forest Country Club, despite some run-ins with road expansion, is a terrific public course, masquerading as a private club. The first hole from the tips measures 707 yards, 625 from the middle tees.

Two courses that have hosted publinx qualifying for nearly twenty years are Pine Tree in Kernersville and Oak Hollow in High Point.

*Metrolina Golf* magazine covers a thirty-mile radius around Charlotte. It's free at 175 locations, including welcome centers. Packed with coupons and an area course map and directory, a subscription is $8 for six issues. Publisher/editor Gil Capps suggests Renaissance Park, Mallard Head, Westport, and Kings Mountain Country Club.

A *Golfer's Guide to North Carolina* is available from the state travel and tourism office (800/847-4862). Golflands USA puts out a freebie annual guide that includes munys and daily-fee courses statewide broken down by region. The North Carolina Golf Coast Association has a free twenty-page brochure to courses between Wilmington and Myrtle Beach (800/426-6644).

*Carolina Golf Today* covers the Research Triangle of Raleigh, Durham, and Chapel Hill (919/781-2752). Fore Better Golf has a Central North Carolina golf map covering Winston-Salem, Pinehurst, and Raleigh-Durham (708/893-8672).

### Discount Cards

American Lung Association Golf Privilege Card. Over 270 rounds at 150 courses. 919/395-5864. $40.

Carolinas PGA Bonus Golf Booklet. Over 120 courses evenly split. Calendar year. 803/399-1PGA. $25.

Golf Links Association of the Carolinas. One free round at 125 courses (about a third in South Carolina.) 800/GLA-1818. $22 for twelve months.

United Golf Relations. Free green fees or half off at fifty-one courses. 919/380-9000. $25 for twelve months.

The World's Golf Capital Card. North Carolina residents only. Discounts on sixty rounds on ten Pinehurst-area courses. Sandhills Golf Association, Box 4596, Pinehurst, NC 28374. $49.

*Shopping*

Between the outlet mall and the manufacturers' outlet center in Burlington, you're talking nearly three hundred stores (910/227-2872 or 910/228-0088). The Carolina Pottery Outlet Center in Smithfield has Bass, Benetton, Duck Head, Nike, and Hathaway (919/934-1157). Blowing Rock has Polo/Ralph Lauren.

## FINDING THE GREEN IN NORTH CAROLINA

Buncombe County Golf Course ($15/$15) 5,929 yds. (67.8/107)
226 Fairway Dr.
Asheville 704/298-1867

Duke University Golf Club ($15/$25*) 6,207 yds. (69.3/119)
Rte. 751 at Science Dr.
Durham 919/681-2288

Finley Golf Course ($16/$22) 6,102 yds. (69.1/117)
University of North Carolina
Old Mason Farm Rd.
Chapel Hill 919/962-2349

Kings Mountain Country Club ($8/$16) 6,143 yds. (69.4/118)
Country Club Ln.
Kings Mountain 704/739-5871

Mallard Head Golf Course ($20/$25) 6,450 yds. (70.5/116)
Brawley School Rd.
Mooresville 704/664-7031

Monroe Golf Club ($12/$17) 6,310 yds. (69.9/116)
Hwy. 601 South
Monroe 704/282-4661

Oak Hollow Golf Course ($12/$15) 6,022 yds. (68.7/118)
1400 Oak View Dr.
High Point 910/883-3260

*Twilight

Paschal Golf Club ($9.50/$12) 2,646 yds. (65.9/103)
555 Stadium Rd.
Wake Forest 919/556-5861

Pine Tree Golf Course ($14/$28) 6,046 yds. (68.0/107)
1680 Pine Tree Ln.
Kernersville 910/993-5598

Renaissance Park Golf Course ($16/$18*) 6,435 yds. (70.3/112)
1525 W. Tyvola Rd.
Charlotte 704/357-3373

Richmond Pines Country Club ($11/$16) 5,800 yds. (na/124)
Hwy. 1 North
Rockingham 910/895-3279

Wake Forest Country Club ($16/$21) 6,109 yds. (71.0/126)
13239 Capital Blvd.
Wake Forest 919/556-3416

Waynesville Country Club ($26/$26*) 27 holes
Carolina/Dogwood Course: 5,395 yds. (64.5/100)
Dogwood/Blueridge Course: 5,258 yds. (63.9/100)
Carolina/Blueridge Course: 5,493 yds. (64.8/100)
Country Club Dr.
Waynesville 704/452-4617

Westport Golf Course ($14.50/$30) 6,200 yds. (70.0/118)
7494 Golf Course Dr.
Denver 704/483-5604

Wilmington Golf Course ($11/$12) 6,250 yds. (69.2/116)
315 Wallace Ave.
Wilmington 910/791-0558

*Twilight

# NORTH DAKOTA

## Local Knowledge

Souris Valley in Minot has hosted publinks qualifying for a number of years. Dennis Doeden at *The Forum* newspaper in Fargo recommends Edgewood, Fargo's muny, regarded as the toughest course in the state. It's an older course right along the river, mature and scenic, a *Golf Digest* Top 5 Best in State. Abe Winter at *The Bismarck Tribune* says twenty-two mature cottonwood trees have been cut down but you hardly notice the difference. He also recommends Tom O'Leary, recently expanded to eighteen holes. Prairie West, across the river from Bismarck in Mandan, and Lincoln Park in Grand Forks are penciled in to host upcoming North Dakota State Golf Association events.

The Tribune puts out an excellent guidebook, *Golf North Dakota,* a fifty-two-page magazine with features and listings for dozens of courses. It's $3, available from Mike Tandy, *The Bismarck Tribune* (Golf ND), Box 1498, Bismarck, ND 58502.

The Tribune's Top 5 public courses in the state are:

1. Edgewood, Fargo
2. Riverwood, Bismarck
3. Souris Valley, Minot
4. Bois de Sioux, Wahpeton
5. Heart River, Dickinson

In Grand Forks, the University of North Dakota's Ray Richards Golf Course is also open to the public.

The *North Dakota State Parks & Recreation Outdoor Adventure Guide* lists course names and city, that's it, not even a phone number. Golf is listed as a nearby attraction with just about every state park, but there are no courses within park boundaries (800/437-2077).

## Discount Cards

American Lung Association Golf Privilege Card. Free or reduced fees at twenty-three courses. 800/252-6325 or 701/223-5613. $20.

Golf for Guardianship/ND. Discounts on over seventy rounds. 701/235-4457 or 800/450-4457. $15.

## FINDING THE GREEN IN NORTH DAKOTA

Bois de Sioux Golf Course ($16/$18) 6,480 yds. (70.1/120)
N. 4th and 13th Ave.
Wahpeton 701/642-3673

Edgewood Municipal Golf Course ($12/$14) 6,050 yds. (68.4/122)
Elm St.
Fargo 701/232-2824

Heart River Municipal Golf Course ($12/$12) 6,440 yds. (69.8/123)
Southwest of City
Dickinson 701/225-9412

Lincoln Park Golf Course ($11.75/$11.75) 6,000 yds. (66.3/107)
Elks Dr.
Grand Forks 701/746-2788

Prairie West ($13/$13) 6,400 yds. (70.2/124)
2709 Longspur Tr.
Mandan 701/667-3222

Ray Richards Golf Course ($11.50/$11.75) 3,165 yds. (69.2/110)
University of North Dakota
Demers Ave.
Grand Forks 701/777-4340

Riverwood Golf Course ($15/$15) 6,400 yds. (69.8/120)
725 Riverwood Dr.
Bismarck 701/222-6462

Souris Valley Golf Course ($13/$13) 6,600 yds. (71.3/124)
2400 Burdick Expy. W.
Minot 701/839-1819

Tom O'Leary Golf Club ($12.50/$12.50) 5,314 yds. (63.7/103)
930 N. Griffin St.
Bismarck 701/222-6531

# OHIO

### Local Knowledge

Recent Ohio sectional publinks qualifying sites include Glenview in Cincinnati, Windmill Lakes in Cleveland, Whiteford Valley in Ottawa Lake, Michigan, and both courses at Kitty Hawk in Dayton.

When they started up a city amateur tournament in Cleveland several years ago, the finals were played first at Sleepy Hollow, the oldest muny. They've since been held at Manakiki, designed by Donald Ross in 1928. I asked George Sweda, whose golf column appears in the Cleveland *Plain Dealer* on Mondays, where he might go to steal eighteen holes on the cheap. He adds Fowler's Mill to the three area courses named above.

In Cincinnati, the seven munys are essentially competing against the six Hamilton County courses, a nice situation for public golfers. Unfortunately, at the third hole at The Vineyard, too many of them were spraying balls into houses and the street. They've had to shorten the hole, but it's still considered a cut (excuse the pun) above. Jack Murray at *The Cincinnati Enquirer* said it'd be a toss-up choosing between The Vineyard and Glenview, the latter often overrun by senior leagues. Since another nine holes have been added, perhaps getting on will be easier.

*MidOhio Golfer* is an exceptional resource with a Columbus focus. The tabloid comes out eighteen times a year, twice a month during the season. Each issue includes course listings. The annual *Course Directory* is terrific. It's available for $1, which happens to be *MOG*'s cover price. A year's subscription is $13.95 (614/888-4567). A summarized version geared to visitors is available from the Columbus Convention and Visitors Bureau (800/345-4386).

*MidOhio Golfer* managing editor Ray Poprocki recommends the Donald Ross–designed Granville Golf Course, about thirty miles east of Columbus. Not only is it a wonderful course, says Ray, the setting's lovely. Three holes have fallen victim to development, prompting debate about whether the added holes detract or improve the design. Nonetheless, it still heads Ray's recommendations. Raymond Municipal is a Robert Trent Jones, Sr., design. Each of the par threes have two holes, a novel attempt at speeding play.

When Winding Hollow Country Club moved out to New Albany,

Columbus took over a venerable course, opened in 1923 and redesigned by Robert Trent Jones. The challenge at Champions, as it's now called, has been to keep up the conditions. PGA Tour player and former Buckeye John Cook designed Cooks Creek with architect Michael Hurdzan. It's also within reach of Columbus, in Ashville. Minerva Lake is in the heart of Columbus, the area's oldest course. Ray says it's a lot of fun—easy and funky, real short with postage-stamp greens and lots of up and down. The converse would be the Players Club at Fox Fire in Lockbourne, a bear.

The LPGA stops at Avalon Lakes in Warren. Not far away, on the Pennsylvania/Ohio border, Yankee Run is a repeated National Golf Foundation Public Golf Achievement Award winner. Kent State's course is open to public play. Miami Shores in Troy was designed by Donald Ross.

Bob Stewart at *The Repository* newspaper said the first stop in and around Canton would have to be Tam O'Shanter, host to U.S. Open qualifying and the Ohio Open. There are two courses. The Hills is about half a shot shorter than the Dales. Both are par seventy. Skyland Pines has served as an Ohio publinks site. Tannenhauf, right outside of Alliance, is 6,600 yards, "kind of long for around here," says Bob, and also recommended. These courses and Seven Hills in Hartville, Bob says, are "all very good."

For some fun you might look in at Lyons Den in Canal Fulton. A labor of love for the longtime greenskeeper at Firestone in Akron, Bill Lyons, it's been expanded to eighteen holes. Well maintained, as you might expect, now by Bill's son, it's got some fun holes, like Devil's Gulch, a very short par five, with carries just long enough to tantalize. Canton and Stark County have an area golf brochure and run various travel packages (800/533-4302).

Ohio has a number of state park courses, the legacy of former governor and avid golfer John Rhodes. Maumee Bay was the number one area course recommendation of Dave Hackenberg of *The Toledo Blade*. Hack described the course, designed by Arthur Hills, as "a blue-light special among resort tracks." Other suggestions in and around Toledo: Riverby Hills, Valleywood, South Toledo, and Ottawa Park. Valleywood's fairways, built atop natural springs, writes Dave, are "among the greenest and lushest to be found." South Toledo and Valleywood "are lush and in near country club condition." The North Course at Whiteford Valley is a "monster," he warns, longer from the whites than the South Course is from the tips.

Other state park courses: Deer Lake in Geneva-on-the-Lake, Shawnee in Friendship, Salt Fork in Cambridge, Punderson in Newbury, Hueston Woods in Oxford, and Deer Creek in Mount Sterling. All are eighteen holes. All run a full slate of packages during the season (800/282-7275). For general tourism information, call 800/BUCKEYE. The Ohio Pass Coupon Book, free with a phone call, includes several golf, state park, and outlet discounts.

In Newark, Dynacraft has opened a free museum. Along with classic photographs, three hundred books and magazines, and what's billed as a very extensive tee collection, the museum's displays feature a number of clubs, some dating back to the 1890s. Hours are eight to five weekdays (614/344-1191). Dynacraft also has a factory and showroom tour and a Newark Golf factory outlet store, 71 Maholm St. (800/423-2968).

Fore Better Golf has a northeast Ohio map, circa 1993, that covers Cleveland, Canton, Akron, and Youngstown. Its southwest map covers Cincinnati, Dayton, and Columbus. They're $3.95 in pro shops (708/893-8672).

### Discount Cards

American Lung Association Golf Privilege Card. At least 160 courses, May–October. 800/232-5864. $30.

### Shopping

In Cleveland, Carolyn Empkey's The Women's Club has, among other things, gloves in colors that manufacturers had to have their arms twisted to produce, as well as handmade bureaus and golf course rugs. It's in Fairview Park; 216/979-0050.

Ohio Factory Outlets in West Lancaster (Exit 65 at I-71 and US 35) has seventy-six stores, among them: Izod, Duck Head, Esprit, Van Heusen, and Fila.

The Old Golf Shop is right downtown in Cincinnati, across from the convention center. The Olmans' books are exceptional resources on golf collectibles and antiques. Their business is open by appointment only: 513/241-7797. And, if you just want to look, or can use some collecting help, that's okay too.

## FINDING THE GREEN IN OHIO

Avalon Lakes Golf Course ($25/$25*) 6,453 yds. (71.7/125)
One American Way
Warren 216/856-8898

Avalon South Golf Course ($15/$17) 6,224 yds. (68.6/112)
9794 E. Market St.
Warren 216/856-4329

Champions of Columbus Golf Course ($25/$27.50) 6,193 yds.
(69.6/123)
3900 Westerville Rd.
Columbus 614/645-7111

Cooks Creek Golf Course ($20/$25) 2,906 yds. (na/na)
16405 US Hwy. 23 South
Ashville 614/983-3636

Deer Creek State Park Golf Course ($13/$17) 6,574 yds. (71.2/113)
20635 Waterloo Rd.
Mount Sterling 614/869-3088

Deer Lake Golf Course ($12/$14.50) 6,104 yds. (67.3/110)
Geneva State Park
6300 Lake Road West
Geneva-on-the-Lake 800/468-8450 or 216/466-8450

Fowler's Mill Golf Club ($22/$22*) 27 holes
Red/White Course: 6,226 yds. (69.5/122)
Red/Blue Course: 6,375 yds. (70.6/126)
White/Blue Course: 6,623 yds. (72.8/123)
13095 Rockhaven Rd.
Chesterland 216/286-9545

Glenview Golf Course ($19/$19) 6,039 yds. (70.5/119)
10965 Springfield Pike
Cincinnati 513/771-1747

Granville Golf Course ($21/$26) 6,217 yds. (69.5/122)
555 Newark-Granville Rd.
Granville 614/587-4653

*Twilight

Hueston Woods State Park Golf Course ($15/$20) 6,727 yds.
(71.8/129)
Brown Rd.
Oxford 513/523-8081

Kent State University Golf Club ($12.50/$17) 5,327 yds. (64.9/107)
2346 State Rd. 59
Kent 216/672-2500

Kitty Hawk Community Golf Course ($15/$15) 36 holes
Hawk Course: 6,396 yds. (69.5/115)
Eagle Course: 6,713 yds. (70.6/116)
3383 Chuck Wagner Rd.
Dayton 513/237-5424

Lyons Den Golf Course ($15/$16) 5,300 yds. (65.0/97)
6347 Manchester
Canal Fulton 216/854-9910

Manakiki Golf Course ($19/$19) 6,192 yds. (70.1/126)
35501 Eddy Rd.
Willoughby Hills 216/942-2500

Maumee Bay State Park Golf Course ($25/$25*) 6,136 yds.
(69.6/122)
N. Curtice Rd.
Oregon 419/836-9009

Miami Shores Golf Club ($11/$13) 6,223 yds. (67.6/97)
Rutherford Dr.
Troy 513/335-4457

Minerva Lake Golf Course ($12/$14.50) 5,638 yds. (65.6/101)
2955 Minerva Lake Rd.
Columbus 614/882-9988

Ottawa Park Golf Course ($14.50/$19) 5,478 yds. (65.1/113)
One Walden Pond
Toledo 419/472-2059

Players Club at Foxfire ($28/$28) 6,507 yds. (72.4/128)
10651 State Hwy. 104
Lockbourne 614/224-3694

*Twilight

Punderson State Park Golf Course ($14/$25) 6,600 yds. (72.0/114)
11755 Kinsman
Newbury 216/564-5465

Raymond Municipal Golf Course ($12.50/$14.50) 6,635 yds.
(69.7/113)
3860 Trabue Rd.
Columbus 614/645-3276

Riverby Hills Golf Course ($15/$19) 6,482 yds. (70.4/121)
16571 W. River Rd.
Bowling Green 419/878-5941

Salt Fork State Park Golf Course ($13/$13) 5,786 yds. (67.0/110)
Rte. 22
Cambridge 614/432-7185

Seven Hills Country Club ($12.50/$21) 5,918 yds. (68.5/116)
11700 William Penn Ave. NE.
Hartville 216/877-9303

Shawnee State Park Golf Course ($15/$15) 6,407 yds. (69.7/114)
Hwy. 52 West
Friendship 614/858-6681

Skyland Pines Golf Club ($18/$14*) 5,944 yds. (68.2/110)
3550 Columbus Rd. NE.
Canton 216/454-5131

Sleepy Hollow Golf Club ($13/$14) 6,004 yds. (67.7/109)
6029 East State Rte. 101
Clyde 419/547-0770

South Toledo Golf Club ($12/$16) 5,953 yds. (67.9/104)
3915 Heathersdowns Blvd.
Toledo 419/385-4678

Tam O'Shanter Golf Course ($20/$20) 36 holes
Hills Course: 6,054 yds. (67.6/103)
Dales Course: 6,249 yds. (68.9/107)
5055 Hills and Dales Rd.
Canton 800/462-9964 or 216/477-5111

*Twilight

Tannenhauf Golf Club ($17/$17) 6,290 yds. (70.2/108)
11411 McCallum Ave.
Alliance 216/823-4402

Valleywood Golf Club ($19/$22) 6,058 yds. (67.4/107)
Airport Hwy.
Swanton 419/826-3991

The Vineyard Golf Course ($21.50/$21.50) 6,254 yds. (70.6/124)
600 Nordyke Rd.
Cincinnati 513/474-3007

Whiteford Valley Golf Course ($15/$19) 36 holes
North Course: 6,263 yds. (na/106)
South Course: 6,560 yds. (na/111)
Old US 223
Ottawa Lake MI 313/856-4545

Windmill Lakes Golf Club ($20/$28) 6,132 yds. (69.7/118)
6544 State Rte. 14
Ravenna 216/297-0440

Yankee Run Golf Course ($18/$21) 6,103 yds. (68.9/116)
7610 Sharon-Warren Rd.
Brookfield 216/448-8096

# OKLAHOMA

*Local Knowledge*

In search of a good steer, I checked in with John Rohde at the *Daily Oklahoman*. Three courses immediately came to mind: Kickingbird in Edmond and the two Lincoln Park courses. Lincoln Park West has hosted tour qualifying, collegiate events, and sectional publinks qualifying. Built back in the 1920s, they are lined with mature trees, to John's mind, "outstanding public courses." The West is a little longer and has more character, the East shorter and more popular with seniors.

*South Central Golf*, the official publication of the South Central

Section of the PGA and Oklahoma Golf Association, is free at Tulsa International, restaurants, visitor centers, and golf courses. It covers Arkansas and Kansas, as well as Oklahoma, and does a great job of mixing news and features beyond a narrow association-news focus. Highly recommended. Single issues are free (you pay the freight) (918/747-6225).

Ken McLeod, *South Central Golf*'s editor, likes Stone Creek, a past host to the national women's public links championship. "It's probably harder than Olde Page and probably prettier," he says. Both are the only public courses in town with zoysia fairways.

LaFortune Park has a strong eighteen-hole course and a lighted par three course. Another area course Ken describes as "a good little test," shorter than LaFortune, but with a lot of trees and water, is South Lakes in nearby Jenks.

Years of sales tax revenues have been earmarked to revitalize the Pecan Valley Course at Tulsa's Mohawk Park. New greens and tee boxes were installed in 1994. The hope is that the improvements, including seventy-five new catch basins, will help with drainage; the course is in a floodplain. Woodbine, also in Mohawk Park, is Tulsa's oldest course.

The idea of a high school having its own course is certainly appealing. Run now by the Cherokee Nation on the grounds of Sequoyah High in Tahlequah, the course was built in 1959 for staff and students. The greens are tiny but bent grass. Sequoyah Golf Course hosts the All Indian Golf Tournament and is open to the public.

So is the University of Oklahoma's course in Norman. The state vacation guide does not include any golf information (800/652-6552). There are, however, several state park courses: Sequoyah in Hulbert, Texoma Resort in Kingston, Fort Cobb, and Fountainhead in Checotah. The nine-hole course in Wewoka is named after the town's favorite nonpracticing optometrist, hometown boy, and PGA tourist, Dr. Gil Morgan.

### Discount Cards:

Tulsa Area Golf Card. Fourteen free rounds of golf from the South Central PGA Section/National Golf Concept. One year from date of purchase. 800/955-4574. $59.95.

American Lung Association Golf Privilege Card. Over fifty courses throughout the state. 405/524-8471. $20.


## FINDING THE GREEN IN OKLAHOMA

Fort Cobb Golf Course ($9/$11) 6,266 yds. (69.8/117)
Fort Cobb State Park
Fort Cobb 405/643-2398

Fountainhead Golf Course ($8.50/$11) 6,489 yds. (69.8/112)
Hwy. 150
Checotah 918/689-3209

Gil Morgan Golf Course ($8/$8) 9 holes/6,470 yds. (69.7/112)
800 E. 7th St.
Wewoka 405/257-3292

Kickingbird Golf Course ($13/$13) 6,305 yds. (71.4/127)
1600 E. Danforth
Edmond 405/341-5350

LaFortune Park Golf Course ($15/$15) 6,484 yds. (70.9/119)
5501 S. Yale
Tulsa 918/596-8627

Lincoln Park Golf Course ($11/$11) 36 holes
East Course: 6,400 yds. (66.5/105)
West Course: 6,501 yds. (69.9/110)
4001 NE. Grand Blvd.
Oklahoma City 405/424-1421

Mohawk Park Golf Course ($13/$15) 36 holes
Pecan Valley Course: 5,849 yds. (66.9/108)
Woodbine Course: 6,577 yds. (70.0/110)
5223 E. 41st St. North
Tulsa 918/425-6871

Olde Page Belcher Golf Course ($13/$15) 6,420 yds. (69.7/116)
6666 S. Union
Tulsa 918/446-1529

Sequoyah Golf Course ($7/$7) 9 holes/5,989 yds. (67.3/110)
Hwy. 69
Tahlequah 918/458-4294

Sequoyah State Park Golf Course ($8/$10.50) 5,860 yds. (66.7/109)
Rte. 1
Hulbert 918/772-2297

Stone Creek Golf Course ($13/$15) 6,104 yds. (69.1/121)
6666 S. Union
Tulsa 918/446-1529

South Lakes Golf Course ($15/$15) 5,839 yds. (67.4/110)
9253 S. Elwood
Jenks 918/746-3760

Texoma Resort Golf Course ($9/$12) 6,400 yds. (68.7/112)
State Hwy. 70
Kingston 405/564-3333

University Golf Course ($12/$12) 6,409 yds. (69.0/111)
University of Oklahoma
One Par Drive
Norman 405/325-6716

# OREGON

## Local Knowledge

In *The Northwest Golfer's Almanac* ($7.95), several top architects were asked how courses in the region compared to the rest of the country. Gene C. "Bunny" Mason's succinct response: "Shorter—prettier—greener. Cheaper."

The Pacific Northwest is equally well served with guides. *Golf Courses of the Pacific Northwest* ($19), by Jeff Shelley, is an accomplishment Webster would admire. Over six hundred pages document the history, upkeep, legal and environmental squabbles, and the playing of golf here. (There's even the admirable inclusion of one's odds of walking on.) Jeff also edited the aforementioned almanac, a delightful read, informative and lively. Both books are in stores and available from Fairgreens Media in Seattle (206/525-1294).

KiKi Canniff, author of *The Northwest Golfer* ($12.95), offers a terrific free service. Anyone who writes her can have a list of "Oregon's Best Golf Bargains, 27 courses where you can play for $6 or less." That's not a misprint. Her book is in stores or available from Ki2 Enterprises, P.O. Box 186, Willamina, OR 97396. (Send a SASE #10 envelope for the list.)

"Because the scenery in this corner of the world is so gorgeous," she writes, "I find that my favorite courses have more to do with the setting than the challenge." She recommends Bandon Face, where the ninth tee is just two hundred yards from the ocean (the encyclopedic Mr. Shelley notes Bandon Face has the distinction of being the westernmost course in the contiguous United States), Hawk Creek in Neskowin ("in a beautiful coastal valley and surrounded by forest"), and Tokatee in Blue River, lauded by *Golf Digest* as "one of the region's prettiest." Other favorites: Crooked River, with a three-hundred-foot gorge, Indian Creek in Hood River (snowcapped mountain views), and Elkhorn Valley in Lyons, "a gorgous place to play with a view of eight mountain peaks."

Instead of putting Idaho, Washington, and Oregon under one cover, Daniel MacMillan chose to divvy up the region's courses into three separate books. *Golfing in Oregon* ($8.95) reproduces course layouts and provides a map on each page to supplement the directions. It's an annual, part of an expanding catalog of guidebooks. For more information, contact Mac Productions, P.O. Box 655, Carnation, WA 98014 (206/333-4641).

Dan played word association on some favorites: Broadmoor ("One of Portland's most popular courses . . . not overpowering to the average golfer . . . good, fair course"), Charbonneau in Wilsonville ("Great 27 hole executive course . . . Great after golf restaurant for the whole family"), Heron Lakes in Portland ("One of the most spectacular public courses in the state. Both the Greenback and Great Blue are very demanding. One of my favorite places to play in Portland"). The Great Blue, past host to amateur publinx, regional PGA qualifying, is the current home of the Northwest Open. It was designed by Robert Trent Jones, Jr. Others: Meadow Lakes in Prineville ("Spectacular with water at nearly every turn. Worth every penny"), Quail Valley in Banks ("Brand new, will be fantastic. Owners want an affordable championship caliber course"), River's

Edge in Bend ("Eats my lunch every year. Greens are tough, three, sometimes four tiers"), Sunset Bay in Coos Bay ("Great nine-hole course with dual tees"), Tokatee in Blue River ("Worth a trip. At this price you won't find a better place to play"), and Trysting Tree in Corvallis ("Great course designed after Scottish links").

The city of Portland's Bureau of Parks and Recreation has an informative packet about its impressive munys. Maps are included (503/823-2223). As it has several times in the past, Eastmoreland will again host the national public links championship in 1997. It has a beautiful setting, surrounded by Crystal Springs Lake, the Rhododendron Gardens, and Johnson Creek. The clubhouse has been redone with a new restaurant and pro shop. (Filet of broiled northwest salmon with lemon butter, served with grilled new potatoes, fresh vegetables, and the special house bread is $13.95. Makes a change from a chili dog at the turn, no?) Of this, one of the nation's finest public, and affordable, courses, MacMillan says simply: "This course is worth a special trip." Ready golf is the order of the day. Plan B might be Glendoveer, sectional publinks qualifying host site in 1994.

Finally, each member of Oregon's golf panel mentioned that west of the Cascades, you can play all year.

### Discount Card

See "Stalking the Elusive Deep Discount" in Finding the Green introduction.

### Shopping

The golf superstore, Fiddler's Green, sends out a free state golf map, although it reserves its most detailed directions for finding Fiddler's Green. (The store also has an eighteen-hole par three course and driving range.) Bring in the map/brochure with an out-of-state license and you'll get a free sleeve of Nitros Poses (800/548-5500 or 503/689-8464).

## FINDING THE GREEN IN OREGON

Bandon Face Rock Golf Course ($13/$14)
9 holes/4,151 yds. (59.6/99)
3235 Beach Loop Dr.
Bandon 503/347-3818

Broadmoor Golf Course ($18/$20) 5,966 yds. (68.4/116)
3509 NE. Columbia Blvd.
Portland 503/281-1337

Charbonneau Golf & Country Club ($18/$20) 27 holes
North Yellow/West Red Course: 3,909 yds. (58.5/83)
North Yellow/East Green Course: 3,967 yds. (59.3/85)
East Green/West Red Course: 4,052 yds. (58.8/84)
32020 Charbonneau Dr.
Wilsonville 503/694-1246

Crooked River Ranch Golf Course ($22/$22) 5,573 yds. (64.7/100)
5195 Clubhouse Rd.
Crooked River 503/923-6343

Eastmoreland Golf Course ($18/$20) 6,105 yds. (70.0/119)
2425 SE. Bybee Blvd.
Portland 503/775-2900

Elkhorn Valley Golf Course ($22/$22) 2,829 yds. (68.8/126)
32295 Little North Fork Rd.
Lyons 503/897-3368

Fiddler's Green Golf Course and Driving Range ($9/$9)
18 holes par 3/2,378 yds. (na/na)
91292 Highway 99 N.
Eugene 503/689-8464

Glendoveer Golf Course ($15/$17) 36 holes
East Course: 5,142 yds. (68.0/116)
West Course: 5,117 yds. (66.2/109)
14015 NE. Glisan St.
Portland 503/253-7507

Hawk Creek Golf Course ($19/$19) 2,343 yds. (63.8/103)
48480 Hwy. 101
Neskowin 503/392-4120

Heron Lakes Golf Club 36 holes
Great Blue Course: ($27/$27) 6,056 yds. (69.4/122)
Greenback Course: ($18/$20) 5,938 yds. (68.4/115)
3500 N. Victory Blvd.
Portland 503/289-1818

Indian Creek Golf Course ($20/$24) 5,356 yds. (67.4/118)
3605 Brookside Dr.
Hood River (503/386-7770)

Meadow Lakes Golf Course ($25/$25) 5,849 yds. (69.1/122)
300 Meadow Lakes Dr.
Prineville 503/447-7113

Quail Valley Golf Course ($25/$25) 6,300 yds. (70.2/118)
12565 NW. Aerts Rd.
Banks 503/324-4444

River's Edge Golf Course ($29/$29) 6,128 yds. (69.8/133)
200 NW. Mount Washington Dr.
Bend 503/389-2828

Sunset Bay Golf Course ($14/$15) 9 holes/6,055 yds. (68.0/na)
11001 Cape Arago Hwy.
Coos Bay 503/888-9301

Tokatee Golf Club ($28/$28) 6,245 yds. (69.7/119)
54947 McKenzie Hwy.
Blue River 503/822-3220

Trysting Tree Golf Club ($23/$23) 6,216 yds. (69.9/122)
34028 Electric Rd.
Corvallis 503/752-3332

# PENNSYLVANIA

## Local Knowledge

Emil Loeffler, for many years the greenskeeper at Oakmont, laid out two terrific public courses, Bucknell University Golf Course in Lewisburg and Tam O'Shanter in West Middlesex. Bucknell's course is terrific, particularly the landscaping; it's like playing inside an arboretum. It opened in 1930. The facility exudes an unpretentious sense of permanence and civility. Members have priority before noon on weekends.

Tam O'Shanter (about an hour northwest of Pittsburgh, slightly longer from Erie or Cleveland) has hosted the state publinks championship several times. Sam Snead's sixty-five on July 13, 1949, still stands.

For the nice touches around the course, for the memorabilia lining the clubhouse walls, for the staff who stop the mowers to let you hit, and for the par three over "Death Valley" with its tombstone dedicated to "the many good scores that died in its depths!"—but most of all for the Kerins family's high standards, Tam is awarded a Golden Apfel Award for Meritorious Service to Apfordable Golf. This is another course that reinforces public golf's silver lining.

Slightly farther off the beaten path, on many levels, is Buhland Golf Course in nearby Sharon. It charges no green fee, requires no cart, no membership, no tee time. There is no starter and no clubhouse, just a sign with scorecards and pencils. Yup, free golf and in surprisingly good shape. A local steel magnate left the course and funds for maintaining it in perpetuity. There are no par fives, but the par threes measure 180, 204, and 237 yards. To walk up and play this course, unburdened by all the encumbrances of modern golf, produces an unsuppressible giddiness.

In the Pittsburgh area, several courses used for Keystone Public Golf Association tournaments include North Park (regional publinks qualifying site for the women), Cedarbrook in Belle Vernon, Butler's in Elizabeth, Black Hawk in Beaver Falls, and Suncrest in Butler. Oakmont East is next door to the Oakmont Country Club, if worlds apart. Built in the forties, the club has purchased the public course and uses it for parking when the Open's in town. It's not as bad as all that. From atop the hills you can see the famed church pew bunkers next door.

The regional tabloid *Keystone Golfer* provides coupons, tips, and local news in western Pennsylvania. It also has a cable show on KBL Sports Network (412/458-0733).

Before leaving Pittsburgh International Airport, snag a copy of the brochure "Public Golf Courses in the Pittsburgh Area" at the Visitors and Convention Bureau desk at ground transportation near the rental car counters. It's got great directions. The Pennsylvania Golf Course Owners produces the free booklet with information on 133 courses, most in the western third of the state. It's also available by calling 412/751-3379.

You've probably never heard of Angelo Spagnolo, but it's safe to say you'd remember him if your paths crossed on the course. Mr. Spagnolo, you see, once shot 257 in a record-setting round at the TPC in Florida in 1985, earning him the title of America's worst avid golfer. (He shot sixty-six on number seventeen, the island green par three.) While he no longer holds the title—a frightening thought—it seems noteworthy to mention his home course, Linden Hall Golf Course in Dawson, outside Pittsburgh.

Penn State's two courses have had to accommodate encroaching university expansion. There's certainly plenty here to entertain the stronger player, particularly on the holes exposed to the wind. Power lines mar the experience on several holes, but this is a typical college course, offering exceptional value for the price. When the dust settles, four nines will be open, and they should be terrific. The nicest course in the area, Toftrees, starts dropping its green fees the day after Thanksgiving. It takes the expected high temperature for the day, divides by four (for a foursome), and that's how much you pay.

In Wilkes-Barre, the muny designed by Geoffrey Cornish is, in the studied opinion of Joe Miegoc of *The Scranton Times-Tribune,* the best course in the area, "better than some clubs." Bob Oliver, who pens "Chip Shots" Mondays in season in the *Bucks County Courier Times,* recommends Five Ponds in Warminster and Penn National in Fayetteville, which has hosted collegiate championships for the Atlantic 10 Conference. It's twenty miles from Gettysburg. There's also a fun, traditional course, one of the oldest in the area, at Caledonia State Park nearby.

Kimberton, near Kennett Square, has hosted the Pennsylvania

State Public Links Championship. Pinecrest in Lansdale has hosted public links events for the Golf Association of Philadelphia. Downing Municipal near Erie was the sectional qualifying site for the USGA Amateur Public Links in 1994.

In Philly, Cobb's Creek and Karakung host sectional publinks qualifying. A paid green fee at one course is good on the same day at the other. If you're over that way, Izett in Ardmore has been making custom clubs the old-fashioned way for decades (215/642-1887).

An easy escape from Center City, Philadelphia, FDR Golf Club is down the street from the Spectrum, right behind the American Swedish Museum. An undistinguished, flat, and open layout, it's a feast for gorillas but has a good practice area.

Center Square, built on land deeded by William Penn, hosted the 1977 and 1980 Women's Public Links National Championship. It's a beautiful course in upper eastern Montgomery County.

It's off the beaten path, but Skippack Golf Course, with its 140-year-old clubhouse and a nice range, is just outside Evansburg State Park, in Skippack. It's a real pleasant setting and the course is now ambitiously tended by American Golf.

T-Time Maps has a detailed statewide golf map for $3.95 (410/667-6738). Two maps of Philadelphia area courses are available for $4.95 each. One is from the Golf Association of Philadelphia (215/687-2340). Fore Better Golf's map includes Reading, Wilmington, Trenton, Allentown, and Willingboro (708/893-8672).

The free tabloid *Pennsylvania Golfer* has coupons and an area course directory (215/269-7670, $7 for nine issues). The Philadelphia Publinks Golf Association might also be a helpful resource (215/525-7439). *Powers Northeast Region Golf Guide* ($14.95) and *Golf Greens* ($9.95) provide extensive course listings and coupons. They're in bookstores and pro shops or available from 800/446-8884 and 800/394-GOLF, respectively.

### Discount Cards

American Lung Association of Central Pennsylvania. Ranges and over fifty courses in York, Bucks, Montgomery, and twenty other counties. 800/351-1512 or 717/845-3639. $30.

American Lung Association of Northwest Pennsylvania. Forty-five courses, May–November. 800/352-0917 or 814/454-0109. $30.

American Lung Association of the South Alleghenies Golf Privilege Card. Twelve courses in Bedford, Cambria, Fulton, and Somerset counties, May–October. 800/732-0099 or 814/536-7245. $25.

The Pocono Golf Pass. Two free rounds at thirteen courses, calendar year. Box 194, Bushkill, PA 18324. $45.

American Cancer Society Pennsylvania Golf Card. Free rounds at over one hundred courses statewide. 800/732-0999. $25.

## Shopping

Reading invented outlet malls, and there are over one hundred stores in the area. For a free coupon book and details, call 800/5-OUTLET. Others are in Lancaster, Morgantown, and Erie. For general tourism and shopping info statewide: 800/VISIT-PA.

## FINDING THE GREEN IN PENNSYLVANIA

Bucknell Golf Club ($21/$26) 5,977 yds. (68.8/125)
Rte. 15
Lewisburg 717/523-8193

Black Hawk Golf Course ($13/$16) 36 holes
Course One and Two: 6,113 yds. (68.0/112)
Course Three and Four: 6,300 yds. (70.0/113)
644 Blackhawk Rd.
Beaver Falls 412/843-5512

Buhland Golf Course (free) 2,364 yds.
Sharon (no phone)

Butler's Golf Course ($17.50/$23*) 6,398 yds. (69.2/113)
800 Rock Run Rd.
Elizabeth 412/751-9121

Caledonia Golf Club ($12/$15) 5,154 yds. (67.1/118)
Caledonia State Park
Golf Course Rd.
Fayetteville 717/352-7271

*Twilight

Cedarbrook Golf Course 36 holes
Red Course: ($15/$21) 5,234 yds. (65.3/115)
Gold Course: ($17/$24*) 6,253 yds. (69.5/130)
Hwy. 51 and I-70
Belle Vernon 412/929-8300

Center Square Golf Club ($17/$23) 6,048 yds. (69.3/114)
Rte. 373
Center Square 215/584-4288

Cobb's Creek Golf Course ($21/$24) 6,130 yds. (69.6/116)
72nd and Lansdowne Ave.
Philadelphia 215/877-8707

Downing Municipal Golf Course ($12/$15) 6,653 yds. (70.6/117)
Troupe Rd.
Harborcreek 814/899-5827

FDR Golf Club ($17/$19) 6,000 yds. (na/na)
20th St. and Pattison Ave.
Philadelphia 215/462-8997

*Twilight

Karakung Golf Course ($15/$17) 5,737 yds. (68.4/114)
72nd and Lansdowne Ave.
Philadelphia 215/877-8707

Kimberton Golf Club ($17/$22) 6,016 yds. (67.6/118)
Rte. 23
Kimberton 215/933-8836

Linden Hall Golf Course ($17/$22) 6,405 yds. (71.2/na)
Linden Hall Rd.
Dawson 412/461-2424

North Park Golf Course ($12/$15) 5,352 yds. (70.2/115)
303 Pearce Mill Rd.
Allison Park 412/935-1967

Oakmont Country Club East ($12/$15) 5,720 yds. (61.0/116)
Rte. 909 and Hulton Rd.
Oakmont 412/828-5335

Penn National Golf Course ($17/$24) 6,451 yds. (71.0/125)
3720 Clubhouse Dr.
Fayetteville 717/352-3000

Penn State University Golf Course 36 holes
Blue Course: ($23/$23) 6,102 yds. (69.9/125)
White Course: ($18/$18) 6,008 yds. (68.7/116)
W. College Ave.
State College 814/865-GOLF

Pinecrest Golf Club ($20/$28*) 6,112 yds. (67.0/118)
101 Country Club Dr.
Lansdale 215/855-6112

Skippack Golf Course ($15.50/$22) 5,914 yds. (67.8/113)
Stump Hall and Cedars Rds.
Skippack 215/584-4226

Suncrest Golf Club ($13/$15) 6,243 yds. (69.3/112)
137 Browndale Rd.
Butler 412/586-5508

*Twilight

Tam O'Shanter Golf Course ($17/$19) 6,047 yds. (67.4/116)
I-80 and Rte. 18
West Middlesex 412/981-3552

Warminster Five Ponds Golf Club ($19/$23) 6,440 yds. (70.6/119)
1225 W. Street Rd.
Warminster 215/956-9727

Wilkes-Barre Golf Club ($16/$19*) 6,409 yds. (70.3/124)
1001 Fairway Dr.
Wilkes-Barre 717/472-3590

# RHODE ISLAND

*Local Knowledge*

How tight is land in Rhode Island? Not only is the Donald
Ross–designed Triggs Memorial the only public course in the city of
Providence proper, it's the *only* golf course within the city limits. The
state recently got its first new course in twenty-five years, Richmond
Country Club, designed by Cornish/Silva.

Triggs is *the* course for public golf in Rhode Island. No surprise
then that despite a magnificent layout, it gets enough play to keep it
from being in the best of shape. Paul Kenyon, who covers golf for
*The Providence Journal,* says the course is in better condition than it
was five years ago and is not nearly as bad as it has been made out
to be. (There is another Ross course open to the public in Rhode
Island, Winnapaug in Westerly.)

Tim Geary, a former winner of the Golf Writers Association of
America Championship, covers the game for the Fall River *Herald
News* in Johnston. He singled out several courses, including Cranston
Country Club ("a nice layout, where you have to hit all the shots"),
Montaup in Portsmouth, right on Montaup Bay ("as good as any pri-
vate course you'll find"), Green Valley, also in Portsmouth ("just a

*Twilight

great golf course"), and Woodland Greens and North Kingston Municipal, both in North Kingston. The muny was a former military course that the town took over when the navy pulled out.

Paul Kenyon also likes the North Kingston muny. The New England Country Club, designed by Hale Irwin, was originally meant to be private. The clubhouse is in Rhode Island; the course is actually in Bellingham, Massachusetts (see "Finding the Green in Massachusetts"). Green Valley also gets a thumbs-up. It gets overlooked because of the "intolerable" forty-minute drive from Providence.

When the conversation turned to good nine-hole courses, the encyclopedic Mr. Geary ticked off several recommendations: Jamestown, Coventry Pines, and Midville in West Warwick. Goddard State Park also has nine holes.

*The Journal* puts out two golf tabloids, including a sixteen-page public course directory that also covers southeastern Massachusetts. It's got all the trimmings, including prices (800/752-9287).

The *Rhode Island Visitors Guide* lists two pages of public course information (800/556-2484 or 401/277-2601). A coupon book, *Powers Northeast Region Golf Guide* ($14.95), features twenty-eight Rhode Island courses (800/446-8884).

Despite the size of their state, Rhode Islanders can bask in the aureated glow of knowing their visitor's map rises above all others. The state map recognizes golf courses, a simple but much appreciated feature. Not only are they denoted, but as befits a state founded on tolerance and freedom of expression, a second flag is used to distinguish public courses, an act deserving of the Golden Apfel Award for Meritorious Service to Apfordable Golf.

### Discount Card

The Rhode Island Lung Association Golf Privilege Card. Free/discounted golf at ten courses. 401/421-6487. $25.

### Shopping

Nothing to rival Mystic in Connecticut or the Mass outlets.

## FINDING THE GREEN IN RHODE ISLAND

Cranston Country Club ($22/$26) 6,261 yds. (69.9/120)
69 Burlingame Rd.
Cranston 401/826-1683

Coventry Pines Country Club ($16/$18) 9 holes/6,340 yds.
(68.0/113)
1065 Harkney Hill Rd.
Coventry 401/397-9482

Goddard State Park Golf Course ($12/$16) 3,021 yds. (na/na)
Ives Rd.
Warwick 401/884-9834

Green Valley Country Club ($22/$27) 6,674 yds. (70.9/120)
371 Union St.
Portsmouth 401/849-2162

Jamestown Golf Course ($15/$16) 3,343 yds. (69.9/110)
245 Conanicut Ave.
Jamestown 401/423-9930

Midville Country Club ($19/$22) 2,768 yds. (68.2/114)
100 Lombardi Lane
West Warwick 401/828-9215

Montaup Country Club ($29/$29) 6,236 yds. (71.2/123)
500 Anthony Rd.
Portsmouth 401/683-9882

North Kingston Municipal ($20/$22) 5,848 yds. (68.3/116)
Quonset Pt. Access Rd.
N. Kingston 401/294-4051

Richmond Country Club ($24/$29) 5,827 yds. (68.5/114)
Switch Rd.
Richmond 401/364-9200

Triggs Memorial Golf Course ($19/$24) 6,394 yds. (71.9/125)
1533 Chalkstone Ave.
Providence 401/272-4653

Winnapaug Country Club ($22/$28) 5,914 yds. (67.9/111)
184 Shore Rd.
Westerly 401/596-1237

Woodland Greens Golf Course ($16.50/$18.50) 5,744 yds.
(68.5/112)
655 Old Baptist Rd.
N. Kingston 401/294-2872

# SOUTH CAROLINA

*Local Knowledge*

Myrtle Beach is a phenomenon, golf served up with a dollop of fat Elvis. Beyond the glitz, the pancake houses offering free tees, and the ubiquitous neon-lit Wings and Eagle stores, with twenty-five-cent sunglasses and hermit crabs, one finds the quality of golf on the Grand Strand a pleasant surprise. It's hard to go wrong wherever you play. Few places are pitched as aggressively or successfully to golfers on a budget. And the beach in Myrtle Beach, somewhat lost in the avalanche of promotion, is very nice indeed—and free.

October, say venerable members of The Dunes Club (one of only a handful of private clubs in Myrtle Beach), is the best time of year to come down. One thing no one tells you: Walking is out for all intents; cart congestion can be analogous to the truly impressive traffic on local roads. Slow play is a problem. But it's hard to get too sore at a town that tries so very hard to please, a place where, God love 'em, the job center has a free practice pitching green on the front lawn, complete with bunker.

Whatever you do, for crying out loud, don't buy the golf maps on sale at the airport and elsewhere. Golf Holiday puts out an arsenal of detailed free guides and brochures. In a town where restaurants hand out complimentary balls with each adult meal (with coupon, not valid with other discounts or promotions), where the golf stores are measured in thousands of square feet, where the stop & gas sells "experienced balls" next to the beef jerky, it's not as if there's no one to ask. What I'm waiting for is the day when the golf ball shops go twenty-four hours. If you'd rather not lug around the Golf Holiday catalog, ask for "Tee Up," a small but informative brochure that lists every course's phone number and has a detailed course locator map on the back cover. (800/445-4653).

The local paper, *The Sun News,* puts out a monthly golf tabloid. It's $9 for twelve issues (800/568-1800). *Golfer's Guide* is a handy quarterly magazine to the area. There's also one for Hilton Head (800/864-6101). For a promotional resort golf planner for Hilton Head, call the Chamber of Commerce (800/523-3373).

When pressed for lesser-known courses outside Myrtle Beach, Dr. Donald J. Millus, "coach" of Carolina University, suggested Conway Golf and Country Club in nearby Conway, "a pretty little course that plays to very tight greens, a real jewel" is how he put it. Golf is alleged to be free here one day a year, although no one would tell me what day that was. Don also likes Rolling Hills in Aynor, under $30 most of the year, including cart.

Harold Martin, a past president of the Golf Writers Association of America, who lives in Columbia, says Hidden Valley in Gaston, is a "good layout, well worth anybody's time." At about $15 for a cart and green fee, heck, yeah. Harold also mentions Northwoods and, if you're headed along I-20, Coopers Creek.

Patriots Point, not far from Charleston in Mount Pleasant, has hosted sectional qualifying for the national publinks. So has Charleston's muny, very open and not too long. Verdae Greens in Greenville has bent-grass greens. The Nike Tour stops here now for the Greater Greenville Classic. You can walk during the week for under $25.

South Carolina has two resort state park courses. Hickory Knob, near the Georgia border, winds its way around Strom Thurmond Lake, where bass, crappie, catfish, and yellow perch are not unknown. Water comes into play on nine holes. There's a range, bent-grass greens, and the trimmings of an upscale park. Cheraw State Park, on Lake Juniper, cuts in and out of a dense pine forest.

Nine holes of a Donald Ross course, Dogwood Hills, just south of Walterboro, are open to the public Monday, Tuesday, Thursday, and Friday. The front side at Fort Mill was designed by Ross, built originally for Spring Maid in 1947. And nine holes at the Lancaster Golf Club in Lancaster are believed to have been designed by Ross in the early 1930s.

South Carolina puts out an exceptional annual golf guide

(800/569-2139, 803/252-2327). Courses are broken down by region and, lo and behold, prices are included with and without a cart.

Additional golf brochures are available for Sumter (800/688-4748), Florence (800/325-9005 or 803/669-0950), Greenville (800/849-IRON or 803/233-2690), Beaufort (803/524-3163), and Santee (800/227-8510 or 803/854-2131). State tourism information is available from 800/346-3634.

### Discount Cards

American Lung Association of South Carolina. 130 courses, many multiple plays. 803/779-5864. $40.
Golf Links Association of the Carolinas. Over 175 rounds, begin anytime. 800/GLA-1818. $22.

### Shopping

The Outlet Park at Waccamaw, just north of Myrtle Beach, has Eddie Bauer, Izod, J Crew, Duck Head, and dozens of others. Reebok is at Low Country Factory Village on Highway 278 in Bluffton.

## FINDING THE GREEN IN SOUTH CAROLINA

Charleston Municipal Golf Course ($9/$11) 6,161 yds. (69.1/110)
2110 Maybank Hwy.
Charleston 803/795-6517

Cheraw State Park Golf Course ($12/$14) 6,130 yds. (70.8/120)
Hwy. 52 South
Cheraw 800/868-9630

Conway Golf and Country Club ($18/$22) 9 holes/6,000 yds.
(67.3/110)
400 Country Club Dr.
Conway 803/365-3621

Coopers Creek ($17/$17) 6,039 yds. (68.4/115)
700 Wagner Hwy.
Pelion 803/894-3666

Dogwood Hills Country Club ($10/$10) 3,000 yds. (68.0/110)
Hwy. 17A
Walterboro 803/538-2731

Fort Mill Golf Club ($17/$20) 6,400 yds. (70.3/118)
101 Country Club Dr.
Fort Mill 803/547-2044

Hickory Knob Golf Course ($12/$16) 5,950 yds. (67.8/113)
Hickory Knob State Resort Park
Hwy. 378
McCormick 803/391-2450

Hidden Valley Country Club ($10/$20) 6,149 yds. (69.4/115)
147 Excalibur Ct.
Gaston 803/794-8087

Lancaster Golf Club ($17/$20) 6,140 yds. (68.6/115)
Airport Rd.
Lancaster 803/285-5239

Northwoods Golf Course ($18/$25) 6,485 yds. (70.4/118)
201 Powell Rd.
Columbia 803/786-9242

Patriots Point Links ($18/$22) 6,274 yds. (70.1/118)
100 Clubhouse Dr.
Mount Pleasant 803/881-0042

Rolling Hills Country Club ($27/$27*) 6,144 yds. (69.0/115)
1790 Hwy. 501
Aynor 803/358-0501

Verdae Greens Golf Course ($20/—) 6,250 yds. (69.1/118)
650 Verdae Blvd.
Greenville 803/676-1500

*Twilight

# SOUTH DAKOTA

### Local Knowledge

Meadowbrook Municipal in Rapid City hosted the Women's Amateur
Public Links Championship in 1984. Elmwood in Sioux Falls was the
sectional qualifying site for the men in 1994. Both come highly recommended from a well-placed source. *Golf Digest* awarded
Meadowbrook four stars in its *Places to Play 1994–95* guide, saying
it was good enough to plan your vacation around. (Well, that and
Wall Drug, maybe.)

Other public courses perennially used for South Dakota Golf
Association events are Willow Run (Sioux Falls), Lakeview (Mitchell),
Hillcrest (Yankton), Moccasin Creek (Rapid City), Hillview (Pierre),
and Brookings (Brookings). Sioux Falls has a new muny, Prairie
Green, with water in play on eight holes.

With the state tourism vacation guide, ask for the sheet of
statewide course information and the year's South Dakota Golf
Association tournament calendar (800/732-5682).

### Discount Card

See "Stalking the Elusive Deep Discount" in Finding the Green introduction.

### Shopping

"What has Wall Drug got?" ask the brains behind *Roadside America*
(surely the definitive road-trip atlas). "Well, for one thing, it's the
only place within a hundred miles that's 'got' anything." Good point.
Anyway, they've got your snake ashtrays, stuffed jackalopes, postcards, etc., etc., all you need for your next garage sale.

## FINDING THE GREEN IN SOUTH DAKOTA

**Brookings Country Club ($19/$25) 6,244 yds. (68.8/125)**
**Brookings 605/693-4315**

Elmwood Public Golf Course ($11/$13) 27 holes
East/West Course: 6,242 yds. (69.5/116)
North/West Course: 6,412 yds. (70.9/126)
North/East Course: 6,326 yds. (69.8/117)
2604 W. Russell St.
Sioux Falls 605/339-7233

Hillcrest Golf & Country Club ($25/$29) 6,530 yds. (70.6/127)
2206 Mulberry
Yankton 605/665-4621

Hillsview Golf Course ($14.50/$14.50) 6,372 yds. (69.4/118)
4201 SD Hwy. 34
Pierre 605/224-6191

Lakeview Municipal Golf Course ($13/$13) 6,280 yds. (69.5/119)
3300 N. Ohlman St.
Mitchell 605/996-1424

Meadowbrook Municipal Golf Course ($18/$20) 6,520 yds. (70.7/133)
3625 Jackson Blvd.
Rapid City 605/394-4191

Moccasin Creek Country Club ($25/$25) 6,602 yds. (70.1/133)
Aberdeen 605/226-0989

Prairie Green Municipal Golf Course ($na/$na) 6,600 yds. (na/na)
E. 69th St. 605/339-6076 or 605/339-7233
Sioux Falls

Willow Run Golf Course ($14.25/$16.75) 6,045 yds. (69.2/123)
Sioux Falls 605/335-5900

# TENNESSEE

*Local Knowledge*

*Nashville Scene* readers have voted Hermitage Golf Course the best in town several years running. It obviously agrees with the LPGA. Many sizzling scores have been shot during the Sara Lee Classic. Except for ads over the urinals, a minor perturbance, this is a country club masquerading as a public course.

A beautiful facility, the course is demanding, with thought-provoking carries (and four tees). No walking is allowed on weekends (after daylight savings). Those who ride do not leave the cart paths, at no time, no how. Ping Eye 2 clones and Spalding woods can be rented for $15. Contrary to every other course I know, the Hermitage has red flags that indicate the pin is in the back of the green, not the front. The Tennessee PGA holds its championship here, as do lots of charity events, from the Shriners to the Floyd Cramer Invitational. No walking on weekends. The yardage book *The Battle Manual,* by George Lewis, who does them for the pro circuit, is $4.95. He draws in fishies and frogmen to point out where the wet stuff is and includes other helpful tips J.I.C.Y.F.U. ("Just In Case You . . .").

*Golfer's Tee Times,* the area's free monthly tabloid, comes out March to December. Best feature: Etonic and Cobra rep Arnie Cunningham's chatty PGA Tour insider's column.

Nashville has seven munys. Two Rivers, near the entrance to Opryland, is white bread muny golf. Both Two Rivers and Harpeth Hills share sectional publinx qualifying. *GTT* publisher Joey Smith describes Harpeth Hills as "a beautiful old course, real nice," with tight fairways and lots of character. He also suggests Nashboro Village. The city championship is contested over all the munys.

Tennessee has excellent state park courses, eight of them. The official travel guide includes bare-bones course listings. Get the state park golf guide instead. It reprints scorecards, has color photos of the courses, and mentions maintenance updates and other pertinent details (800/836-6200).

Fall Creek Falls is in a wonderful area that only normally gets twenty days over ninety degrees. (The greens did get fried several years ago during a freak heat spell, but they should be back.) The concept of the resort state park does verge on the absurd here. There's a "motor nature trail," for instance. Talk about your oxymorons. But the falls are truly spectacular, and the golf is very nice indeed with bunkers and big 'uns all the way around. As many as 250 rounds are recorded on the weekends in season. The course is also home to a very popular summer junior golf camp.

T. O. Fuller State Park, in Memphis, was built by the only black company in the Civilian Conservation Corps, the 490th. The course was originally developed as Shelby Bluffs State Park for Negroes, just north of Boxtown, near Highway 61. It's next door to the Chuckalissa Indian Museum. Readers of *The Commercial Appeal* have plenty to say about the number one handicapped hole, a nasty par three of 196 yards. The approach on "Eagle's Nest" is narrow and guarded by a bunker. Anything long falls off the table into a valley. Wrote one reader:

> I've played golf 41 years, been a member of nine country clubs and played hundreds of courses. This is the toughest par 3 in the world. I haven't played at Fuller in at least 20 years, but I'll never forget that hole.

At "Hooker's Hell," hit it too good and you'll have a shot at knee level 250 yards from the green. Bowl-shaped fairways curl upward like ski slopes, and small greens make the course challenging and engaging.

Before Cary Middlecoff made good, and still today, Overton Park is where Memphis golfers learn to play. Galloway is flat and easy to walk. Davy Crockett, albeit in a deteriorating neighborhood, is on a beautiful piece of property. David Field, an active freelance writer, describes it "as one of the prettiest golf courses I've ever played." The hilly terrain tends to keep play down. "You can drive over there any weekend and tee off," Dave says. It's twenty minutes from the Peabody Hotel. Edmund Orgill may not have as spectacular a layout, but it enjoys a reputation as one of the best-conditioned courses in the area.

Fox Meadows, a former country club, Audubon, and Galloway are venues for the City of Memphis Publinks Championship. Stonebridge and Audubon have hosted public links and U.S. Open qualifying. A brochure to Memphis-area courses with a map and cursory information is available at the visitor center. The freebie tabloid *Mid South*

*Golfer* has your coupons and Memphis local knowledge (901/452-1496).

In Knoxville, *On the Green* magazine correspondent Walter Galyon recommends Willow Creek, where the annual Nike Knoxville Open is played, Three Ridges ("one of the most . . . if not the most . . . popular course in the area"), and Whittle Springs, the oldest and shortest in Knoxville and easy to walk.

Somewhat off the beaten path, Graysburg Hills in Chuckey was designed by Rees Jones. It's a family-owned operation, Walter says, "comfortable and friendly." In Chattanooga, Moccasin Bend holds publinx qualifying. The University of the South has a course in Sewanee.

## Discount Cards

American Cancer Society Golf Card. One round at about 100 courses, January 1–December 31. 901/382-9500. $35.
Tennessee PGA PassKey. One free weekday round at 60 courses, January 1–December 31. 615/790-7600. $39.98.

## Shopping

Look for outlets in Pigeon Forge (Tanger); Sevierville (Five Oaks), and Chattanooga (Warehouse Row). Factory Stores of America are in Blountville, Crossville, and Union City.

The club-making Dargie family of St. Andrews, Scotland, has been at it since 1908. They opened a store in Memphis in 1924. They're still there at 1749 Cherokee Blvd. (901/744-3133).

## FINDING THE GREEN IN TENNESSEE

**Audubon Golf Course ($9/$11) 6,075 yds. (68.9/108)**
4160 Park Ave.
Memphis 901/683-6941

**Brainerd Golf Course ($11/$13) 6,112 yds. (68.1/116)**
5203 Old Mission Rd.
Chattanooga 615/855-2692

Buford Ellington Golf Course ($16/$16) 6,604 yds. (71.2/122)
Henry Horton State Park
4358 Nashville Hwy.
Chapel Hill 615/364-2319

Davy Crockett Golf Course ($8/$10) 6,024 yds. (na/na)
4380 Rangeline Rd.
Memphis 901/358-3375

Edmund Orgill Golf Course ($12.50/$13.50) 5,814 yds. (66.8/109)
9080 Bethuel Rd.
Millington 901/872-3610

Fall Creek Falls State Park ($16/$16) 6,391 yds. (70.8/121)
State Hwy. 30
Pikeville 615/881-5706

Fox Meadows Golf Course ($11/$12) 6,275 yds. (68.7/105)
3064 Clarke Rd.
Memphis 901/362-0232

Frank G. Clement Golf Course ($16/$16) 6,091 yds. (69.3/121)
Montgomery Bell State Park
800 Hotel Ave.
Burns 615/797-2578

Galloway Golf Course ($11/$12) 5,844 yds. (67.4/109)
3815 Walnut Grove Rd.
Memphis 901/685-7805

Graysburg Hills Golf Course ($18/$21) 27 holes
Fodderstack/Knobs Course: 6,341 yds. (69.6/119)
Fodderstack/Chimneytop Course: 6,234 yds. (na/na)
Knobs/Chimneytop Course: 6,319 yds. (na/na)
Hwy. 93
Chuckey 615/234-8061

Harpeth Hills Municipal ($14/$14) 6,481 yds. (71.2/122)
2424 Old Hickory Blvd.
Nashville 615/862-8493

Hermitage Golf Course ($14.50/$17*) 6,483 yds. (70.8/119)
3939 Old Hickory Blvd.
Nashville 615/847-4001

Moccasin Bend Golf Club ($12/$14) 6,086 yds. (68.0/107)
381 Moccasin Bend Rd.
Chattanooga 615/267-3585

Nashboro Village Golf Club ($5/$5*) 6,400 yds. (71.6/129)
2250 Murfreesboro Rd.
Nashville 615/367-2311

Old Stone Fort State Park Course ($8/$16) 3,077 yds. (68.7/112)
Country Club Dr.
Manchester 615/723-5075

Overton Park Golf Course ($8/$10) 2,087 yds. (na/na)
2080 Poplar Ave.
Memphis 901/725-9905

Paris Landing State Park Golf Course ($16/$16) 6,407 yds. (70.1/124)
US 79 and Rte. 1
Buchanan 901/644-1332

Sewanee Golf & Tennis Club ($10/$15) 9 holes/6,136 yds.
(70.4/122)
University of the South
Hwy. 64
Sewanee 615/598-1104

Stonebridge Golf Course ($18/$30) 6,249 yds. (70.7/122)
3049 Davies Plantation Rd. South
Memphis 901/382-1886

Three Ridges Golf Course ($15/$18.50) 6,000 yds. (69.3/119)
Wise Springs Rd.
Knoxville 615/687-4797

T.O. Fuller State Park Golf Course ($8/$12) 5,986 yds. (71.0/117)
Mitchell Rd.
Memphis 901/543-7771

*Twilight

Two Rivers Golf Course ($14/$14) 6,230 yds. (69.8/116)
3140 McGavock Pike
Donelsen 615/889-2675

Warriors Path State Park Golf Course ($14/$16) 6,078 yds.
(68.8/113)
Fall Creek Rd.
Kingsport 615/323-4990

Whittle Springs Golf Course ($9.75/$12) 5,600 yds. (66.4/101)
3113 Valley View Rd.
Knoxville 615/525-1022

Willow Creek Golf Course ($22/$28) 6,500 yds. (71.0/121)
12003 Kingston Pike
Knoxville 615/675-0100

Winfield Dunn Golf Course ($16/$16) 6,284 yds. (69.3/na)
Pickwick Landing State Park
Hwy. 57
Pickwick Dam 901/689-3149

# TEXAS

*Local Knowledge*

Why has Texas nurtured so many great golfers? My own preference
is to side with those who believe the answer is blowing in the wind.
With it, against it, under it and around it, dealing with all its conse-
quences, several generations attest that if you can play well in Texas
you can play well anywhere.

For golf information in Houston, look for a copy of *Golf Houston*
magazine. From anywhere, try its fantastic fax service. Dial in the
number 713/591-2223, then a three-digit number (999 gets you the
directory), and you can receive daily coupon specials (would you
believe three pages' worth?), public or resort course listings and
directions, and more. You receive only what you request.

*Golf Houston* publisher Harry Phillips offers to personally assist golfers in finding the right fit. He'll arrange tee times, help with hotels, even get you onto courses you'd otherwise not be able to play. Did I mention the service is free?

Kevin Newberry's "Golf Notebook" appears in Sunday and Tuesday's *Houston Post*. Charlie Epps teaches golf on the radio during "Sports Beat" on KTRH–740 AM, Friday evenings from seven to eight. He's also got a TV show Sunday mornings on Channel 39. Ed Sehl hosts a golf show on KSEV–700 AM, Sunday mornings from eight to nine.

*Shell's Golf Guide to Greater Houston* ($14.95) devotes nearly five hundred pages to its subject. The almanac reprints scorecards with color reproductions of each hole and full-page reviews of one hundred courses. There are also coupons, stats, history, instruction, and a new edition covering Austin and San Antonio. To order: Shell, P.O. Box 572274, Houston, TX 77257.

*Great Texas Golf* ($14.95) by Pat Seelig, is the first updated statewide course guide in years. It also offers a passel of coupons and gets specific about prices.

*Golf Courses of Texas* ($4.95) is a magazine guide with detailed course listings, prices, features, and attractive graphics. The free tabloid *Par Fore* covers Dallas and Fort Worth. Along with tips from the inventive John Rhodes (see "1,001 uses for Home and Golf Swing" in Saving the Green), there's also lots of coupons and area news.

Associate editor Tom Willhoite prefers the West Course at Tennison Park and also suggests Squaw Valley in Glen Rose, about thirty to forty minutes south of Fort Worth. Tom commends the owners for having had the good sense to give the course a chance to grow in before opening in 1992. The two nines are like playing two different courses, he says.

Some other suggestions from Tom in the metroplex: Hank Haney's Golf Ranch (McKinney), Plantation (Frisco), Sleepy Hollow (Dallas), Grapevine (Grapevine), Riverside (Arlington), and Sugar Tree (Dennis). *Par Fore* comes out the first week of each month (817/654-2544), free at courses.

The *Fort Worth Star-Telegram*'s monthly special section, "Fairway Golfer's Guide," is also free. *Gulf Coast Golfer* is a statewide tabloid in two regional editions. For a pocket-sized guide to amateur tournaments and courses within a two-hour radius of the metroplex, look for a copy of *The North Texas Sandbagger*. The quarterly is free, if you can find it; a year's subscription is $9.95 (817/543-9102).

*Hispanic Golfer Magazine* focuses on getting exposure for top young golfers and raising scholarship money and awareness. It also covers the pro circuit. Subscriptions are $19.95 for 12 issues. Plans are in the works to expand the horizons beyond Texas (713/941-7261). Fore Better Golf has relatively recent maps covering Dallas and Houston, $4 by mail (708/893-8672).

Wednesday is golf day in the *The Dallas Morning News.* There are complete Tour stats, Jack Nicklaus's comic strip, and features on the pros and the Texas amateur scene. The newspaper's statewide annual golf tabloid pulls together a distinguished panel of judges.

Tennison Park in Dallas, Hermann Park in Houston, and Firewheel in Garland perennially flip-flop top honors for best municipal course. They're joined by a strong supporting cast of munys, daily-fees, and state parks.

Tennison Park, Lee Trevino wrote, "had a tremendous influence on my play, and my life. It always will be one of my favorite courses." He called the East Course "the hardest 'easy' course I ever played."

First-leg qualifying for the PGA Tour and the Texas State Open have repeatedly been held at Firewheel's Old Course. Hermann Park hosted the Houston Open for years, spawning a succession of golf legends. Two north Texas caddies who did pretty well themselves started out at Glen Garden in Fort Worth, a private course which accepts limited public play. Call for openings. Ben Hogan and Byron Nelson battled for the caddy championship as boys (Nelson won in a play-off).

Cedar Crest, a muny in the Oakcliff section of Dallas, hosted the PGA Championship in 1927. Young Byron followed the favorite around the Tillinghast course that year. In a story to warm the hearts of Hollywood, he proffered his school cap to his hero, Walter Hagen, who was having trouble battling the glare. Hagen's eventual triumph had to be savored in private. Eager to avoid some impatient bill collectors, he pocketed the take in the clubhouse basement and vamoosed. Cedar Crest hosted the 1954 Amateur Public Links Championship. City publinx events are still contested here.

Another Tillinghast muny is Brackenridge Park in San Antonio. The site of the first PGA Tour event in 1922, the cavernous Tudor-style clubhouse is a treasure trove of golfing lore. There's the megaphone that called the players to the tee at that first tournament and withered columns about record rounds, including Jug McSpaden's fifty-nine. My favorite is the large oil painting of Queenie the dog, who used to hang around the first tee. Parallel fairways require some attentiveness, but the course still has much to commend it. Cedar Creek and Olmos Basin host sectional publinks qualifying in San Antone.

The Masters course at Bear Creek in Houston hosted the 1981 Amateur Public Links Championship. It's where PGA Tour player Jodie Mudd won his second consecutive publinks title. It's under $30 during the week; there are also two other courses, the Presidents course, and the Challenger. Southwyck in Pearland is the University of Houston's home course.

Jimmy Clay Municipal in Austin defines a well-managed muny. Staff is conscientious about pace of play. The course is longish but not bearish, and offers good practice facilities. A second course, Kizer, is positioned as an upper-niche muny, open with lots of water. Lion's Municipal hosts the city championship and an astonishing number of tournaments. It also gets the lion's share of local play.

Although considerably altered, Riverside was the Austin Country Club when sprouts named Kite and Crenshaw were learning the ropes. It still has some special holes. The original nine from the first Austin Country Club, where Harvey Penick cut his teeth, is Hancock Municipal. In sight of the University of Texas, it's one of several courses that claim to be the state's oldest (1899).

Del Lemon travels central Texas's golf byways for the *Austin American-Statesman*. He takes a particular delight in finding small-town gems that dot the scenic hill country. He loves the two town courses in Seguin, about an hour's drive from Austin: Max Starcke Park and Chaparral Country Club.

Bastrop State Park, a Civilian Conservation Corps project in an area known as the Lost Pines, is part of an enjoyable network of state park courses. Find them in Inks Lake, Lubbock (MacKenzie), San Felipe (Stephen F. Austin), and Lockhart.

Other recent pearls from *The Dallas Morning News*'s Best 25 Municipal Courses:

Indian Creek's Creek Course, Carrollton
Ross Rogers East Course, Amarillo
Hogan Park, Midland

In El Paso, Ascarate and Painted Dunes host qualifying for the national publinks. There are also a slew of college courses at Texas

*The "Arthritis Special" at the Texas Golf Hall of Fame.*

A&M in College Station, Texas Woman's University in Denton, Temple Junior College in Temple, Western Texas College in Snyder, and San Jacinto College in Pasadena.

The Texas Golf Hall of Fame, at The Woodlands, has a growing collection of fun state-related memorabilia. A favorite is the "Arthritis Special," a prehistoric golf cart (1948, actually) that features a partially upholstered cast-iron park bench. The museum is open every day, 10 A.M. to 3 P.M. (713/364-7270).

The Babe Zaharias Museum in Beaumont honors one of sport's great personalities. There's footage of Babe playing golf. Her Olympic and AAU medals are also on display. The museum is open every day but Christmas, 9 A.M. to 5 P.M. (409/833-4622).

UST, a leading shaft maker in Dallas, is one of the diminishing number of manufacturers that offers a factory tour (800/621-6728 or 214/869-1993).

### Discount Cards:

American Cancer Society Texas Golf Card. Free green fees at over 135 courses (300 rounds) calendar year. 800/227-2345. $25.

American Lung Association Golf Privilege Card. Free green fees and
specials at over 122 courses. 800/252-5864. $35.

Junior Achievement Golf Lover's Card. One free round at seven central Texas courses, two calendar years. 512/837-5252. $35.

Southern Texas PGA Golf Pass. Discounted green fees at ninety-six
courses, calendar year. 713/363-0511. $59.95.

Texas Society to Prevent Blindness Golf Fore Sight Card. One free
round at twenty courses in central Texas, July 1– June 30. 512/338-
9668. $35.

## *Shopping*

There are outlets in San Marcos, Conroe, and Hillsboro. An Ashworth
outlet is in a growing complex in San Marcos (512/396-8366). And
how many golfers have a mall named after them? In El Paso, just take
the Lee Trevino Drive exit off I-10 West.

GolfSmith International, north of Austin off I-35, is a revelation if
you've never been in a golf superstore before. It offers a factory tour
and has a range and putting green to test-drive clubs (512/837-4810).
Empowered Women's Golf, a golf shop for women, has a store at
5344 Beltline Rd. in Dallas, and another in the works (214/233-8807).

## FINDING THE GREEN IN TEXAS

**Ascarate Park Golf Course ($8/$10) 6,185 yds. (67.7/110)**
6900 Delta Dr.
El Paso 915/772-7381

**Bear Creek Golf World 36 holes**
Masters Course: ($27/—) 6,188 yds. (68.9/123)
Presidents Course: ($17/$20) 6,115 yds. (67.6/107)
Challenger Course: ($17/$20) 4,907 yds. (62.5/99)
16001 Clay Rd.
Houston 713/859-8188

**Brackenridge Park Golf Course ($14/$16) 5,767 yds. (66.0/118)**
2315 Avenue B
San Antonio 210/226-5612

Cedar Creek Golf Course ($18/$20) 6,650 yds. (66.5/125)
8250 Vista Colina
San Antonio 210/695-5050

Cedar Crest Park Golf Club ($11/$14) 6,140 yds. (69.2/116)
1800 Southerland
Dallas 214/670-7615

Chaparral Country Club ($14/$28) 6,000 yds. (70.5/115)
300 Chaparral
Seguin 210/379-6314

Firewheel Golf Park ($16/$24)
Old Course: 6,617 yds. (71.6/125)
Lakes Course: 6,116 yds. (69.5/119)
600 W. Blackburn Rd.
Garland 214/205-2795

Glen Garden Golf & Country Club ($20/—) 6,100 yds. (69.4/113)
2916 Glen Garden Dr.
Fort Worth 817/535-7582

Grapevine Golf Course ($13/$15) 6,400 yds. (69.8/113)
3800 Fairway Dr.
Grapevine 817/481-0421

Hancock Municipal Golf Course ($6/$7) 2,427 yds. (na/na)
811 E. 41st St.
Austin 512/453-0276

Hank Haney's Golf Ranch ($7/$10) 3,000 yds. (na/na)
4101 Custer Rd.
McKinney 214/542-8800

Hermann Park Golf Course ($13/$16) 5,600 yds. (66.0/100)
6201 Golf Course Dr.
Houston 713/526-0077

Hogan Park Golf Course ($8.50/$13) 27 holes
Holes 1–18: 6,320 yds. (67.5/108)
Holes 10–27: 6,250 yds. (68.4/108)
Holes 19-9: 6,230 yds. (68.0/107)
3600 N. Fairground
Midland 915/685-7360

Indian Creek Golf Course 36 holes
Creek Course: ($12/$18) 6,094 yds. (70.9/116)
Lakes Course: ($15/$21) 6,102 yds. (70.3/118)
1650 W. Frankfurt
Carrollton 214/492-3620

Inks Lake State Park ($8/$10) 2,700 yds. (na/na)
Park Rd. 4 (3 miles south of Rte. 29)
Inks Lake 512/793-2859

Jimmy Clay Municipal Golf Course ($11/$12.50) 6,368 yds.
(69.8/119)
5400 Jimmy Clay Dr.
Austin 512/444-0999

Lion's Municipal Golf Course ($11/$12) 5,642 yds. (67.2/115)
2901 Enfield Rd.
Austin 512/477-6963

Lockhart State Park Course ($7/$8) 9 holes/5,978 yds. (70.0/110)
Hwy. 20 West
Lockhart 512/398-3479

Lost Pines Golf Course ($11/$15) 3,122 yds. (69.9/114)
Bastrop State Park
State Park Rd. 1
Bastrop 512/321-2327

Mackenzie State Park Golf Course ($9/$12) 36 holes
Meadowbrook Course: 6,100 yds. (69.0/117)
Squirrel Hollow Course: 5,900 yds. (71.0/113)
I-27 and 4th St.
Lubbock 806/767-2455

Max Starcke Park Golf Course ($9/$11) 6,400 yds. (70.2/112)
1400 S. Guadalupe St.
Seguin 210/401-2490

Olmos Basin Golf Course ($14/$16) 6,100 yds. (71.0/118)
7022 N. McCullough
San Antonio 210/826-4041

Painted Dunes Desert Golf Course ($13/$16) 6,162 yds. (70.5/129)
12000 McCombs Rd.
El Paso 915/821-2122

Plantation Resort Golf Course ($25/—*) 5,945 yds. (68.1/117)
4701 Plantation Ln.
Frisco 214/335-4653

Riverside Golf Course ($12/$15) 6,121 yds. (68.3/115)
1020 Grove Blvd.
Austin 512/389-1070

Riverside Golf Course ($27/—*) 6,400 yds. (68.4/119)
3000 Riverside Pkwy.
Grand Prairie 817/640-7800

Ross Rogers Golf Course ($8/$10)
East Course: 6,200 yds. (69.2/109)
722 NW 24th St.
Amarillo 806/378-3086

Roy Kizer Municipal Golf Course ($16/$21) 6,412 yds. (na/na)
5400 Jimmy Clay Dr.
Austin 512/444-0999

San Jacinto College Course ($4/$6) 2,638 yds. (na/na)
8060 Spencer Hwy.
Pasadena 713/476-1880

Sherrill Park Municipal Golf Course ($14/$17) 36 holes
Course One: 6,511 yds. (72.0/121)
Course Two: 5,843 yds. (66.0/113)
2001 E. Lookout Dr.
Richardson 214/234-1416

Sleepy Hollow Golf Course ($16/$27)
River Course: 6,450 yds. (70.7/118)
4747 S. Loop 12
Dallas 214/371-3433

*Twilight

Southwyck Golf Course ($19/$29) 6,010 yds. (69.4/116)
University of Houston
2901 Clubhouse Dr.
Pearland 713/436-9999

Squaw Valley Golf Course ($22/$26*) 6,284 yds. (69.6/119)
Hwy. County Rd. 51 45B
Glen Rose 800/831-8259 or 817/897-7956

Stephen F. Austin State Park ($11/$18) 5,500 yds. (66.7/114)
Park Rd. 38
San Felipe 409/885-2811

Sugar Tree Golf Course ($15/$19) 5,826 yds. (69.8/126)
Hwy. 1189
Dennis 817/441-8643

Temple Junior College Golf Course ($5/$6) 2,763 yds. (na/na)
S. 1st St.
Temple 817/773-0888

Tennison Park Golf Course ($11/$14)
East Course: 6,404 yds. (70.8/113)
3501 Samuel Blvd.
Dallas 214/670-1402

Texas A&M Golf Course ($13/$16) 6,020 yds. (68.5/118)
Bizzell St.
College Station 409/845-1723

Texas Woman's University Golf Course ($9/$11) 5,675 yds.
(67.0/na)
Clubhouse Dr.
Denton 817/898-3163

Western Texas College Golf Course ($8/$13) 2,754 yds. (66.2/na)
S. College Ave.
Snyder 915/573-9291

*Twilight

# UTAH

*Local Knowledge*

An anomaly compared to the rest of the country, the overwhelming majority of courses in the state of Utah are government-owned: public, well maintained, subsidized by tax dollars. Green fees are kept artificially low. Jeff Waters, a frequent contributor to *Utah Fairways,* the state golf association's official magazine, sums up the good news: "Outside of Park City and Saint George, which are destination areas, you can play—with a cart—for under $30 on virtually every course in the state." Actually, you can even play affordably in Park City, and the muny comes highly recommended.

Kurt Kragthorpe, who writes the "Golfing" column for the Salt Lake City *Tribune,* says simply: "This is a great public golf state."

The other important thing to keep in mind about Utah golf is the concentration of the majority of courses between Provo and Ogden.

In and around Salt Lake City, Kurt recommends Valley View, about twenty-five minutes away, in Layton. It's got "real spectacular views of the Great Salt Lake" and lots of elevation changes with a good variety of holes. He also likes the "links-style" Wingpointe, an Arthur Hills course, right in town. The "old staple" of Salt Lake City golf is Bonneville. Kurt calls it "a classic old course" with "great, great greens." The layout may be vanilla, but the setting and condition of the course commend it.

The Utah Golf Association's annual *Book of Golf* is another bargain, packed with useful information: a detailed course directory, maps, index, tee-time guidelines, and phone numbers. There are also instate tournament listings for the USGA, UGA, and Utah PGA Section events, a favored tip sheet to divining better courses. It's a great resource, and the price is right. Yup, it's free (801/532-7421).

A smattering of courses used for events of the aforementioned organizations are Homestead in Midway, Tri-City in American Fork, Mount Ogden in Ogden, Davis Park in Kaysville, Eagle Mountain in Brigham City, Wolf Creek in Eden, and East Bay in Provo. Davis Park and Glendale in Salt Lake City have hosted sectional USGA publinks qualifying. Green Spring in Washington was once tabbed as a Top 5 *Golf Digest* Best New Course.

Utah has three state park courses. Wasatch Mountain has twenty-seven holes up in the mountains, not far from Park City. Palisade, next to the seventy-acre Palisade Reservoir, draws golfers, swimmers, anglers, and nonmotorized boaters. Jordan River is in Salt Lake City, a nine-hole, par-three course. The University of Utah also has nine holes.

For package and course information on seven courses in the Saint George region, call 800/869-6635. For a copy of *Utah Fairways,* call 801/299-8421.

## Discount Card

See "Stalking the Elusive Deep Discount" in Finding the Green introduction.

## Shopping

Component club maker UT Golf has a store in Salt Lake City, its headquarters (2346 W. 1500 South, 801/975-0096). Factory Stores of Park City has Nike, Brooks Brothers, Geoffrey Beene, and Great Outdoor Clothing (801/645-7078). Factory Stores of America, south of Salt Lake City on I-15, has twenty stores (801/572-6440); Zion Factory Outlet in Saint George has Izod, Polo/Ralph Lauren, Bugle Boy (801/674-9800).

## FINDING THE GREEN IN UTAH

**Bonneville Golf Course ($15/$17) 6,431 yds. (69.0/116)**
954 Connor St.
Salt Lake City 801/583-9513

**Davis Park Golf Course ($15/$15) 5,922 yds. (67.4/112)**
1074 E. Nichols Rd.
Kaysville 801/544-0401

**Eagle Mountain Golf Course ($15/$15) 5,546 yds. (65.1/103)**
760 E. 700 South
Brigham City 801/723-3212

**East Bay Golf Course ($13/$15) 6,400 yds. (66.0/108)**
160 E. Bay Blvd.
Provo 801/379-6612

Glendale Golf Course ($15/$16) 6,470 yds. (69.3/114)
1560 W. 2100 South
Salt Lake City 801/974-2403

Green Spring Golf Course ($27.50/$27.50) 6,293 yds. (69.3/118)
588 N. Green Spring Dr.
Washington 801/673-7888

Homestead Golf Course ($15/$20*) 6,159 yds. (68.8/122)
700 N. Homestead Dr.
Midway 800/327-7220 or 801/654-1102

Jordan River Golf Course ($5/$5) 9 holes/1,200 yds. (na/na)
1200 N. Redwood Rd.
Salt Lake City 801/533-4527

Mount Ogden Golf Course ($15/$15) 5,888 yds. (67.5/115)
3000 Taylor Ave.
Ogden 801/629-8700

Palisade State Park Course ($13/$13) 9 holes/6,068 yds. (66.9/107)
Palisade State Park
Manti 801-835-4653

Park City Golf Course ($26/$26) 6,400 yds. (69.9/124)
Lower Park Ave.
Park City 801/521-2135

Tri-City Golf Course ($13/$13) 6,710 yds. (68.3/112)
1400 N. 200 East
American Fork 801/756-3594

University of Utah Course ($8.50/$8.50) 9 holes/2,300 yds.
(63.1/104)
Salt Lake City 801/581-6511

Valley View Golf Course ($15/$15) 6,223 yds. (69.2/116)
2501 E. Gentile
Layton 801/546-1630

Wasatch Mountain State Park Golf Course ($15/$15) 27 holes
Canyon/Lake Course: 6,322 yds. (69.2/123)
Lake/Mountain Course: 6,172 yds. (69.2/123)

*Off season

Canyon/Mountain Course: 6,192 yds. (69.2/125)
1281 Warm Springs Dr.
Midway 801/654-0532

Wingpointe Golf Course ($16/$18) 6,096 yds. (69.0/121)
3602 W. 1st North
Salt Lake City 801/575-2345

Wolf Creek Resort ($16/$18) 6,200 yds. (70.4/126)
3900 N. Wolf Creek Dr.
Eden 801/745-3365

# VERMONT

## Local Knowledge

In considering this obstinate game in this obstinate state with its obstinate climate and its obstinate natives, *Vermont Golf Journal* ($3.95) is indispensable. Equal parts travel guide, historical quarterly, and association journal, it also has a dash of Vermont life. Every state should be so well served. The annual edition ($4.95) includes updated particulars for courses statewide. *The Vermont Golf Atlas* reprints scorecards with luscious signature-hole spreads. *VG* also sells logoed Cross Creek golf shirts for under $30. The cost of a three-year subscription will please even the most penurious Vermonter ($8.50) (802/864-6115).

*Vermont Golf Courses: A Player's Guide* ($15) by Bob Labbance and David Cornwell provides a more companionable guide, admirably fulfilling the title's mandate. Some guides leave you wondering whether the author even plays the game, but not this one. Others tediously detail shot by shot, blow by blow, which makes reading them as absorbing and confusing as bad erotica, but not this one. Though dated (1987), the book still provides facts with a long shelf life. When someone writes, "This is a short course with abundant insect life" or "We swear the ball will break uphill when putted on certain locations of the eighteenth green," the reader recognizes a credible voice (802/234-9200).

*New England Golf Guide* ($14.95) has the skinny on 49 courses.

Scorecards are reprinted and coupons are a part of the deal (800/833-6387).

The words "country club" do not automatically preclude admittance, especially in Vermont, a state with a streak of independence so pronounced it hesitated joining the Union. Most but not all courses welcome outside play. According to Ben Hale, publisher of *Vermont Golf,* the state is only just getting its first munys. Sherburne's Green Mountain National Golf Course is slated to open in July 1996. Signs of a small but pronounced percolation in new course development are evident. Cedar Knoll in Hinesburg, built by a farmer with a penchant for thrift, could, in Ben's opinion, turn out to be "the nicest public course in Chittenden County."

There are scads of older courses. The original holes at Saint Johnsbury Country Club were designed by Willie Park, Jr., a two-time winner of the British Open. From one of the great Scottish club-making families, Willie, Jr., can legitimately be said to have put offset into irons, invented a revolutionary putter, and, among other things, developed a grooved recovery wood identical to those still on the market. A second nine, designed by Geoffrey Cornish, was added a couple of years ago. Ben describes it as "absolutely gorgeous." One of the Top 10 Best in State, Saint Johnsbury outdistances many of the higher-profile courses that are charging real money for green fees.

Ben also notes Williston, near Burlington, although it is one of the state's busiest courses. "Maintenance-wise," he says, "it's gorgeous and very reasonably priced. They don't try to gouge you."

Malletts Bay has Marble Island, designed by Mr. Tillinghast (keep an eye out for "Champ," Lake Champlain's Nessie).

Middlebury College, where Patty Sheehan's father coached skiing, baseball, and football, has its own ski resort. It also has its own course, Ralph Myhre Country Club, which annually hosts a number of Vermont Golf Association tournaments. "Pretty wide open, it's just a nice course," recommends Ben.

For other lesser-known gems, Ben suggests Proctor-Pittsford near Rutland, Newport in Newport, and Tater Hill in Chester, "always known as the nicest nine-holer in the state." Lake Morey Country Club in Fairlee, opened in 1915, annually hosts the Vermont Open. And, finally, an unimpeachable source was effusive about the cheeseburgers at Bellows Falls, made from fresh ground beef daily, and even more memorable French fries. But Dave, what about the golf?

## Discount Cards

Vermont Golf Links Card. No green fees at eleven resort courses, and you also receive the *Vermont Golf Journal and Directory* and other discounts. 800/639-1941. $55.

Vermont Lung Association Golf Privilege Card. Free round at over forty courses. 800/642-3288 or 802/863-6817. $50.

## Shopping

Look for Dexter Shoe factory outlets in Bennington (North Side Drive), Rutland (Rte. 4 East), Manchester (Rtes. 11 and 30)—a spawning outlet mecca—and Shelburne (Shelburne Road). Manchester is also where tony labels like J Crew, Benetton, Brooks Brothers, and Pendleton have set up outlet shops. They're along Route 7-A and on 11 and 30.

You'd have to have spent some time in the Northeast Kingdom, a stark and rugged section of the state, to truly appreciate the incongruence of including Newport, Vermont, with Hilton Head, New York, Paris, and Tokyo. There is some common ground, however. Bogner, whose ski clothing adorns the slopes of Aspen and Saint Moritz, has, along with many traditional ski makers, found golf. Newport is Bogner of America's headquarters, and it has an outlet store there.

## FINDING THE GREEN IN VERMONT

Bellows Falls Country Club ($16/$21) 9 holes/5,702 yds. (67.0/109)
Rte. 103
Bellows Falls 802/463-9809

Cedar Knoll Country Club ($17/$17) 5,903 yds. (67.4/117)
Rte. 116
Hinesburg 802/482-3186

Lake Morey Country Club ($24/$29) 5,809 yds. (68.6/108)
Rte. 5
Fairlee 802/333-4800

Marble Island Golf Course ($11.50/$15.50) 9 holes/5,086 yds.
(65.6/110)
150 Marble Island Rd.
Colchester 802/864-6800

Newport Country Club ($21/$21) 6,219 yds. (69.2/117)
Pine Hill and Mount Vernon
Newport 802/334-2391

Ralph Myhre Country Club ($27/$27) 6,014 yds. (69.6/126)
Middlebury College
Rte. 30
Middlebury 802/388-3711 ext. 5125

Proctor-Pittsford Country Club ($25/$25) 5,680 yds. (67.9/117)
Corn Hill Rd.
Pittsford 802/483-9379

Saint Johnsbury Country Club ($22/$24) 9 holes/6,064 yds.
(69.2/114)
US 5/Memorial Dr.
St. Johnsbury 802/748-9894

Tater Hill Country Club ($15.75/$15.75*) 9 holes/6,794 yds.
(71.4/124)
Popple Dungeon Rd.
Chester 802/875-2517

Williston Country Club ($18/$18) 5,206 yds. (66.6/113)
N. Williston Rd.
Williston 802/878-3747

*Twilight

# VIRGINIA

*Local Knowledge*

Chandler Harper was an eight-time winner on the PGA Tour. He's remembered for a particularly fateful twist of misfortune. In 1953, Harper appeared to have the Tam O'Shanter Tournament in Chicago in the bag. The first prize was a whopping $25,000, and with it came a year's worth of exhibitions at $1,000 a pop. As Harper was accepting congratulations, Lew Worsham stole the bacon, holing out for an eagle on the eighteenth hole.

Harper retired shortly thereafter to Portsmouth, where he built a course, Bide-A-Wee. The fourth hole, he told Al Barkow in *Getting to the Dance Floor,* is called "Wedgie" "because it's 140 yards long, which is close to the distance Worsham holed out from."

The *Virginia State Golf Association Member Club Directory* is an excellent resource. It's got directions, ratings, and slope from each set of tees and a list of amenities at each VSGA member course. Sadly, green fees are not included. It's available for $10 (804/378-2300). The Virginia Golf brochure from the Tourism Development Group is not as juicy, but it is free (800/93-BACK-9). The packet of information from Virginia Beach lists those courses participating in the city's Golf Package Program (804/437-4700).

The Crossings in Richmond has hosted public links qualifying and is considered one of the best courses in the state, public or private. The Woodlands, right in the heart of Hampton, was designed by Donald Ross, although only a couple of original holes remain. Kinderton Country Club in Clarksville, on the border with North Carolina, was also designed by Ross, in 1947.

Several writers recommend the Newport News Golf Club in Newport News, which regularly hosts USGA events. There are two courses, Cardinal and Deer Run. "Conditioning is always good," Dave Field, a freelancer who lives in Hampton, told me. Both courses run through totally secluded forest.

One of golf's preeminent museums is at the James River Country Club in Newport News. Don't miss Harry Vardon's seven clubs and the bag he used to win the 1900 U.S. Open. The museum is closed Mondays (804/595-3327).

Other suggestions: Reston National, Shenandoah Valley, and The

Hamptons, built on top of a landfill. The three nines of The Hamptons, designed by Michael Hurdzan, are each distinct. The Woods runs through oaks and pines, The Lakes skirts a ten-acre lake, and The Links, up on a plateau, conveys the openness associated with Scotland.

Shenandoah Valley also has three nines. Tuesday, Wednesday, and Thursday, the club runs an excellent special, including cart. Walking's even cheaper. It's a *Tee Time* magazine Top 10 winner. So is South Wales in Jeffersonton, lauded as "one of the state's best golf secrets" whose "pleasant atmosphere is surpassed only by the challenge of the gently rolling course." A Better than Par rating (conveying "diamond in the rough" status) went to Caverns Country Club in Luray in 1993.

*Tee Time*'s sixteen-page color annual course directory to the Mid-Atlantic States is available for $3.50. It's included with a subscription, $13 for six issues. *Tee Time* is also on sale at courses, shops, and newsstands. Back issues are $4.50 (301/913-0081).

*Metro Golf* magazine mixes capital-region golf news and travel with area pro tournament coverage. Some of the toughest public courses in Virginia, determined on the basis of slope and course rating, are Pohick Bay in Lorton and Royal Virginia in Hadensville. *Metro Golf* is free at courses. A year's subscription of eight issues is $14.95 (202/663-9015). Finally, Virginia Tech's course in Blacksburg is open to all friends of the Hokie.

Women interested in mixing a little business with pleasure in the Hampton Roads area should know about the Career Women's Golf Association. Bridget Pendergast, head pro at Honeybee in Virginia Beach, started the organization in 1990. Members play nine holes every Tuesday evening. Dues are $30 a year plus discounted green fees for events (804/471-2768).

### Discount Card

American Lung Association of Northern Virginia. Over sixty courses. 703/591-4131. $25.

### Shopping

In Newport News, stop in to peek at the museum and classic clubs for sale at American Golf Classics (12842 Jefferson Ave.). Bob Farino has some interesting stuff on display from the late 1700s to the present. There's also original artwork and more golf ducks (wood club heads turned into duck decoys) than you can imagine. Mention this book and his classic club price guide, regularly $35, is discounted.

Williamsburg has Brooks Brothers and Polo/Ralph Lauren (804/565-0732). Potomac Mills in Prince William is monstrous. A sampling: Eddie Bauer, Nordstrom, Benetton, Levi's, Alexander Julian, Calvin Klein, Nike (800/VA-MILLS). Factory Merchants Outlet is north of Wytheville at the junction of I-77 and I-81. There's more. All you need to know is available in the annual travel guide (800/VISIT-VA or 804/786-4484).

## FINDING THE GREEN IN VIRGINIA

Bide-A-Wee Golf Course ($7.50/$9) 6,308 yds. (68.7/123)
Bide-A-Wee Lane
Portsmouth 804/393-5269

Caverns Country Club ($18/$24) 6,299 yds. (69.7/115)
Airport Road Rt. 647
Luray 703/743-7111

The Crossings Golf Course ($25/$30) 6,229 yds. (69.7/123)
800 Virginia Center Pkwy.
Glen Allen 804/266-2254

Newport News Golf Club ($20/$21) 36 holes
Cardinal Course: 6,282 yds. (69.1/114)
Deer Run Course: 6,757 yds. (72.4/118)
Fort Eustis Blvd.
Newport News 804/886-7925

The Hamptons ($14/$17) 27 holes
Woods/Lakes Course: 6,002 yds. (68.3/108)
Woods/Links Course: 5,577 yds. (65.3/98)
Lakes/Links Course: 5,863 yds. (67.6/107)
320 Butler Farm Rd.
Hampton 804/766-9148

Kinderton Country Club ($15/$25) 6,108 yds. (69.7/119)
Kinderton Dr.
Clarksville 804/374-8822

Pohick Bay Golf Course ($18/$22) 5,897 yds. (69.2/126)
10301 Gunston Rd.
Lorton 703/339-8585

Reston National Golf Club ($20/$20*) 6,480 yds. (71.2/123)
11875 Sunrise Valley Dr.
Reston 703/620-9333

Royal Virginia Golf Club ($24/$30) 6,789 yds. (71.8/127)
3181 Duke's Rd. (Rte. 606)
Hadensville 804/457-2041

Shenandoah Valley Golf Club ($12/$12*) 27 holes
Red/White Course: 5,687 yds. (67.8/113)
Red/Blue Course: 6,027 yds. (68.9/113)
White/Blue Course: 5,892 yds. (68.5/114)
Rte. 2
Front Royal 703/636-2641

South Wales Golf Club ($15/$20) 6,578 yds. (71.0/118)
Rte. 229
Jeffersonton 703/937-3250

Virginia Technical Golf Course ($14/$16) 6,131 yds. (68.2/104)
Duckpond Dr.
Blacksburg 703/231-6435

The Woodlands Golf Club ($10/$14) 5,191 yds. (63.9/96)
9 Woodland Rd.
Hampton 804/727-1195

*Twilight

# WASHINGTON

*Local Knowledge*

Dan MacMillan, author of *Golfing in Washington, The Complete Guide to Washington's Golf Facilities* (nine editions and counting), graciously offers the following insights on some of his favorite courses.

Avalon Golf Club in Burlington is a twenty-seven-hole Robert Muir Graves–designed course that offers spectacular views of the Skagit Valley and surrounding countryside: "Worth every penny. The food in the 'Sweet Bite Cafe' is worth the trip alone". Dungeness Golf & Country Club in Sequim is Dan's favorite course in the state for several reasons: "1. Sequim only receives an average of 14 inches of rain a year. 2. Very affordable all year long. 3. Tough championship course that plays much longer than the yardage indicates. 4. Great greens that are always in excellent condition. 5. The Olympic Peninsula is a favorite for weekenders and tourists; you can plan weekend trips here. 6. Great on-course restaurant and lounge that overlooks the golf course."

Gold Mountain Golf Course in Gorst, he says, is a "great course that has hosted many public links tournaments." He calls it "one of the finest public courses in the state." If you want spectacular views of Mount Rainier, Dan says, "this is the course to visit. Towering cedars line the fairways on many holes. The facility also has an executive nine that is a real challenge. Great on-course restaurant for after." Indian Canyon in Spokane is "one of the best eastern Washington golf courses, always rated in the Top 75 public golf courses by *Golf Digest*" (and host to several national publinx championships). Kayak Point in Stanwood is a "tough, tough course. Local pros," says Dan, "call it one of the toughest in the state" (and it was a 1994 sectional publinks qualifying course). Just outside of Spokane, Dan also recommends Liberty Lake, Meadow Wood, and Valley View in Liberty Lake, Mint Valley in Longview ("Great short course. Excellent greens all year long"), Mount Si in North Bend ("Great public course. The views of Mt. Si alone are worth the trip"), Snohomish ("Tough long course located in a very scenic area of Washington. Can eat you up if you stray from the fairway. Great homemade food in the restaurant. The course is famous for its

PIE!!!!!"), and Tumwater Valley in Tumwater ("Tough, tough, tough, tough").

*Golfing in Washington* is in stores and available by calling 206/333-4641.

KiKi Canniff, author of *Washington Free: A Guide to the Best of the State's Cost Free Attractions* and *The Northwest Golfer,* can be expected to know a bargain when she sees one. Here's another. KiKi will send out a free list of Washington's Best Golf Bargains, twenty-three courses where you can play for $6 or less, to anyone who sends her a self-addressed, stamped #10 envelope: P.O. Box 186, Willamina, OR 97396. She recommends Carnation Golf Course in Carnation, Skyline in Cathlamet (where you may see elk), and the two courses in the San Juan Islands: Lopez and San Juan.

One of several impressive facets of Jeff Shelley's *Golf Courses of the Pacific Northwest* ($19.95) is the attention he devotes to the not inconsequential question of climate. Even when considering some of the more expensive courses, he notes that courses in Washington and Oregon west of the Cascades are open all year. It's worth a check for off-season specials, even at Semiahmoo and Port Ludlow, topnotch, nationally recognized resort courses.

Leo Chandler, a correspondent for *Back Nine* magazine, says golf in Spokane is a steal. The munys (Downriver, Esmeralda, The Creek at Qualchan, and the aforementioned Indian Canyon) are "equal to or better than most national private tracks." There are also eleven other privately owned daily-fee courses in Spokane, for which info is available by calling 800/248-3230.

College courses: Moo U. (Washington State University) has a nine-hole course about which Dan MacMillan has nice things to say; so does Pacific Lutheran University in Tacoma. Jeff Shelley notes that the original course (1926) has been pared by development. He describes it as "a quiet suburban-type course," flat with tall evergreens. U Dub (The University of Washington) only has a driving range. Two state parks have courses: Lakewoods near Bridgeport State Park, not far from Coulee Dam, and Sun Lakes. For seasonal travel guides call 800/544-1800, ext. 001. For general tourist information, call 206/586-2088 and 800/562-0990.

*Discount Card*

See "Stalking the Elusive Deep Discount" in Finding the Green introduction.

*Shopping:*

North Bend has Great Northwest Factory Stores. Burlington has the Pacific Edge Outlet Center. The Peace Arch Factory Outlet is in Custer: 206/366-3127.

## FINDING THE GREEN IN WASHINGTON

Avalon Golf Club ($19/$19*) 27 holes
North/South Course: 5,994 yds. (69.1/122)
North/West Course: 5,786 yds. (69.1/122)
South/West Course: 6,206 yds. (69.1/122)
1717 Kelleher Rd.
Burlington 206/757-1900

Carnation Golf Course ($20/$22) 5,503 yds. (65.1/104)
1810 W. Snoqualmie River Rd. NE.
Carnation 206/333-4151

The Creek at Qualchan ($21/$21) 6,023 yds. (68.8/121)
301 E. Meadowlane Rd.
Spokane 509/448-9317

Downriver Golf Course ($17/$17) 6,021 yds. (68.5/115)
N. 3225 Columbia Circle
Spokane 509/327-5269

Dungeness Golf & Country Club ($19/$23) 6,013 yds. (68.8/117)
1965 Woodcock Rd.
Sequim 206/683-6344

Esmeralda Golf Course ($17/$17) 6,071 yds. (68.2/112)
E. 3933 Courtland
Spokane 509/487-6291

*Twilight

Gold Mountain Golf Course ($16/$20) 6,146 yds. (69.0/116)
7263 Belfair Valley Rd.
Gorst 206/674-2363

High Cedars Golf Club ($21.50/$27) 6,384 yds. (68.7/118)
14604 149th Court East
Orting 206/893-3171

Indian Canyon Golf Course ($21/$21) 5,927 yds. (69.3/123)
4304 West Dr.
Spokane 509/747-5353

Kayak Point Golf Course ($25/$30) 6,109 yds. (70.3/128)
15711 Marine Dr.
Stanwood 206/652-9676

Lakewoods Golf Course ($14/$15) 5,642 yds. (66.7/115)
Hwy. 17
Bridgeport 509/686-5721

Liberty Lake Golf Course ($17/$17) 6,153 yds. (68.7/118)
24403 E. Sprague Ave.
Liberty Lake 509/255-6233

Lopez Island Golf Course ($14/$14) 2,701 yds. (62.8/105)
Airport Rd.
Lopez Island 206/468-2679

Meadow Wood Golf Course ($17/$17) 6,398 yds. (71.4/124)
E. 24501 Valley Way
Liberty Lake 509/255-9539

Mint Valley Golf Course ($13/$17) 5,800 yds. (67.9/115)
4002 Pennsylvania St.
Longview 206/577-3395

Mount Si Golf Club ($25/$25) 5,793 yds. (66.0/108)
9010 Meadowbrook/North Bend Rd. SE.
Snoqualmie 206/391-4926

Port Townsend Golf Course ($17/$17) 9 holes/5,604 yds. (65.8/114)
1948 Blaine St.
Port Townsend 206/385-0752

San Juan Golf & Country Club ($25/$25) 6,508 yds. (70.9/118)
2261 Golf Course Rd.
Friday Harbor 206/378-2254

Skyline Golf Course ($12/$12) 2,255 yds. (62.7/111)
20 Randall Dr.
Cathlamet 206/795-8785

Snohomish Public Golf Course ($19.50/$24.75) 6,315 yds.
(70.0/121)
7806 147th SE. Ave.
Snohomish 206/568-2676

Sun Lakes State Park Golf Course ($9/$11) na yds. (na/na)
Hwy. 17
Coulee City 509/632-5583

Tumwater Valley Golf Club ($17/$24) 6,531 yds. (70.7/121)
4611 Tumwater Valley Dr.
Tumwater 206/943-9500

University Golf Club ($13/$13) 9 holes/5,371 yds. (64.4/100)
Pacific Lutheran University
754 124th Street S.
Tacoma 206/535-7393

Valley View Golf Course ($12/$12) 9 holes/4,095 yds. (58.0/na)
off Liberty Lake Rd.
Liberty Lake 509/928-3484

Washington State University Golf Course ($9/$9) 9 holes/5,785 yds.
(65.4/110)
off Fairway Dr.
Pullman 509/335-4342

# WEST VIRGINIA

*Local Knowledge*

The Speidel Course at Oglebay Park in Wheeling garners its share of praise. The Robert Trent Jones course has, after all, hosted the LPGA for over a decade. *Golf Digest* rates it just behind The Greenbrier in the state's Top 5. Heady company for a muny.

Part of an attractive tourist centerpiece, Oglebay is legitimately a resort course at public course prices. It does take a beating. Visitors play from the wrong tees, drive carts hither and yon, don't bother replacing divots. The "Hey, I'm on vacation" syndrome seems to be a problem. Ditto with slow play. Would you believe two hours and forty-nine minutes for nine holes? "It's like this every Saturday and Sunday," a marshal told me in August. "We want 2:15, but we never get it."

Oglebay has also received national acclaim for its innovative caddie program. (Be advised: They don't work Mondays and not after 11 A.M. on Sundays.) There's also a great yardage book.

The locals leave Speidel to the tourists and stick to the cheaper and easily missed Crispin Course nearby. Too bad. Perhaps it's a legacy of its Civilian Conservation Corps heritage, but the course is less formal, less resorty. Considered the town course, it's also a delight and golfers treat it tenderly. It gets just as much maintenance as Speidel, it's just cheaper and less crowded.

For fifty years, top players from the region gathered at Crispin for The Bernharts, a tournament named for a local clothing store. Arnold Palmer still holds the record: sixty-two. (He didn't birdie a par three but feasted on the short par fives, of which the front side has three.)

Henry Bober, who supervised some of the construction, grows his vegetables along the eighteenth fairway. He describes his course by saying: "The only level place is on the tee." He's not exaggerating. The course meanders over devilish grades. Club selection is a guessing game. "You'll use every club in your bag," Henry says. I did. The courses are almost right next to each other. Play both.

Each state park course in West Virginia is prettier than the next. These really are tremendous values, designer labels with gorgeous scenery, unbeatable amenities and prices. Canaan Valley and Capacon (Robert Trent Jones) each draw on its own sources of

water, repelling the occasional drought. The season is short, April 15
to November 15, but at Canaan Valley, in summer, "We have more
days in the fifties than the high eighties." Pipestem (Geoffrey
Cornish) has hosted the West Virginia Open and offers inspiring
views. It's rated in the Top 10 by *Tee Time* magazine.

Pipestem does have a slight goose problem. Capacon can get
buggy. Pipestem showed signs of the vacation syndrome. But these
are minor irritants. If you're feeling flush at Capacon, you can always
hit the spas in Berkeley Springs. (Even if you're not, you will after
you come out of the springs.) Twenty-seven dollars will cover a soak
and massage. Oglebay and Pipestem also have par three courses.

The annual state tourism publication has only course names and
phone numbers, but detailed state park information is available by
calling 800/CALL-WVA. (This number, miracle of miracles, also
works in-state and can be used to connect directly with any state
park.) Reservations are taken a year in advance at Pipestem, which
gives an idea of its popularity. Plan accordingly.

On Route 220, between Moorefield and Petersburg, is another
pleasant course. Valley View has water on nine holes; it's short but
frisky, with nice views of the surrounding hills. The clubhouse dates
to 1840 and is in *The National Register of Historic Places*.

### Discount Cards

American Cancer Society Golf Package. Fifty percent off green fees
at over 1,600 courses nationwide, four or more plays at most
courses, two-for-one driving-range discounts. 800/ACS-2345. $30.
American Lung Association Golf Privilege Card. Complimentary
green fees at thirty-eight courses, discounts at three state parks.
304/342-6600. $40.

### Shopping

Blue Ridge Outlet in Martinsburg advertises fifty "authentic" manufacturers outlets (800/445-3993). There's also a Tanger Factory Outlet
Center nearby (800/727-6885).

*The unusual practice green target at Capacon.*

## FINDING THE GREEN IN WEST VIRGINIA

Canaan Valley Resort State Park ($24/$24) 6,436 yds. (na/119)
Hwy. 32
Davis 304/866-4121

Capacon Resort State Park Course ($19/$22) 6,410 yds. (70.0/116)
Rte. 522
Berkeley Springs 304/258-1022

Oglebay Park Golf Course
Crispin Course: ($19/$19) 5,670 yds. (66.6/103)
Speidel Course: ($30/$30) 6,085 yds. (68.6/118)
Oglebay Park
Wheeling 304/242-3000

Pipestem Resort State Park Course ($19/$22) 6,131 yds. (69.7/123)
Rte. 20
Pipestem 304/466-1800

Twin Falls State Park Golf Course ($19/$22) 5,978 yds. (68.3/119)
State Rte. 97
Mullens 304/294-4000

Tygart Lake State Park Golf Course ($13/$16) 6,019 yds. (68.0/113)
Rte. 50
Grafton 304/265-3100

Valley View Resort State Park ($16/$19) 5,661 yds. (65.6/101)
Rte. 220
Moorefield 304/538-6564

# WISCONSIN

### Local Knowledge

The Wisconsin State Golf Association's attractive annual directory goes for $5. It lists slope, ratings, and yardage from every set of tees for some three hundred member courses. Also handy is the complete list of public course tournament sites (414/786-4301).

The state tourism development division mails out free copies of *Wisconsin Golf* magazine's annual *Directory of Courses* (800/432-TRIP). With regional quadrant maps and directions, it's got everything you'd expect but prices. Fore Better Golf has a '93 edition map that covers southeast Wisconsin, including Milwaukee, Madison, Green Bay, and Beloit. Check for more recent editions. It's $3.95 in pro shops or from 708/893-8672.

*Par Excellance* magazine focuses on Greater Milwaukee and Chicago. A year's subscription is $12 for five issues. The first issue every season features a comprehensive statewide course directory, with prices. It's free to subscribers or can be picked up at courses and retail golf stores. Order your copy for $1.95 by mail. The magazine also publishes a sixteen-page full-color calendar and a course directory for northern Illinois. Best feature: the "unburied treasure"

course reviews. This is one magazine worth making the effort to find
(414/327-7707).

Publisher Doug Neumann recommends Nagawaukee, a twenty-
five minute drive west on I-94 from downtown Milwaukee, in
Pewaukee. Doug calls it "probably the best public course in the state
of Wisconsin owned by a county or city." He did say it was very hard
to get on unless you're a single.

The Golf Course Owners Association of Wisconsin offers a terrific
free service with a personal travel planning touch. Tell the association where you're headed and it will pull together and send appropriate course brochures and scorecards. Call 608/847-7968.

Courses hosting recent state qualifying for the USGA Public Links
Championship include, in Milwaukee, Brown Deer Park (home of
the PGA Tour's Greater Milwaukee Open), Oakwood, and Dretzka
Park; New Berlin Hills in New Berlin; and Ives Grove Links in
Racine. Other courses where state and local public links associations
have held their championships include Grant Park in South
Milwaukee, Currie Park in Wauwatosa, Whitnall Park in Hales
Corners, and Yahara Hills in Madison, which hosted the National
Women's Publinx Championship in 1977.

University courses are open to the public at George Williams
College in Williams Bay and at the University of Wisconsin in Green
Bay. National Golf Foundation Public Golf Achievement Award win-
ners, drum roll please, include Muskego Lakes Country Club in
Muskego, Cherry Hills in Sturgeon Bay, and Johnson Park in Racine.
Wisconsin has one state park golf course, Peninsula in Fish Creek,
built in 1921. The scenery looks gorgeous. Beware tournaments the
first week of August.

### Discount Cards

American Lung Association Golf Privilege Card. 130 courses, either
   free with a cart or two-for-one without a cart, or the choice.
   800/242-5160 or 414/782-7833. $35.
Golf Wisconsin Coupon Book. Two-for-one green fees at over seventy courses, free cart rentals at a handful of others, and a bunch
   of related benefits, from the Golf Course Owners of Wisconsin.
   608/847-7968. $34.95.

## Shopping

National outlet stores from Brooks Brothers, Polo/Ralph Lauren, and others are in Kenosha at Lakeside Marketplace and in Appleton at the Fox River Mall.

## FINDING THE GREEN IN WISCONSIN

Brown Deer Park Golf Course ($21/$25*) 6,390 yds. (71.0/129)
7835 N. Green Bay Rd.
Milwaukee 414/352-8080

Cherry Hills Golf Course ($23/$23) 5,901 yds. (68.0/119)
5905 Dunn Rd.
Sturgeon Bay 414/743-3240

Currie Park Golf Club ($15/$16) 6,095 yds. (68.6/115)
3535 N. Mayfair Rd.
Wauwatosa 414/453-7030

Dretzka Park Golf Club ($13/$14) 6,443 yds. (70.5/120)
12020 W. Bradley Rd.
Milwaukee 414/354-7300

George Williams College Golf Club ($15.75/$20) 5,066 yds.
(63.4/102)
350 Constance Dr.
Williams Bay 414/245-9507

Grant Park Golf Club ($15/$16) 5,174 yds. (64.1/103)
100 Hawthorne Ave.
South Milwaukee 414/762-4646

Ives Grove Golf Links ($17/$18.25) 6,413 yds. (70.3/124)
14200 Washington Ave.
Sturtevant 414/878-3714

Johnson Park Golf Course ($14.25/$15.75) 6,380 yds. (69.5/115)
6200 Northwestern Ave.
Racine 414/637-2840

*9 holes only

Muskego Lakes Country Club ($18/$25) 6,057 yds. (69.6/121)
S100 W14020 Loomis Rd./Hwy. 36
Muskego 414/425-6500

Nagawaukee Golf Course ($21.75/$25.75) 6,453 yds. (70.4/122)
1897 Maple Ave.
Pewaukee 414/367-2153

New Berlin Hills Golf Course ($17.50/$18.50) 6,209 yds. (69.9/123)
13175 W. Graham St.
New Berlin 414/782-5005

Oakwood Golf Club ($17/$20) 6,658 yds. (71.1/118)
3600 W. Oakwood Rd.
Franklin 414/281-6700

Peninsula State Park Golf Course ($16/$16) 5,844 yds. (67.5/118)
Hwy. 42 between Fish Creek and Ephraim
Ephraim 414/854-5791

Shorewood Golf Course ($12.25/$14.25) 2,792 yds. (67.4/117)
University of Wisconsin
2420 Nicolet Dr.
Green Bay 414/465-2118

Whitnall Park Golf Club ($17/$20) 6,169 yds. (68.6/114)
6701 S. 92nd St.
Hales Corners 414/425-7931

Yahara Hills Golf Course ($17.50/$18.50) 36 holes
East Course: 6,564 yds. (69.5/110)
West Course: 6,399 yds. (69.6/114)
6701 E. Broadway
Madison 608/838-3126

# WYOMING

*Local Knowledge*

With nine months of winter and three months of bad skiing, Wyoming golfers have to get their golf in on the run. Wind can be a real problem. Wayne Cummings at the Casper *Star-Tribune* lays it all out: "If you can't play the wind here, you might as well get out your bowling ball." His favorite courses, not surprisingly, offer some protection from the elements. He likes Kendrick in Sheridan. "For a community course, it's real challenging. It's got a little bit of everything," he says, "uphill, downhill" and—music to the ears—"you'll use every club in your bag." The front-side greens were redone in 1994. Buffalo Golf Club (about thirty miles south of Sheridan) fared well in *Golf Digest's* Places to Play ratings.

For an out-of-the-way course, Wayne loves the nine holes in the small town of Sundance. It's got some real tough holes, and the wind is rarely a problem.

The *Star-Tribune* runs a special "Best Holes" list that is determined by its readers. It comes out in early May (307/266-0500).

Jim Core, president of the Wyoming State Golf Association, calls White Mountain in Rock Springs "probably the best public course we've got." Olive-Glen in Cody, Bell Nob in Gillette, and Green Hills in Worland have also hosted top WSGA events. In the foothills of the Bighorns, Dayton has nine very tough holes. Horseshoe was designed by Pete Dye, part of a project that went belly-up before completion.

Jackson Hole Golf & Tennis Club hosted the 1994 National Amateur Public Links Championship. The best you can do there is nine holes after 4 P.M. for under $30—barely.

Airport, Cheyenne's muny, has hosted the state amateur. So has the University of Wyoming's Glenn "Red" Jacoby Golf Course in Laramie.

Not much on golf in the state vacation guide. Instead, ask for the WSGA's wallet-size tournament schedule, which includes a statewide course directory and handicap information (800/CALL-WYO or WSGA 307/265-8445).

*Shopping*

Sierra Trading Post is headquartered in Cheyenne. It's got an outlet store to complement its mail-order catalog of discounted outdoor wear and equipment. The store is off I-80 at Exit 364, East Lincoln Way. The address is 5025 Campstool Rd. Hours: 10 A.M. to 7 P.M. Monday through Saturday (307/775-8000).

## FINDING THE GREEN IN WYOMING

Airport Golf Club ($11/$11) 6,121 yds. (67.1/99)
4801 Central Ave.
Cheyenne 307/637-6418

Bell Nob Golf Course ($15/$15) 6,449 yds. (68.1/113)
4600 Overdale Dr.
Gillette 307/686-7069

Buffalo Golf Club ($15/$15) 6,214 yds. (68.4/114)
W. Hart St.
Buffalo 307/684-5266

Glenn "Red" Jacoby Golf Course ($13.50/$13.50) 6,030 yds.
(65.7/104)
30th and Willett
Laramie 307/745-3111

Green Hills Golf Course ($14/$15) 6,052 yds. (na/na)
1455 Airport Rd.
Worland 307/347-8972

Horseshoe Golf Course ($16/$18) 9 holes/5,688 yds. (67.0/116)
100 Paisan Ave.
Dayton 307/655-9525

Jackson Hole Golf & Tennis Club ($25/$25*) 6,783 yds. (70.3/124)
5000 N. Spring Gulch Rd.
Jackson 307/733-3111

*Twilight

Kendrick Golf Course ($15/$15) 6,532 yds. (70.0/113)
Big Goose Rd.
Sheridan 307/674-8148

Olive-Glen Country Club ($21/$21) 6,515 yds. (69.9/120)
802 Meadow Lane
Cody 307/587-5308

Sundance Country Club ($na/$na) 2,930 yds. (na/na)
(east of city)
Sundance 307/283-1191

White Mountain Golf Course ($15/$15) 6,741 yds. (na/118)
1501 Clubhouse Dr.
Rock Springs 307/382-5030

# APPENDIX

## A

Accessory Golf
   8810 West 131st Place
   Overland Park, KS 66213
   913/681-8713

H. Arnold Wood Turning
   Box 278
   875 Mamaroneck Ave.
   Mamaroneck, NY 10543
   914/381-0801

Artistic Greetings
   One Artistic Plaza
   Elmira, NY 14925
   607/733-9010

Atlas Pen and Pencil Corp.
   3040 N. 29th Ave.
   Hollywood, FL 33022
   800/327-3232

Augusta National Golf Shop
   P.O. Box 268
   Augusta, GA
   706/667-6200

Austad's Golf
   4500 E. 10th St.
   P.O. Box 5428
   Sioux Falls, SD 57196-0001
   800/759-4653 (to order)
   800/444-1234 (customer service)

Avon Golf Grips
   c/o Technical Department
   603 W. 7th St.
   Cadillac, MI 49601
   800-33GRIPS

## B

BJ Designs
   489 Richmondville Ave.
   Westport, CT 06880
   800/253-2247

Sarah Baddiel Golf Gallery
   Grays-in-the-Mews
   B-10
   Grays Antique Market
   Davies Mews
   London W1
   071-408-1239

Mike Baier
c/o Bayou Chevrolet-Pontiac
2020 W. Airline Hwy.
La Place, LA 70068

Barr's Postcard News
70 S. Sixth St.
Box 310
Lansing, IA
800-397-0145

Eddie Bauer
P.O. Box 3700
Seattle, WA 98124
800/426-8020 (to order)
800/426-6253 (customer service)

The Best for Less Newsletter
14 Washington Place
NY, NY 10003-6609
212/673-6297

Bogner of America
Bogner Drive
Newport, VT 05855
800/451-4417

The Boundary Waters Catalog
105 N. Central Ave.
Ely, MN 55731
800/223-6565

Brooks Brothers
Catalogue Fulfillment Center
350 Campus Plaza
Edison, NJ 08818
800/274-1815 (to order)
800/274-1816 (customer
service/get list of outlets)

## C

CHO-PAT, Inc.
Mount Holly Industrial Commons
Lippincott Ln., Unit 6
Mt. Holly, NJ 08060
800/221-1601

Cambridge Golf Antiquities Ltd.
P.O. Box 965
Pebble Beach, CA 93953
408/626-3334

Campmor
810 Route 17N
P.O. Box 997-P
Paramus, NJ 07653-0997
201/445-5000 (for free catalog)
800/526-4784 (to order)
201/445-9868 (to order in NJ)

Cayman Golf Co.
1705 Radium Springs Rd.
Albany, GA 31705
800/344-0220

The Center Shop/Pittsburgh Center
for the Arts
Fifth Avenue Place
120 Fifth Ave.
Pittsburgh, PA 15222
412/261-3855

Checks in the Mail
5314 N. Irwindale Ave.
Irwindale, CA 91706
800/800-2432

Chesal Industries
2120 W. Florist Ave.
Milwaukee, WI 53209
800/832-8772

Marilyn Clark, Inc.
P.O. Box 24
Kent, OH 44240
800/356-0020 or 216/678-6476

The Classics of Golf
68 Commerce Rd.
Stamford, CT 06902
203/348-4514

Competitive Edge Golf
526 W. 26th St., 10th floor
New York, NY 10001
800/344-8586

Consumer Advantage
40074 Eagle Dr.
Sterling Heights, MI 48310
800/462-1667

Cubic Balance
30231 Tomas Rd.
Rancho Santa Margarita, CA
92688
800/858-1855 (to order)

Current Checks
P.O. Box 19000
Colorado Springs, CO 80935-9000
800/533-3973

**D**

Dennco Inc.
16 Industrial Way
Salem, NH 03079
603/898-0004
800/336-6242

Richard E. Donovan Enterprises
P.O. Box 7070
Endicott, NY 13760
607/785-5874

**E**

Eastern Golf Corp.
RD #2
Golf Park Drive
Hamlin, PA 18427
800/482-7200

Ecco/Green Packaging
24 Compello Rd.
Framingham, MA 01701
508/875-1430

Exclusive Design Products, Inc.
7226 W. Colonial Dr.

Orlando, FL 32818
407/578-8400

**F**

Factory Outlet Newsletter
11 Tory Lane, Rt. 3
Newton, CT 06470
203/384-2500

Fore Better Golf
177 Lockwood Lane
Bloomingdale, IL 60108
708/893-8672

Fuller Brush Co.
P.O. Box 1247
One Fuller Way
Great Bend, KS 67530
800/523-3794

Chuck Furjanic Inc.
P.O. Box 165892
Irving, TX 75016
800/882-4825

**G**

John Gates
35 Ocean Trace Rd.
St. Augustine, FL 32084
904/461-8408

Gifts Fore the Golfer
23 Wilshire Dr.
Albany, NY 12205
518/869-7103

Golden Golf
1100 Summit Sq., Suite 109
Plano, TX 75074
800/433-1342

The Golf Bookshopper
403 Stringtown Rd.
Williamsburg, KY 40769
606/549-4827

Golf Collectors Society
P.O. Box 20546
Dayton, OH 45420
513/256-2474

Golf Day
375 Beacham St.
Chelsea, MA 02150-0999
800/669-8600

Golf Fore Women
P.O. Box 2471
St. Louis, MO 63114
314/426-3397

Golf Gifts and Gallery
219 Eisenhower Lane S.
Lombard, IL 60148-5407
708/953-9087

Golf Haus
700 N. Pennsylvania
Lansing, MI 48906
517/482-8842

GolfHer Inc.
16716 Shea Lane
Gaithersburg, MD 20877
800/424-2262

Golf Pride Grips
Hwy. 401 N.
Laurinburg, NC 28352
910/277-3771

GolfRite
P.O. Box 12068, Dept. A
Alexandria, LA 71315-2068
318/473-2849
800/259-3673

Golf's Golden Years
P.O. Box 842
Palatine, IL 60078-0842
708/934-4108

Golf Shop Collection
P.O. Box 14609
Cincinnati, OH 45250
800/227-8700

GolfShots
Riverbend Office Park
9 Galen St., Ste. 020
Watertown, MA 02172
617/926-0940

GolfSmart
P.O. Box 1688
Cedar Ridge, CA 95924-1688
800/637-3557

GolfSmith International
11000 N IH35
Austin, TX 78753-3794
800/456-3344

Golf Specialtees of Scotland
11585 Paramus Dr.
N. Potomac, MD 20878-4282
800/GR8-SCOT

The GolfWorks
P.O. Box 3008
Newark, OH 43058-3008
800/848-8358 (to order)
800/562-5829 (customer service)

Ed Granados
2855 West Avenue 34
Los Angeles, CA 90065
213/259-5005

Grant Books
Victoria Square
Droitwich
Worcestershire
England WR9 8DE
0905 778155

Great Lakes Golf Ball Co.
4527 Southwest Hwy.
Oaklawn, IL 60453
800/367-4518

## H

Greg Hall
24717 E. Oakland Rd.
Bay Village, OH 44140
216/871-9319

Garry Hauk
1624 Trendley
St. Charles, MO 63301-2629

The Herb Bar
200 West Mary
Austin, TX 78704
800/766-4372

House of Bruce
26 Three Pence Lane
Charleston, SC 29414
803/763-1360

## I

Imprint Products
P.O. Box 1330
Binghamton, NY 13902-1330
607/723-1071

International Golf Philatelic Society
P.O. Box 2183
Norfolk, VA 23501

Izod Club Golf and Tennis
Airport Industrial Park, Rt. 183
Reading, PA 19605
800/522-6783

## J

J Crew
One Ivy Crescent
Lynchburg, VA 24513-1001
800/562-0258 (to order)

800/782-8244 (to receive catalog)
800/932-0043 (services)

Bob Jones
Box 582
Pebble Beach, CA 93953

## K

Kiss My Face
P.O. Box 224
Gardiner, NY 12525
800/262-KISS

## L

L. L. Bean
Freeport, ME
800/341-4341 (orders)
800/221-4221 (customer service)

LPGA
2570 Volusia Ave., Suite B
Daytona Beach, FL 32114
904/254-8800

LPGA Merchandise Center
c/o Spectator Sports Services,
Inc.
5029-A West W. T. Harris Blvd.
Charlotte, NC 28629
800/945-7223

La Golfeur
1484 Town Line Rd.
Mundelein, IL 60060
800/894-9603

The Leadbetter Collection
Golf Training Systems
3400 Corporate Way, Suite 9
Duluth, GA 30136
800/772-3813

Left Handed Golfer
P.O. Box 7445
Charlotte, NC 28241

800/488-5338
704/588-7594

Lefties Only
1972 Williston Rd.
S. Burlington, VT 05403
800/533-8437

Leisure Outlet
421 Soquel Ave.
Santa Cruz, CA 95062
800/322-1460

George Lewis Golfiana
P.O. Box 291
Mamaroneck, NY 10543
914/698-4579

The Lighter Side
4514 19th St., Court East
Box 25600
Bradenton, FL 34206-5600
813/747-2356

Links Graphics, Inc.
8200 E. Pacific Pl. #201
Denver, CO 80231
303/750-0397

Logisoft
274 N. Goodman St.
Rochester, NY 14607
800/554-2991
716/442-0030

## M

M&S Publishing
1320 Egret Rd.
Homestead, FL 33035
305/247-8985

Maryco Products
7215 Pebblecreek Rd.
W. Bloomfield, MI 48322-4172
800/334-7757

Maxwell's Bookmark
2103 Pacific Ave.
Stockton, CA 95204
209/466-0194

Memphis Net & Twine Co., Inc.
P.O. Box 8331
Memphis, TN 38108
800/238-6380
901/458-2656

Mochrie's Maniacs
8499 S. Tamiami Tr. #1
Sarasota, FL 34238
813/966-0150

## N

Newark Golf Company
99 S. Pine St.
Newark, OH 43055
800/222-5639

The Jack Nicklaus Collection
55 West Court
Mandeville, LA 70448
800/229-2447

Nike, Inc.
One Bowerman Dr.
Beaverton, OR 97005
503/671-6453

Ann Norling
P.O. Box 1440
Mill Valley, CA 94942
800/483-6722

## O

The Oklahoma Library for the
Blind and Physically
Handicapped
300 NE. 18th St.
Oklahoma City, OK 73105
405/521-3514

Old Chicago Golf Shop
4977 Arquilla Dr.
Richton Park, IL 60471
708/747-1045

## P

PGA Tour
Sawgrass
Ponte Vedra, FL 32082
904/285-3700

PGA of America
100 Avenue of the Champions
Box 109601
Palm Beach Gardens, FL 33410-9601
407/624-8400

Palmer Magic
23 Duane #6
Redwood City, CA 94062

Paper House Productions
Woodstock, NY 12498
914/679-4700

Parsons Technology
One Parsons Drive
P.O. Box 100
Hiawatha, IA 52213-0100
800/223-6925

Patagonia
1609 W. Babcock St.
P.O. Box 8900
Bozeman, MT 59715
800/336-9090 (to receive catalog)
800/638-6464 (to order)

Pimpernel International
P.O. Box 6
Consett County
Durham DH8 8LY
England

Pin High
10085 Rio San Diego Dr., Suite 348
San Diego, CA 92108
619/281-9717

Gary Player Golf Equipment Co.
3300 PGA Blvd., Suite 100
Palm Beach Gardens, FL 33410
407/624-0300

Pocketec, Inc.
3 S. Newport Ave.
Ventnor City, NJ 08406
800/669-5239

Practicorp Inc.
26 Maplewood Dr.
Danbury, CT 06811-4211
203/792-2812

Pro Shop World of Golf
8130 N. Lincoln Ave.
Skokie, IL 60077
708/675-5286

## Q

Quantum
754 Washington St.
Eugene, OR 97401
800/448-1448

## R

REI
1700 45th St. East
Sumner, WA 98352-0001
800/426-4840
800/828-5533 (customer service)

Rare Sportsfilms
1126 Tennyson Lane
Naperville, IL 60540
708/527-8890

Reebok
  100 Technology Center Dr.
  Stoughton, MA 02072
  617/341-4603 (outlet store)
  617/341-5000

Nason Richmond
  215 McClellan St.
  Schenectady, NY 12304

S

Sandbagger Enterprises Inc.
  P.O. Box 2404
  Lewistown, ME 04241
  800/659-9607

Sierra Trading Post
  5025 Campstool Rd.
  Cheyenne, WY 82007
  307/775-8000

Howard Smith
  5122 Vance Jackson Rd.
  San Antonio, TX 78230
  210/344-5615

Jerry Snyder
  American British Golf Card
  Connection
  98885 E. Watermill Circle
  Boynton Beach, FL 33437

Sporting Designs
  250 South Rd.
  P.O. Box 557
  Rye Beach, NH 03871
  603/964-4079

Sportcard
  Box 817
  Newport, RI 02840
  401/847-5848

Sports Products Co.
  405 Main St.
  Parkville, MO 64152

The Styles Co.
  15916 Manufacture Lane
  Huntington Beach, CA 92649
  800/356-0353

Sun Mountain Sports
  301 N. 1st
  Missoula, MT 59802
  800/227-9224

T

Tandy Leather
  P.O. Box 791
  Fort Worth, TX 76101
  817/551-9620

Telepro Golf Shop
  17642 Armstrong Ave.
  Irvine, CA 92714-5728
  800/333-9903

Tender Buttons
  143 E. 62nd St.
  New York, NY 10021
  212/980-3540

TerraForm
  P.O. Box 92
  Dalton, MA 01227
  413/684-9771

Tin Pan Annies
  c/o Babcock Audio & Video
  P.O. Box 136113
  Ft. Worth, TX 76136
  817/677-2016

Titleist
  P.O. Box 965
  Fairhaven, MA 02719-0965
  800/225-8500

Tour Golf Co., Inc.
  102 S. Tejon St., Suite 1100
  Colorado Springs, CO 80903
  719/526-3324

B.J.S. Turner Golf Art
  4500 Colt Drive
  West Des Moines, IA 50265
  515/225-2532

## U

USGA Catalog from Golf House
  P.O. Box 2000
  Far Hills, NJ 07931-2000
  800/336-4446

UT Golf
  2346 West 1500 South
  Salt Lake City, UT 84104
  800/666-6033

UP 2 Par
  Golf Shop for Women
  41770 12th St. West, Suite A

Palmdale, CA 93551
800/237-4727

## V

Irwin R. Valenta
  4405 Bromley Dr.
  Greensboro, NC 27406

Variety International
  1977 Otoole Ave., Suite B 106
  San Jose, CA 95131
  408/383-1666

## W

Edwin Watts Golf Shops
  20 Hill Avenue
  Ft. Walton Beach, FL 32548
  800/874-0146

# ABOUT THE AUTHOR

Freelance writer JIM APFELBAUM edits *Bottom Dollar Golf: The Consumer Value Golf Guide*. He plays out of Peter Pan West in Austin, Texas. His ambition is to become sneaky long.